M

Changing Faces of Madness

WITHDRAWN
UTSA LIBRARIES

Mary Ann Jimenez

Changing Faces of Madness

Early American Attitudes and Treatment of the Insane

Published for Brandeis University Press by
University Press of New England
Hanover and London, 1987

University Press of New England
Brandeis University
Brown University
Clark University
University of Connecticut
Dartmouth College
University of New Hampshire
University of Rhode Island
Tufts University
University of Vermont

Printed in the United States of America

Library of Congress Cataloging-in-Publication Data
Jimenez, Mary Ann.
   Changing faces of madness.
   Bibliography: p.
   Includes index.
   1. Mental illness—New England—Public opinion—History—18th century.   2. Mental illness—New England—Public opinion—History—19th century.
   3. Mentally ill—Care and treatment—Massachusetts—History—18th century.   4. Mentally ill—Care and treatment—Massachusetts—History—19th century.
   5. Public opinion—New England—History—18th century.
   6. Public opinion—New England—History—19th century.
   7. New England—Social conditions.   I. Title.
   RC455.2.P85J56   1986   362.2'0974   86-40112
   ISBN 0-87451-375-8

Thanks to Essex Institute, Salem, Mass.; Massachusetts Historical Society; American Antiquarian Society; and New England Genealogical Society for permission to use material from their archival deposits.

Contents

Preface   vii

Introduction   1

1. The Supernatural Face of Madness   12

2. A Familiar and Pitiful Sight   31

3. Non Compos Mentis in Colonial Massachusetts   49

4. The Medical Face of Madness   65

5. Dangerous to Go at Large   90

6. The Place for Lunatics   106

Epilogue   131

Notes   141
Bibliography   193
Index   209

Preface

My interest in the history of insanity began several years ago when I was a social worker involved with chronically disturbed clients in a medical setting. I was surprised and saddened at the inability of any of us on the staff, psychiatrists or social workers, to make a meaningful difference in the lives of those we sought to help. I began wondering how the contemporary view of madness had come to be the dominant one, when it seemed clear, to me at least, that it had very little to offer the seriously mentally disturbed, especially those who had been institutionalized for long periods of time. As a graduate student, I continued to pursue this question by looking at the treatment of the insane before the introduction of the asylum. As the history of insanity in the colonial and post-Revolutionary periods unfolded in my research, I realized that the story was far more complicated than I had imagined. The medical view of madness that developed in this country in the nineteenth century was in many ways more humanitarian and efficacious than what it replaced, at least in New England, where the post-Revolutionary generation had confined the insane in local jails and almshouses, often under punitive conditions. On the other hand, the proscriptive aspects of the medical approach, initially only a minor note in the search for cure, eventually developed into its dominant theme in the custodial mental hospital of the nineteenth and twentieth centuries. The return of the mentally disordered to the community in the wake of the Community Mental Health Centers Act was in many ways a recognition of the inhumanity of the custodial asylum, which has been noted repeatedly in the last thirty years by sociologists and historians as well as by mental health professionals. Yet this turning away from the asylum has also resulted in an abandonment of the seriously mentally disordered, since

few alternatives have been offered to them. The apparent un-
raveling of the medical model of madness is no longer the source
of satisfaction to me that it might have been in an earlier and
more naive period; rather, it is a painful sign that my generation
is unlikely to witness the reemergence of serious efforts to help
the insane.

I have deliberately used the terms *madness* and *insanity* in this
history rather than the commonly accepted one, *mental illness*,
since I want to trace the evolution of attitudes to a phenomenon
rather than substitute one understanding of it for the phenomenon itself. Since the notion of mental illness was not widely
accepted in colonial New England, madness or insanity seemed
to embody a more objective lexicon, although I regretfully acknowledge the pejorative connotation these terms sometimes
carry outside historians' circles.

There are many people who were intimately connected with
the process of writing this book in one way or another, and
whom I now wish to thank. David G. Gil, my graduate school
advisor in social policy at the Florence Heller School, Brandeis
University, encouraged the project from its inception; his uncommon analytical abilities were invaluable in helping me sift
through the earlier inchoate forms taken by my interest in phe-
nomenology, social policy, and history. His humanity and his
conviction about the possibility of the creation of a more just
social order are fundamentally important in shaping the thinking of everyone who works with him. David Hackett Fischer, my
thesis advisor in the American Civilization Department at Brandeis, was the key figure guiding my research and was ultimately
responsible for shaping my career as a historian. His insistence
that there is something real to know about history and his excitement in the pursuit of it have caught me and many others
up in a lifelong love of the discipline. Some of the ideas in this
book are a product of our scholarly collaboration; I hope he is
happy with the final version. John Demos shared his ideas about
madness in the colonial period with me and was of vital importance in the process of converting a dissertation into a book. He
carefully read more than one version of the manuscript and

shared his elegant mind and unique ability for historical insight on more occasions than either of us would like to remember. Most importantly, he was always unfailingly encouraging in his conviction that a book would eventually emerge. The process of revision was aided immeasurably by Charles E. Rosenberg, Barbara Gutman Rosenkrantz, Andrew Scull, and Robert D. Gross, who read various versions of the manuscript and offered critical and helpful comments. All this invaluable help has not absolved me of sole responsibility for the book's limitations.

The final draft of the manuscript was skillfully and cheerfully typed under great pressure by Stella Vlastos and Beverly Scales; without question I owe them a great deal. My good friend and fellow historian Louis Piccarello read the entire manuscript in several incarnations and provided unfailing scholarly advice as well as very significant personal support through the various down times. Others important to the summoning of will and energy necessary for completion of the book through several years of full-time teaching were Gene Taylor, Allen Greenberger, Sidney Bergman, Erika Sloane, Beverly Scales, and Paula Louise Mochel. My husband, Daniel Jimenez, was very important to every stage of the process, in both professional and personal ways unique to him. I also want to thank G.L. Harrington for his enormous help, faith in the project, and shared vision of the suffering of the insane.

This book is for him, without whom it would never have been completed.

Los Angeles, California   M. A. J.
March 1986

Changing Faces of Madness

Introduction

This book is a study of the changing response to madness in Massachusetts from 1700 to 1840. It seeks to explore the relationship between the social reaction to madness and wider social, political, economic, and cultural changes during this period. Massachusetts is particularly appropriate as a focus of research on madness both because of the relative availability of records there for the eighteenth and early nineteenth centuries, and because it played a pioneering role in asylum building and in the creation of other public provisions for those considered mentally disordered. A dramatic change overtook both ideas about madness and the treatment of the insane in Massachusetts during this period, a change that resulted in a significantly altered life experience for most of the insane there. The reactions of the residents of Massachusetts Bay Colony, the post-Revolutionary generation, and the reformers of the Jacksonian period to madness were different from one another. This book will describe those changes in attitudes and explore the reasons for the transformation in the reaction to madness.

While this study tells the story of madness in one geographic area, the questions it poses suggest a broader relationship between madness and the social order. Does the response to madness depend on the degree of complexity of the society? Or on the financial resources available to meet problems of deviance and dependence? Or on the development of humanitarian sentiments? Or on the necessity for social order? Historians have suggested all these factors as significant in shaping the social response to madness in American history.[1]

Another way of viewing the history of madness is to see the social reaction to insanity itself as a mirror reflecting deeper issues in the society. What is the meaning of madness in a culture? Is it universally feared, or is it less frightening in some historical periods than in others? What are the reasons for the threat insanity may pose? What dimensions of the past does the reaction to madness illuminate?

The history of insanity has an intrinsically compelling quality and consequently has attracted several important historians in the attempt to unravel its complexities. Perhaps the most influential contributor to this history is Michel Foucault. In *Madness and Civilization,* a work that continues to be controversial, he argued that up to the seventeenth century in Western Europe the mad were involved in a dialogue with the sane in which they experienced little opprobrium, neither were they singled out for special treatment. Somewhere in the seventeenth century, according to Foucault, this dialogue was terminated, and the insane inherited the stigmatized role of lepers and lost their freedom to move freely through society. This new confinement of the insane was functional for the larger society, he argued, for it provided a means of dealing with the rising problems attendant on the spread of the market economy and the values associated with new demands for economic behavior. Staggering cycles of unemployment then besetting France and England necessitated new responses to deviant behavior; madness became inexorably linked with nonproductivity—with an incapacity for work—and thus the insane were banished from the larger society. Foucault used little archival evidence to support his argument, relying instead largely on literary evidence and medical writing from France and England to describe shifts in attitudes. In spite of the rather narrow base of this evidence, he has made a great impact on the history of madness, partly because he cast his history in highly dramatic—some might say even romantic— terms.[2]

George Rosen has argued in *Madness in Society: Chapters in the Historical Sociology of Mental Illness* that in medieval and Renaissance Europe "forms of unreason were considered fundamental elements in the fabric of the universe and of man."[3] In the seventeenth and eighteenth centuries, a shift in social attitudes toward madness took place: "Folly and madness were no longer to roam aimlessly. Order was necessary, and the mentally and emotionally deranged were to be subjected to discipline in institutions created for this purpose." Like Foucault, Rosen viewed the repression of idleness as crucial in the seventeenth century, particularly among those concerned with economic productivity. Thus institutions were created whose purpose was to deal with all kinds of antisocial behavior. Madness now became a social problem, and the insane, who were thought to have gone mad through their own volition, were confined.[4]

English beliefs about madness from the sixteenth through the mid nineteenth centuries are chronicled in Richard Hunter and Ida Macalpine, eds., *Three Hundred Years of Psychiatry, 1535–1860*.[5] The primary sources presented in this work are accompanied by rich editorial comments, which reveal the indebtedness of the English observer of insanity to Galen's humoral doctrine, both in explanations of madness and in efforts to treat the insane. The documents attempt to clarify various kinds of madness and offer mixed notions of causation, including religious, physical, and psychological, that coexisted for most of the seventeenth and eighteenth centuries.

Michael MacDonald provided an intense look at madness in one area of seventeenth-century England in *Mystical Bedlam: Madness, Anxiety, and Healing in Seventeenth Century England*, in which he set out to show how "popular beliefs about insanity and healing illuminate the mental world of ordinary people."[6] His evidence is centered on the records kept by one astrological physician, Richard Napier, in which MacDonald found a richly textured image of madness that combined religious beliefs, magical beliefs, scientific attitudes, and astrological ideas. In seventeenth-century England this eclectic mixture was seen as a unified cosmological model, not as a number of competing explanations. Efforts at healing the mad were equally eclectic, with religious, psychological, astrological, and medical techniques being offered freely, sometimes by the same healer. MacDonald argued that in the eighteenth century, the ruling classes, in a rejection of sectarian enthusiasms, began to prefer more secular models of insanity and turned away from the quasi-religious, quasi-magical notions offered by practitioners like Napier. While ordinary men and women continued to view madness from the point of view of older cosmology in the eighteenth century, the trend was moving in the other direction. With the secularization of madness came the ascendancy of medical practice and finally the confinement of the mad in public and private madhouses.

Andrew T. Scull has argued in *Museums of Madness: The Social Organization of Insanity in Nineteenth Century England* that a dramatic change overtook the social reaction to the mad in England in the early nineteenth century.[7] During this period, the insane were "incarcerated" in a state-supported asylum system where their condition was newly defined as a medical problem and their lives were under the jurisdiction of the medical profession. Scull pointed to "the changing structure of the English economy from the late eighteenth century onwards," in which the older economic paternalism was replaced with a self-regulating market, which in turn led to the extension of wage labor and the continual cycles of boom and bust as the major cause of the confinement of the insane.[8] Scull argued that the mad were placed in asylums because, as nonproductive members of the lower classes, they could no longer be absorbed into the family or parish relief system under the exigencies of this new economic system. They were then separated from the rest of the population and became the raison d'être of a new "growing market or trade in lunacy," operated by a growing psychiatric profession that claimed scientific expertise in the cure of madness.[9]

Scull acknowledged that the disruptive behavior of the insane made their absorption into the social fabric doubly difficult, but his is essentially a social control thesis. While more insistent on this perspective than either Foucault or Rosen, Scull presented a similar argument: that it was largely deep structural changes in the economic organization of society that led to the separation of the mad from the rest of the population. For these historians, the confinement of the insane was the watershed in the history of madness.

American historians similarly have been most interested in the confinement of the insane, focusing most of their attention on the antebellum reform movement to establish asylums for them. These historians have placed less emphasis on economic factors in accounting for the changing response than have their European and English counterparts. Instead, they have pointed to broader cultural influences in their discussions of the creation of the asylum. The new look at the contemporary mental hospital provided by the Community Mental Health movement of the 1960s is no doubt responsible for at least some of the recent historical interest in the origins of the American asylum. The contemporary rejection of the curative functions of the mental hospital has clearly had some influence on the telling of its history.

One historian not influenced by contemporary doubts about the efficacy of the mental hospital was Albert Deutsch, the only American historian to provide a more detailed account of the history of insanity before the era of the asylum. In his *Mentally Ill in America*, published long before the mental hospital became a subject of intense controversy, the colonists were portrayed as largely ignorant, sometimes cruel people who mistreated the insane. A decidedly Whig interpretation of the subject was offered by Deutsch, who argued that medical science rescued the mad from this inhumane treatment in the early nineteenth century through the establishment of the asylums. He argued that the medical profession's recognition of madness as a disease gave new hope to its victims.

The crucial chapter of asylum building in the Jacksonian period has received far more attention than any other in the history of madness in America. Gerald Grob and David Rothman tell the story from different points of view, but both emphasize the ineluctable shift from a more benign era of moral treatment in the early phases of the asylum to a final deterioration of those original reform impulses by the middle of the nineteenth century.

The movement from treatment to custody at Worcester State Lunatic Hospital in Massachusetts is presented in compelling detail by Gerald Grob in *The State and the Mentally Ill*. Grob suggested that growing numbers of insane and an increasing population density caused tensions in Massachusetts society, tensions that were resolved when medical science was wedded to a reform movement that created asylums. In *Mental Institutions in America; Social Policy to 1875,* an impressively rich work that presents a broader analysis of asylum building across the country, Grob documented a decline from the original mission of asylums wherever they appeared. More interested in this decline than in the reasons for the creation of the asylum, he argued that institutional imperatives were largely responsible for the transformation of the asylum from a place of care to a place of custody. Eschewing a structural-functional analysis, he described pressures on the asylum in the form of increasing admissions, cultural differences presented by immigrants, and underfunding by states as the most significant factors in their failure. Yet originally the asylums were a product of a genuine reform impulse, according to Grob, one that led the asylum builders to view their solution as a deeply humane one.

David Rothman, in *The Discovery of the Asylum: Social Order and Disorder in the New Republic,* a penetrating analysis of the origins of asylum building, argued that the movement to confine the insane was a reaction to the unstable, disordered world of Jacksonian America. According to Rothman, the asylum represented society's attempt to impose order and stability on the deviant to compensate for the wildly changing social order. Rothman did not insist that individual reformers acted out of personally malevolent motives; in fact, he allowed them the sincerity of their beliefs. Instead, he maintained that in spite of their good intentions, the ultimate significance of all asylums erected in this period was to provide Jacksonian society with mechanisms of social control. Like Grob, he described the decline of the mental hospital from a place of moral treatment early in its history to a place of often punitive confinement. In Rothman's analysis this shift was inevitable, a result of the meaning and function the asylum had for Jacksonian America.

Norman Dain, in *Concepts of Insanity in the United States, 1789– 1865,* viewed the opening of the asylum in the Jacksonian period as the triumph of an enlightened, progressive spirit, yet he went beyond this to recognize a cyclical pattern of reform and neglect in the treatment of the insane in the nineteenth and twentieth centuries.[10] Dain's book is an important study of how the ideas about the nature and causes of madness developed in the nineteenth century, especially within the medical profession. He demonstrated that the growing conviction about the curability of insanity that developed in the nineteenth century was at least partially responsible for establishment of the asylums. Dain provided a detailed exposition of the ideology of asylum superintendents, from the establishment of the asylum through the Civil War, which highlights the growing pessimism about curability that overtook many in this group as their hospitals became overcrowded with pauper immigrants and patients considered incurable.

Nancy Tomes, in *A Generous Confidence: Thomas Story Kirkbride and the Art of Asylum-Building, 1840–1883*, has argued that a major impulse behind the establishment of the Jacksonian asylum was the desire of families of the insane to transfer the burden of care to the asylum keepers.[11] This new discomfort with family care was, according to Tomes, the result of both a new faith in the asylum's efficacy in curing the insane and a heightening of the importance of domestic life in nineteenth century America. Focusing on the story of Thomas Kirkbride and his years as asylum director at Pennsylvania Hospital, she emphasized the moral and religious dimensions of asylum treatment, portraying Pennsylvania Hospital as a place where a set of complex transactions maintained a careful balance among psychological, social, and moral reasons for confinement.

With the exception of Deutsch, no American historian has done extensive research on the period before the opening of the asylum. Tomes presented material on the first Pennsylvania Hospital, which began treating the insane in the mid eighteenth century, but her evidence did not take her outside the walls of the asylum.[12] Most historians have assumed a continuity from the colonial period to the Jacksonian era, in which the mad were cared for privately by their families until other imperatives made it necessary to move to asylum care. The major transition in the history of madness has generally been seen as taking place in the 1820s and 1830s, with the rise of the asylum.[13] The evidence presented here suggests another, earlier transition in the history of madness, not linked to the asylum. After the American Revolution, the confluence of social, economic, and cultural changes in New England colored madness with a vivid significance and led to a break with earlier ways of responding to the insane. This new reaction was largely a fearful one and resulted in a move to confine the insane, not in asylums, but in local jails, almshouses, and even private homes. Before the Revolution, the insane in Massachusetts were as a rule not confined but were largely left alone to live out their lives with little interference. The asylum builders in nineteenth-century Massachusetts were rescuing them not from the cruelty and neglect of the colonists but from an anxiety about insanity in the post-Revolutionary period that led to the separation of the insane from the rest of society. The reformers of the Jacksonian period were not the first, but rather the second generation of nineteenth-century Americans to see in madness a troubling problem.

The role of madness itself in the history of the response to it has not been fully elaborated. In Rothman's work it is not the force of madness that provides the impulse for confinement; rather, it is broader social variables. Madness is merely one of many deviant states that could not be tolerated in the chaos of Jacksonian society. Other historians do not directly address this issue either, although Grob came closer to seeing madness as a real force when he suggested that population density may have been a significant factor in the rise of the asylum, because insane behavior cannot be tolerated as easily under such circumstances. Tomes recognized that the definition of what behaviors constituted madness broadened with the opening of the Jacksonian asylum in Pennsylvania, but she did not view insane behavior as a critical determinant in the changing social response to it. In contrast, this history is written from the assumption that madness has a force, an impact of its own. Madness itself is a significant actor in the drama that unfolds around it.

While no definitive understanding of the nature or causes of madness has been reached, the epistemological dilemma suggested by the mysterious nature of insanity can be avoided in a history that recognizes that it is real, whatever its causes, whatever its ultimate nature. Because madness is real, it makes an impact on those who are sane in ways that may vary in different cultures and in different historical periods.

The behavior of the insane can offer a severe challenge to the socially constructed meanings and ritualized behaviors of the sane. Insane behavior is apparently meaningless; it has no clear referent that is accessible to others. This behavior seems alien because it is based on a private world of meaning, rather than on a socially shared one. Although much of reality (except for a handful of biological and physical imperatives) is socially constructed, few of us perceive its relativity and human origin. On the contrary, we mostly see the social world we inhabit as inevitable, for the social constructions have become reified and legitimized so that they are viewed as the natural way. Perhaps the most profoundly important kind of socially constructed meaning is at the most primitive level, what phenomenologists call the reality of everyday life. Here are the ritualized ways of behaving, the ordinary routines of daily life, the level of ordinary social interchange, of gestures, language, greetings, dress, common courtesies—the specific cultural boundaries that define what it is to be human. While this level of reality has human origins, it is least likely to be perceived in this way; rather, it is seen as the normal and inevitable state of affairs. By behaving in ways that seem contrary to these accepted natural or normal ones and therefore seem meaningless, the insane can threaten the inevitability of this necessarily most fiercely defended socially constructed reality.[14] At this fundamental level of meaning, the boundaries of self are defined, and existential isolation is reduced through participation in common rituals. The belief in the reality of these social meanings is crucial to the ability to function and survive in the human world.[15] Confrontation with a dissenter from the reality of everyday life may suggest to the observer doubts about the inevitability of this reality. Madness can be an uncomfortable and even deeply threatening experience for the sane.

Insane persons can also be threatening because their behavior suggests that they are not in control of themselves. This potential loss of self-control can be unacceptable in some societies but may be less of a problem in others. There is likely to be a wide range in the reaction to madness and the amount of anxiety it causes. Some of this variation may be related to the kind of society in which the insane live.[16] The relationship between madness and society is a dynamic one; the tensions created by the mad reveal much about what is important in a particular period, and the reaction to insane behavior is the most important measure of that conflict.

Throughout American history various explanations about the nature and causes of madness have been fashioned. The need to explain madness has always existed as a means of disarming the anomalous and potentially disrupting effect of the behavior of the insane.[17] During the period covered here, the medical explanation of madness triumphed over earlier versions of its meaning; the consequences for the insane in the early nineteenth century were mixed and continue to be so today.

The so-called medical model of insanity has been the cause of considerable controversy in the last twenty years. Criticisms include the arguments that madness has not been shown to be a disease or even biologically based; that the medical profession has too much control over the lives of the mentally disordered; and that treatment has remained largely ineffective.[18] Mental health professionals, on the other hand, generally view the history of insanity as a progressive movement toward a clearer scientific understanding of madness and continue to look for an eventual solution to the still stubborn mysteries.[19] It is my hope that this history will prove useful to both camps. I am also hopeful that the story of how the mad fared before the medical model took hold may serve to illuminate alternatives to our present policies.

Finally, a word about the limitations of this history. The study focuses on one geographic area, the colony and later the state of Massachusetts, largely because this was a very important place in the history of madness. Massachusetts was the pioneer in public provisions for the insane in the nineteenth century. One of the first—and perhaps the most influential—of the early public mental hospitals was established there in 1833. Dorothea Dix, Samuel Gridley Howe, and Horace Mann, all nationally known reformers from Massachusetts, concerned themselves with the plight of the insane at various points in their careers. Its leadership role in establishing public mental hospitals meant that Massachusetts served as a model for other states; it therefore played a significant role in the development of a broader response to insanity in nineteenth-century America. In this sense the history of an earlier reaction to madness there takes on special meaning. Massachusetts asylums were established for reasons at least partly based on what had gone on before: earlier reactions necessarily influenced the way citizens went about asylum building. Since a great deal is already known about the history of Worcester State Lunatic Hospital, it seems important to look back to the period before its creation to fill out the history of insanity in Massachusetts. An understanding of the colonial and early nineteenth-century reaction to madness may shed new light on a question that has not been finally answered: Why were the asylums established?[20]

While the subject of the reaction to the insane is intrinsically significant, evidence from which to make a judgment about it is painstakingly gathered and necessarily limited. Even in Massachusetts, whose colonial and Revolutionary archives are perhaps the best preserved of any state, it is very difficult to find evidence about an issue that was (for whatever reason) not perceived to be a significant one. Madness crops up occasionally in all sorts of places: court records, records of the overseers of the poor for various towns, private diaries, and newspapers. The best information is available for those who were in the public eye or in public facilities, such as jails or poorhouses. There were doubtless some insane folk who have eluded my careful research, who are the permanently anonymous of history. Nonetheless, I am convinced that the general outlines of the story are correct and that this history has some significance for the broader history of madness in America. The relationship in this story between madness and society is not confined to the boundaries of one state but rather suggests a universal tension that speaks to our profoundest nature as human beings.

1 The Supernatural Face of Madness

Cotton Mather, the great Puritan divine, was perhaps the most literate and certainly the most famous observer of madness in colonial Massachusetts. His speculations about its nature and causes suggest the complexity of the colonial effort to understand insanity, in which religious, biological, and moral explanations were woven into a unified model of madness in which God, devil, and human actors all played various roles.[1]

Mather's earliest writings about madness emphasized the satanic connection, as in a sermon where he suggested that "there is an unaccountable and unexpressable interest of Satan often times in the Distemper of madness." He rather poetically described how this "interest of Satan" works: "It is often some Devil, which takes advantage of the Poisonous Fires which madness is inflamed with, to carry on the hideous Hurly Burly's that are in the minds of the distempered."[2] How does Satan work through the human body? Mather thought that some men "afford a bed wherein busy and bloody devils have a sort of lodging provided for them." The "bed" is a "mass of blood . . . disordered with some fiery acid," and "juices, ferments and vapours."[3] Alternatively, something may be awry with the humors, which "yield the steams when Satan does insinuate himself until he has gained a sort of possession in them, or at least an opportunity to shoot into the mind as many fiery darts as may cause sad life to them."[4] Of course, Satan was implicated in many untoward occurrences in colonial Massachusetts, most notably witchcraft, but he was also thought to have the power to drive or tempt a person into madness. The responsibility to resist the importuning of the devil rested with those so beset; however, the failure to win the struggle was not necessarily a cause for shame.

William Thompson, a melancholy minister in late seventeenth-century Massachusetts, became so debilitated by his mental state that he had to resign his ministry. Mather wrote of him sympathetically in *Magnalia Christi Americana* in 1702, recalling that Satan became "irritated by the evangelic labours of this holy man" and "obtained the liberty to throw him into a Balneum Diaboli." Mather assured his readers that Satan had obtained this "liberty" from God, who finally saved Thompson from his madness, thanks to the prayers of his congregation.[5] While Mather's need to find a moral lesson in Thompson's story has him restored to reason after his congregation's prayers, other accounts have him going to his grave insane.[6]

Resisting the devil's assault on one's sanity was a very strenuous task. In a collection of poems written after his death by Thompson's family and friends, the minister is described as courageously trying to thwart the devil's efforts, as he "vexed his mind with diabolical assaults and horrid, hellish darts." These devilish attacks left Thompson resembling "the lively portrature of Death / A walking tomb, a living sepulcher / In which black melancholy did inter." Although the devil was the primary actor in the onset of Thompson's madness, the poet was careful to acknowledge the ultimate authority of God in allowing the devil to tempt him, for "he hath let the devil loose / me strongly to oppose." While Mather's account of Thompson's suffering leaves the reader with a strong impression of the latter's innocence, in these poems the suggestion appears that Thompson "swerved from the duties of his calling" and so brought on Satan's assaults himself.[7] Here the moral implications of madness are summoned; its appearance could signal some earlier flaw that had given the devil a foothold, just as Mather, on another occasion, suggested that some men offer Satan an easy "bed." Madness, like anything calamitous that might befall the colonist, was a rich source of moral instruction.[8]

In 1719 Mather pointed out another way in which the devil

might be responsible for madness, when he began fretting over his third wife's behavior, which he described as consisting of "furious and froward pangs." He worried whether they were the result of a "distraction or a possession." *Distraction* was the most common name for ordinary madness in colonial Massachusetts, while *possession* suggested a more serious form and implied a direct takeover of an individual's will by Satan. During one "prodigious return of her pangs upon her," Mather's wife Lydia scolded her husband with a "thousand unrepeateable invectives" and "got into a horrid rage," causing him to judge her behavior "Little short of a Proper Satanical Possession."[9]

Possession by the devil might be suggested by the more extreme forms of madness, but such behavior could also summon the specter of witchcraft, a distinct form of Satanic intervention in human affairs. Colonists usually made a distinction between possession and bewitchment, since the latter meant, for one thing, the necessity of finding a witch to prosecute. Mather was probably not worried that his wife was bewitched. He had, after all, witnessed several cases of bewitchment in the course of his ministry and knew that there were "distinct and formal fits of witchcraft" that accompanied true bewitchment.[10] Colonists drew a very clear line between madness, which might or might not be caused by possession, and bewitchment, as evidenced by the efforts of witnesses in cases of suspected bewitchment to rule out madness. The behavior of the bewitched was far more dramatic than that of the merely distracted; in fact, there was an expectation that something "preternatural" should be performed by one who was truly bewitched.[11] Being under the spell of a witch was clearly not the same as being distracted; one dissenter from the Salem witchcraft trials argued that the Salem girls were not bewitched but were merely "poor distracted children," or perhaps "a parcel of possessed, distracted or lying wenches."[12] As Mather knew well, the colonists did not view any part of the witchcraft drama as a sign of anyone's insanity, whether witch or bewitched.[13]

Cotton Mather may not have known how to account for his wife's behavior, but if he *had* really believed that the devil was responsible for her outbursts, he might have been less inclined to blame her. In the case of a minister of Mather's acquaintance whom Satan drove mad, Mather was exceedingly sympathetic. In *Magnalia Christi Americana*, Mather recounted the story of John Warham, a pious man whom Satan "threw into the deadly pangs of melancholy," and who suffered "terrible temptations and buffetings," which were relieved only at his death. Mather was concerned about a growing number of "pious" New Englanders who "have contracted these melancholy indispositions which have unhinged them from all service or comfort." Explaining the madness of apparently good people was occasion for calling upon the "unsearchable judgements of God," who allowed the devil to drive such persons mad.[14] The melancholy forms of madness may have been viewed in a more sympathetic light than were the raving kinds. In another sermon written in 1717, Mather argues that melancholy madness, the kind suffered by those with "troubled minds," was likely to be a test by God of the patience and resolve of an otherwise holy person.[15]

Mather found insanity somewhat easier to explain when the afflicted person clearly had been guilty of some moral transgression. In *Magnalia* he pointed out the case, "which many hundreds among us know to be true," of a layman who, upon being asked to preach a sermon for an absent minister, took the opportunity to attack the exclusive right of the clergy to preach. Mather warned the reader that this sin of pride was immediately punished, when "God smote him with a horrible madness; he was taken ravingly distracted: the people were forced with violent hands to carry him home." He lived the rest of his life in total madness, according to the minister's account.[16] Here the raving madness of an obvious sinner was easily translated into a moral lesson.

Sin was not the cause only of insanity in Mather's cosmology, but of all human suffering. It was, he argued in "Insanibilia," the cause of "all the grievous things" that come from God. This view of sin as an all-purpose agent of human misery was shared by Mather's contemporaries in the early eighteenth century, yet their emphasis on human responsibility for suffering did not eliminate the role of Satan, for he still had a "hand in All grievous Things which darken the world."[17]

Mather combined supernatural actors, personal sin, and human biology to explain madness in the early eighteenth century. His causal scheme was flexible; the distraction of the saint was understood as another of God's tests of his followers, while the sinner could be blamed for bringing on his own insensibility by invoking God's punishment. The devil could be summoned in either case: as a way of blaming those who did not resist his blandishments, or as the overpowering force that swept aside the rationality of an unwilling victim.

Mather was writing as a Puritan minister, one who would be eager to explain insanity in religious terms. His views are important not only because of his eminence in colonial Massachusetts, but also because they were probably shared by most of his contemporaries. The Massachusetts Bay colonists were very likely to believe in the reality of the supernatural order invoked by Mather, and they had much evidence of the direct power of God and the devil in their lives. What we would call superstitious beliefs in witchcraft, in signs and portents, were widespread in the colony in this period, in urban as well as in rural areas. These beliefs were part of a complex framework of causality in which all happenings, including those with natural causes, such as earthquakes and storms, were seen in a supernatural light. The colonists believed that God's hand was in all events, and they were particularly eager to point to this in the case of anything untoward.[18]

Mather's explanations of madness were fashioned out of a traditional model that included a powerful demonology, a strong sense of sin, and an acceptance of God's ultimate power. His speculations about madness remind us that the division between secular and religious reality that characterizes modern thinking was not so important in colonial thinking. Calvinism provided a symbolic structure that lent supernatural meaning to all human activities.[19] This ability to explain the everyday aspects of reality in supernatural terms was especially important when no other clear explanation existed. The rational basis of Puritanism did not completely eliminate the belief in the basic inscrutability of God, which allowed every event, no matter how untoward, to be absorbed into the predominant symbolic order of Calvinist theology. The notion of Providence was an all-encompassing concept that explained God's mysterious intervention into human affairs. Puritans believed that God's Providence was not passive but consisted in the direct operation of His will in the natural order.[20] God's inscrutability as well as His glory was therefore magnified by the appearance of the unusual. In the last analysis, madness was another way this lesson could be learned more profoundly.

The idea of God's Providence was to become increasingly important in explaining madness in the eighteenth century, as the role of the devil receded. By 1724, for instance, Mather had retreated to a vaguer argument that "maniaks are more or less demoniaks."[21] The diffuseness of the explanation offered by God's Providence was more acceptable by the mid eighteenth century, as interest in demonology began to wane in New England.

To argue for the power of this symbolic world is not to claim that all members of Massachusetts society were involved with theological questions. The issue is one of faith, not dogma. The colonist had a place to turn his mind when he needed explanations. No colonist could escape the fact that the vast majority of his friends and neighbors believed firmly in an elaborate overarching structure of supernatural meanings that both absorbed and dwarfed human reality.[22]

Cotton Mather's model of madness was not idiosyncratic, for it was the only logical one that could have existed within the Puritan symbolic world. Furthermore, his and other ministers' speculations about madness would have been taken seriously by their congregations because clergymen had a strong influence in New England through much of the colonial period. This influence could and often did extend beyond the bounds of theology, although clearly that was their greatest point of persuasion.[23] As long as madness was embedded in a theological context, the explanation of it offered by ministers was likely to find wide acceptance. The explanations in this period were entirely consistent with the supernatural belief system of the colonists. Insanity, no matter how mysterious, was not unfathomable.

Cotton Mather was clearly interested in speculating about the biological side of madness, even as he took pains to point out the religious implications of the disorder. In his mind, of course, there was no disjunction between natural and supernatural orders, for they were wedded together to form what Mather and his contemporaries considered to be reality. In this sense, explanation of the biology of madness in no way diminishes its supernatural aspects; instead, such efforts at explanation could only serve to magnify God's power in the world.

One of the first Puritans in Massachusetts to speculate about the biological aspects of insanity was Michael Wigglesworth, the seventeenth-century diarist who worried frequently about his mental state. He complained of being "much troubled with the spleen these divers days." The "spleen" could be a disorder brought on by that organ, which was thought to be the seat of melancholy humors and morose feelings; it had exposed Wigglesworth to several kinds of miseries: "to much frothyness and unsavoury discourse, . . . weariness of religious duties, . . . carnal lusts by reason of the abundance of flatulent vapours that annoy me . . ." and "melancholy scrupulosity and a multitude of distractions that way."[24] This was not madness exactly, but rather a set of troublesome physical and emotional anxieties plaguing Wigglesworth. By the mid eighteenth century the concept of spleen was less equivocal and more clearly linked to insanity. One anonymous author described it as a "painful Folly of the mind," thus foreshadowing later debates about the nature of madness when he confessed to some difficulty in deciding whether the "spleen" was an actual disease or a condition, somehow analogous to a disease, which "makes us sick without a disease." The most salient characteristic of the "spleen" was that it allowed "fancy" to overrule reason. The reader was cautioned not to be angry at the "splenetick," for such a person acts out of "suspended reason" and is punished through his own "crazy" actions.[25]

Colonists like Wigglesworth and Mather had access to a wide range of speculations about the nature and causes of madness in English writings on the subject. English ideas about insanity in the seventeenth and eighteenth centuries were far more extensive and systematic than anything offered by the colonists.

These writers relied on the ancient system of explanation inherited from the Greeks, known as humoral doctrine, which revolved around the idea that impurities or excesses in the four body fluids (known as humors) led to all somatic dysfunctioning and underlay all diseases.[26] As early as 1633, the Englishman John Hawkins published a book on "hypochondriac melancholy" that featured a list of symptoms including "twitching of the stomach, rumbling in the guts, palpitation of the heart" and linked this disorder to the disturbed humors.[27] The most famous of these early English writers was probably Nicholas Culpeper, who in *The English Physician* (1669) discussed the morbid states of the melancholy humors, suggesting mostly herbal cures.[28]

In the 1720s a speculative pathology, which, like humoral doctrine, was inherited from the Greeks, was revived in England. This approach rested on the assumption that illness was primarily due to a condition of tension in the nervous and vascular systems. Nicholas Robinson's *New System of the Spleen, Vapours and Hypochondriak Melancholy* . . . , published in London in 1729, applied that theory directly to madness. Robinson thought the cause of insanity could be found in "alterations in the motions of our nervous fibers" leading to "irregular motions, irregular sensation and irregular perceptions in the mind." These combined to cause "Wrong Turn of Thoughts and Judgment, under the spleen vapours and melancholy"—all viewed by Robinson as stages of madness.[29] Though humoral pathology continued to be an important part of Robinson's theory, it was his emphasis on a more mechanistic explanation of madness that was to be influential in colonial thinking in Massachusetts in the middle of the eighteenth century.[30]

Mather and other colonists relied on the writing of these and other English physicians for remedies and speculations, since they wrote little on medical matters themselves. The art of medical practice in the colonies was not nearly as sophisticated as it was in England at this time.[31] Although there were physicians practicing medicine in the colonies, the professionalization of the medical role was not evident until the end of the eighteenth century. The practice of the healing art was shared by a variety of people, including ministers and women, who also did other things. Medicine and religion were not necessarily seen as separate vocations, and ministers freely offered medical advice.[32]

It is not surprising, then, that it was Cotton Mather who made the first real attempt in the colonies to offer a fully elaborate theory of madness, one that sought to unite its biological and the supernatural aspects. That Mather was familiar with English writing on insanity is evident in his *Angel of Bethesda*, written in 1724.[33] In this quasi-medical textbook that discussed various diseases and physical calamities common in the colonies, Mather attempted to weave together various contemporary ideas about madness. While in 1693 he had singled out the devil as the moving force behind insanity, in 1724 his explanations took on a more naturalistic cast. Although Mather had always acknowledged the role of human biology in his speculation about madness, bodily processes had played a rather minor role in his previous comments. The inclusion of a discussion of insanity in a work that dealt with physical illness is one indication of the direction in which his thinking was moving. In a larger sense, *The Angel of Bethesda* also suggests that Mather was becoming increasingly curious about the physical aspects of the human condition.

Since he did not view supernatural and natural explanations of madness as competing ones, Mather continued to give the supernatural dimensions respectful attention in *The Angel of Bethesda*. The devil was given his due as being responsible for some cases of insanity, as Mather did not want to forego the possibility that "there is often a Degree of Diabolical possession in the Melancholy." He reminded his readers that they had all sinned sufficiently to be "Smitten with Madness" and argued once again that sin was the greatest madness. Therefore, from a godly point of view, the whole world was mad.[34] Mather clearly saw no reason to give up the instructive value of madness. Yet while these themes remained in *The Angel of Bethesda*, he seemed more interested in discussing the various "natural" remedies that had been useful in extinguishing the "Fury of the Animal Spirits." He suggested the heroic remedies and herbal treatments that were popular in English folk medicine, such as "Living swallows, cut in two, and laid hott reeking unto the shaved Head."[35] The fact that Mather was now apparently more interested in the treatment of insanity than in its causes signals another shift toward a more naturalistic view.

Mather warned his fellow ministers to take signs of madness in their congregations seriously, for they had a responsibility to intervene in such cases. He urged ministers plagued by melancholics not to "Make Light of the Matter," providing that the sufferer was really "under Awakenings From the SPIRIT of God, and under Apprehensions of the Wrath." That sort of *"Trouble of Mind,"* he reminded his reader, was not "a *Mechanical Business* in our Animal Spirits," but involved the ultimate relationship with the supernatural. This kind of melancholia would be cured only if the minister could "carry *a Troubled Sinner* through the Process of Repentance." The sinner should make a "Confession of his Guilt, and Impotency, and Unworthiness." Here, in contrast with what Mather wrote earlier, melancholy is directly linked to sin and the devil is given no role in its onset. However, the message of prayer in the face of an ultimate dependence on God's power is the same. Yet he also suggested that the causes of melancholy were related to "*Flatulencies* in the region of the *Hypochondria*," while mania was caused by "Animal Spirits inflamed." The multiple framework that he had used earlier to explain madness had not been dismantled; he had merely given the biological aspects of it new emphasis.[36]

Mather viewed his own suggestions for intervening in the biology of madness as perfectly compatible with the idea that the disorder was intimately tied to supernatural realities. Although he wanted the reader to be sure to see the religious implications of madness and especially the implications for righteous behavior, he also believed that God provided natural remedies for insanity, and he insisted that it was up to humans to search them out. In this work Mather's thinking was transitional between the older indeterminate conception of the causes of insanity and the newer, more determinate naturalistic notions. *The Angel of Bethesda* is also significant because in it Mather made the first effort in the colonies to forge systematic links between human behavior and human biology.

Mather's taxonomy of madness in *The Angel of Bethesda* included the categories of *mania* and *melancholy*. Mania was thought to be a state of insanity characterized by excitement, frenzy, and possibly violence, while melancholy was characterized by sullenness and low spirits. Both these terms were commonly used in England in this period, and Mather clearly borrowed them from English writings.[37] However, they were not widely used in eighteenth-century Massachusetts. Instead, *mad, crazy,* and *lunatic* were more common ways of describing insanity, especially in private correspondence and diaries. By far the most likely term for an insane person, however, was *distracted*. That word appears along with the more formal legalism, non compos mentis, in most public documents.[38] *Distracted* was used more loosely than *non compos mentis* as a description for madness, for the latter had to be determined legally by the courts or by town officials. The term *distracted* is itself a rather mild one. It suggests a person whose mind is occupied outside present reality, not a person in danger of losing control or becoming violent. Whether this indicates that forms of insanity were in fact gentler in the colonial period than later is a fascinating but elusive question that cannot be determined from the historical evidence left to us.

In his efforts to classify madness, Cotton Mather had generally reserved the term *melancholy* for a state of distraction that involved despair over the state of one's soul, as in his sermon in 1717 when he warned again that "a melancholy condition" was becoming a "common problem" in New England. The "troubled soul wrongfully concludes that God holds one his enemy or hides his face from me." "Persons of a melancholy nature and much alone" were most susceptible to this condition, he concluded.[39]

Mather apparently was correct in his sense that religious melancholy was a "common problem." Ebenezer Parkman, a minister from western Massachusetts, also described cases in his diary throughout the 1730s and 1740s of persons, usually women, "under great Trouble of mind" over the state of their souls—persons clearly driven to madness because of anxiety about their salvation. Deborah Brigham, a member of Parkman's congregation often called on the minister to visit her. He usually found her in a distracted and frenzied condition, which she claimed was due to the "distress of her soul concerning her Eternal Condition."[40] In 1741 Samuel Chandler, a minister in York, Maine, described another distracted woman in such despair over the state of her soul and her fate in the next world that, after five years of suffering, she hanged herself with a fishing line. "Some weeks she never slept a wink," Chandler wrote; at other times she "has laid down on the hearth with the fire to prepare her for hell. Her distress was so great that she would sweat and it would roll down from her head to her toe as though water was poured on her head." It was "generally thought," by her friends and neighbors, "that she was beside herself," for she would not go to meetings and omitted prayers because of her "melancholy."[41] These melancholy women clearly were not responsible for their madness but were among those suffering from the "unsearchable judgements of god." Mather had appeared to link melancholy with sin in *The Angel of Bethesda;* here no such connection was made by the attending ministers. Melancholy, like all forms of insanity, could invoke blame or pity, depending on the circumstances of its appearance. It seems to have been more likely, however, to elicit sympathy.

While the relationship of the distracted person to God or the devil was central to the understanding of madness for much of the colonial period, in the middle of the eighteenth century the supernatural context in which it had been securely located began to diminish in potency. Instead, failure to live within certain moral limits came to be seen as the cause, and the role of God and the devil began to fade as the supernatural aspects moved from center stage. Though these moral limits ultimately were rooted in the divine law, they were increasingly discussed in the context of natural law, a law accessible to human reason. Men and women were becoming capable of going mad on their own, with little help from God and none from the devil.

In mid-eighteenth-century Massachusetts, madness began to be explained as the result of moral irregularities or excess passions that could be overcome by renewed efforts at self-control. While such moral irregularities were clearly connected to earlier notions of personal sin, those elaborating the new ideas unlike an earlier generation, did not discuss them in the language of theology. The issue of faith was no longer as central to the discussion. Behavior, not belief, was the linchpin around which the newer theory of madness was fashioned.

Passions had been important to English explanations of insanity since the early sixteenth century, when Sir Thomas Elyot wrote the "first manual of popular . . . medicine in the vernacular." In it he argued that "affects and passions of the mind . . . do not only annoy the body, and shorten the life, but also do impair and sometimes lose utterly a man's estimation. . . . They bring a man from the use of reason."[42] Edward Reynolds, writing in the seventeenth century, also was convinced that excess passions caused mental derangement.[43] William Harvey, the famous English physician, linked passions to problems with circulation of the blood and agitation of the heart.[44] Yet these theories about the role of passions do not appear in discussions of madness in Massachusetts until the middle of the eighteenth century. Before then, religious explanations had more power than matters of human psychology over the New Englanders' imagination.

Massachusetts continued to be a strongly religious society in the years before the Revolution, so the shift to ethical imperatives in explaining madness was first presented by the still powerful ministers.[45] The explanations of insanity had not lost their proscriptive tone; rather, this theme now had a more secular cast. More secular, but not completely so, for while madness was no longer discussed as a punishment from God, it was still seen as the natural result of breaking God's law. This law presumably could be known through reason. Enlightenment thought had clearly begun to be important in the discourse about madness.

The new emphasis on moral turpitude and irregular habits first appeared in Massachusetts in 1740 in a sermon by Solomon Williams, who introduced these themes in a broader religious context at the burial of a suicide. According to Williams, distraction arises when, "through the ignorance and perverse desires of the Mind, the bodily motions are become irregular, and through the Inordination of the animal motions, irregular desires are continually excited in the Mind," so that "tis vainly and wickedly pursuing its happiness in the gratification of its tentative appetites to the neglect of God." In this way "Man thereby continually increases his own Disorder." These irregular bodily motions lead to a condition wherein "the Blood and other Fluids move too slow or too fast; From whence Pain, melancholy, stupor and distraction ensue."[46] Williams combined contemporary English medical explanations of madness, especially humoral theories and the "irregular motions" idea of Nicholas Robinson and others, with his own version of the newer moral perspective. God is mentioned as a passive figure who is neglected, not as an active cause of insanity. Clearly, these immoral habits were sins, though Williams did not call them such. Instead, his causal sequence moved from moral lapses to physical irregularities, which in turn affected reason. As in Mather's *The Angel of Bethesda*, the way in which those different orders—moral, physical, and mental—were linked was not explored, since their unity was assumed.

Williams delivered his sermon at the burial of David Trumble, a young man who had drowned himself. The congregation must have been confused as to whether David died in guilt or innocence. After linking insanity with "perverse desires of the mind," Williams proceeded to assure the boy's parents that since he was in a "state of distraction," God would not punish him for his suicide. According to this sermon, while madness might be brought on by one's own failures, suicide while in the state of madness was not a matter of moral responsibility.[47]

The fatalism that had been a leitmotiv in earlier discussions of madness was still present, for Williams was not optimistic about the reversibility of insanity. He believed that "according to the ordinary and standing Laws of Nature it was impossible that his Reason could have been restored." Death, he added, was preferable to life in "that state." Reason was the supreme gift of God, and its loss was the greatest of all calamities.[48] Williams's glorification of reason is a further indication of the impact of the Enlightenment in Massachusetts. Reason did not have an exalted place in Puritan theology. Instead, Puritan divines taught that it had been corrupted by the Fall, and unless redeemed by grace, reason could be man's enemy as easily as his friend.[49] Williams's sermon suggests that the Calvinist view was beginning to be eclipsed by a newer one.

In 1752 Charles Chauncey gave his Boston congregation a mixed message about insanity and other unfortunate conditions. Although he did not mention the insane directly, they were likely to have been included in his category of "disabled persons." On the one hand, Chauncey wished these "disabled persons," to be condemned, because their "follies and Vices" had brought them to their present "incapacity for labor." He lamented that "it is very unhappy indeed when this is the Case, as God knows it too often is. . . . And such Persons have infinite Reasons to look back upon their past mad and sinful conduct with grief and shame." Yet, in spite of their responsibility for bringing on their own condition, they were to be forgiven. They were, suggested Chauncey, "the proper objects of Charity." He concerned himself only with those poor disabled persons who were "naked and destitute" and exhorted his congregation to "give them those things which are needful to the Body."[50] He was attempting to distinguish between the worthy and unworthy poor. He placed "disabled persons" in the former category because of their incapacity for work, even though their condition was caused by past transgressions. Like Williams, Chauncey apparently believed that, while distraction itself was the result of personal failings, the behavior of those who were insane could not be judged.

Ministers would naturally take every opportunity to point out the moral implications of insanity and had done so since the seventeenth century. The question of what the rest of the residents of the Massachusetts Bay Colony thought about madness is more elusive. Although such evidence is limited, there is some suggestion that the growing connection between madness and personal culpability was not confined to the ministry.

The lay view of David Trumble's madness can be found in the newspaper article describing his death. In it his distraction was described as having been brought on by "too much study and a recent case of the measles." The paper reported that David was brought home to Boston from Yale when he first felt a "Disorder of Mind coming on"—a disorder that soon "turned into a Distraction." He was kept home until his suicide.[51] Here madness is caused by both personal excess and physical illness. This article suggests that degrees of insanity were recognized in this period, as evidenced by the various stages of disintegration suffered by young Trumble.

Samuel Coolidge, about whom we will hear more later, was a Harvard College graduate, ne'er-do-well, and sometime schoolteacher. He was supported by the overseers of the poor of Watertown as a distracted resident in the 1740s and 1750s. When his madness struck him, he was given to wandering and boisterous behavior. At these times the Watertown selectmen charged with responsibility for the insane Coolidge exhorted him several times to "behave well" and to "reform."[52] Similarly, in 1749 Joseph Belcher wrote to his nephew concerning another nephew, Simeon Stoddard, also mad and also a Harvard graduate, who was from a very respectable family in Boston, "I Pity your poor Unhappy Brother and pray God to restore him to his Reason and give him an awakening Sense of his Wicked Life."[53] These bits and pieces of evidence, all that have survived, suggest that the notion of personal responsibility for insanity seems to have been growing among the lay population as well. However, the most important evidence about how the average folk thought about madness can be found in the way they responded to their insane friends and neighbors, a subject explored in the next chapters.

In a suicide sermon delivered by another minister in 1767, the causes of madness have become almost completely emptied of their religious content. In this homily, Samuel Philips distinguished between sinful suicide resulting from temptation by the devil and suicide as a result of a "disorder of the mind." Like Chauncey and Williams, he believed that those "wholly bereaved of reason" who killed themselves were not guilty of sin and did not deserve to be punished. Most suicides acted out of distraction, according to Philips, who suggested a homely list of "ways to avoid suicide" and, by implication, distraction. These included "don't worry too much about your body, don't despair; don't miss Sabbath or sleep during meetings; and be careful of drinking too much." In general, warned Philips, "avoid bad habits."[54] Unlike Williams, who gave his sermon twenty-seven years earlier, Philips never mentioned God as either an active or passive cause of insanity. Still, his list included religious as well as physical and psychological factors, its mixed nature suggesting that the older religious views had not been completely discarded. There was clearly a difference, though, as insanity was no longer thought to be visited upon the victim by God or the devil, but was instead considered to be the result of a personal choice that assaulted certain religious, biological, or ethical imperatives. "Hypochondria" was mentioned several times as a precipitator of distraction; perhaps it was particularly common in mid-eighteenth-century New England.

An important shift signaled by the sermon lies in Philips's admonition to his congregation to call a physician for those "under Trouble of Mind." Philips urged, "Don't say, as many do, that no Physician can relieve us because our Trouble is altogether a Trouble in Mind, and the Body is not at all affected." This attitude is wrong, according to Philips, "because Trouble of Mind often starts with Trouble in the Body."[55] The distracted should seek the help of a physician, but if he cannot find a bodily cause of the melancholy, a minister *may* be able to help. This is the first indication that a physician was to be preferred to a minister in solving the thorny problem of distraction. It indicates something even more important—a new sense that madness could be interrupted, that its course could be stayed. While Williams had been highly pessimistic about the possibility of help for the mad, Philips was encouraging, even insistent. He saw insanity as having natural as opposed to godly or satanical causes, and therefore he was convinced that it had natural, as opposed to prayerful, remedies.

It would be more than twenty years before the medical profession offered a fully developed theory of madness that linked the disparate moral, psychological, and biological elements tentatively advanced in the middle of the century. In the meantime, the changes that took place in the conception of madness in the middle of the eighteenth century did not involve a complete abandonment of the supernatural dimension but rather led to a softening and blurring of it. By 1770 God's Providence would be acknowledged as the final cause of madness, but in a way that was too general to offer much explanatory power.[56] The natural order was still linked to the supernatural one, but the emphasis had shifted so profoundly that the supernatural dimension was referred to only in a perfunctory way; instead, attention focused on the more interesting and accessible natural sphere.

The theme of increasing personal responsibility for madness and a diminishing role for supernatural actors is perhaps the most crucial element in this change first suggested by sermons in the mid eighteenth century. This new emphasis on individual responsibility was also appearing in other aspects of life in the Bay Colony: the Great Awakening had given an increased role to individuals in their own salvation; self-interest was increasingly characterizing economic relationships in Boston; the Enlightenment itself offered the possibility of human control over hitherto unthinkable frontiers. The structure of causality was changing everywhere in the Colonies around the time of the Revolution, as human referents for actions began to replace Providential ones.[57] The new understanding of madness was to be only one reflection of this change.

As a result of this shift toward individual responsibility, madness could be explained apart from the direct actions of God or the devil; insanity was beginning to come under human control. Yet the belief that madness was a matter of human responsibility could lead to an increasing suspicion that the distracted were culpable. While the earlier way of explaining insanity had exonerated the holy man and woman and blamed the sinner, it was now becoming a matter of general shame, since under the new rubric no such flexibility remained. The moral content of madness had not been emptied; instead, it was increasingly based on reason and natural law rather than on theology; it rested on a new, secularized notion of sin. The instructive value of insanity, carefully cultivated since the seventeenth century, was not lost; it was merely redefined. After the Revolution, New Englanders would turn completely away from the supernatural in their effort to understand madness and focus instead on the relationship between the moral and physical aspects of man's nature.

But for a good deal of the colonial period, Massachusetts residents had a surety about their understanding of madness that would not be replicated later. Insanity was explained in the same way as many things were explained: as a result of a combination of supernatural and natural forces that were part of an interlocking and unitary framework of causality. This explanation of madness was a powerful one simply because it was embedded in the overarching symbolic world that gave meaning to all events. For those who believed, and many did, madness was mostly God's business.

2 A Familiar and Pitiful Sight

Samuel Coolidge, Harvard College graduate and Watertown schoolmaster, lived out much of his life a thoroughly insane man. The reaction that he elicited in those who knew him in eighteenth-century Massachusetts indicates the range of responses to madness that existed in this period. Coolidge first appears in the records as a student librarian at Harvard, where his distracted and unruly behavior brought him much trouble, though he was not formally asked to leave the school. After he left Harvard as a graduate in 1738, "a place was found for him as Chaplain of the Garrison on at Castle William."[1] While there, he continued to act in unusual ways, as is illustrated by a letter he wrote to a Boston publisher. "For Dust we all are and by a Just and irrevocable Decree of the Almighty unto Dust we must return there is Scripture you Dog you."[2] His madness increased. He returned to Harvard to work but was dismissed after three years for misbehaving "as a Vagabond . . . , carrying himself in an insolent and outrageous manner, indulging himself in Cursing and Swearing profanely, in drinking to Excess, in a rude and indecent Behavior at Divine Worship . . . , Insulting and reproaching to Governors of this house, Hindering the Students from their Business and abusively endeavoring to force himself into their chambers."[3] Coolidge was banished from Cambridge in 1743 and became a "familiar and pitiful sight" in his hometown of Watertown, having wandered there from Cambridge. Since he had no means of support, town selectmen took up a collection to furnish him with winter clothing. He managed to eke out an existence there for nearly a year, depending on the goodwill of his neighbors. A place was found for him as a school-master in Westborough, but he could not keep the job and he sank into "great Horrors and Despairs," leaving there in 1744 "being far gone in Despair, sordidness and viciousness." At the Harvard commencement in 1745, Coolidge appeared in "his Distractions and Delirium" and was "plucked out of the president's Chair in the Meeting House and dragged out on the Ground by a Negro like a Dead Dog in presence of all the Assembly." He returned to Watertown as a vagrant in 1749, and the selectmen there agreed to pay his board and give him clothing if he would serve as their schoolmaster. For the rest of his days Coolidge was a charge of his hometown and taught school there whenever he was able to function. In his bad periods he would wander through the streets of Watertown and Cambridge disheveled and half-naked, often disrupting classes at the college. After one of his Cambridge visits, he was taken before a justice of the peace, who ordered Watertown selectmen to keep him in his hometown. He was later arrested in Boston for disorderly behavior and returned to Watertown by the constables of Charlestown. In 1750 Coolidge was confined to the town jail for a week because no one in the town would keep him. He soon escaped and continued his wandering. The desperate selectmen tried to get him into the Boston workhouse, agreeing to reimburse that town for the cost of his keep. That scheme failed, and Watertown accepted final responsibility for Coolidge. His brushes with the law in neighboring towns always resulted in his being returned there, sometimes after being physically retrieved by Watertown selectmen. He lived at various homes in Watertown in his last years at town expense, teaching school when he could. Selectmen sometimes locked him in the schoolhouse at night to ensure that he would be there to perform his duties the next day. When he was most unruly, the town paid someone who "had to remain at home to keep a hand on him." His condition worsened in 1763 and he became wilder. After that, the townsfolk refused to board him, so he was locked up in a room in a private home, where he lived another year until his death in 1764.[4]

Coolidge's madness did not eliminate his responsibility to repay Watertown residents for their support. He was expected to function as town schoolmaster (for no pay) in spite of his distraction. Town fathers were not happy at having to support him; they repeatedly exhorted him to behave and urged him to cease his wanderings.[5] But they made little attempt to interfere with his mad behavior until he became completely obstreperous at the end of life.

Coolidge was not the only insane schoolmaster in eighteenth-century Massachusetts. Nathan Prince was fired from Harvard in 1741 for "rude and ridiculous gestures" and for generally disturbing the studious atmosphere of the college with his bizarre conduct. During his appeal of his dismissal to the General Court, Prince became "temporarily Disordered in the Brain" and lost his case. He was subsequently asked to leave Boston on the grounds that he might be a financial charge, but was again granted residency in the town several months later. At that time, though his madness was clearly evident, he was granted permission to establish a school. When that arrangement did not work out, he moved to Stratford, where he taught school again. His madness periodically plagued him during his years as a schoolmaster.[6]

Colonial Massachusetts residents were probably far more accustomed to the sight of distracted persons wandering around town and countryside than were later generations. Coolidge was a familiar sight, as was Noyes Parris, son of Samuel Parris, leading participant in the witchcraft hysteria. After a successful ministry of several years, Noyes began to go mad and went to live with his brother in Sudbury in the late 1730s. From there he had the habit of roaming throughout the countryside, returning regularly to his brother's house.[7]

Ministers provide perhaps the most startling examples of madmen generally able to live out their lives in external, if not internal, peace. Joseph "Handkerchief" Moody, minister and graduate of Harvard College, was probably the most famous of these distracted ministers in early eighteenth-century Massachusetts.[8] Immortalized in a short story by Nathaniel Hawthorne, Moody began wearing a handkerchief over his face in 1738 because he felt himself unfit for the company of others. When dining with members of his congregation, he sat at a separate table and turned his face toward the wall. While leading his congregation in prayer at his church in York, Maine, he stood with his back turned toward them. Only after three years of this behavior did the church council remove him as their official minister. Even so, for the next ten years Moody preached occasionally, until he found it impossible to speak aloud in public and had to be persuaded by friends to mime his prayers in morning visits to his congregation.

Samuel Chandler, another minister in York, was a friend of Moody's who sought to help him. In 1746 he wrote in his diary, "I went down to town and preached for Mr. Moody and administered the Sacrament at his desire and consent of the Church, he being broken and shattered."[9] In 1750 Chandler participated in a day of prayer for Moody organized by the distracted minister's congregation. "Today was observed as a day of fasting and prayer in the second church in York to humble themselves under Divine powers having had two pastors and both living and both as to them useless, save that Mr. Moody was not present, the fast was further to pray for his restoration and to seek for direction," he wrote.[10] Prayer and fasting were the only recourse open to Moody's congregation, who, though they may have found him "useless," allowed him to continue ministering to them as best he could. He died at the age of 53 still wearing his handkerchief, and still occasionally tending his flock.[11] While his madness certainly interfered with his career, it did not end it. Moody's son, Samuel, seems also to have been distracted. The younger Moody, a schoolteacher in eighteenth-century Massachusetts, had the habit of wandering through town in a green flannel gown and tasselled stocking cap, begging for bread. He finally quit his job as schoolmaster and devoted his full time to wandering about the countryside.[12]

The congregation of the Reverend Samuel Checkley showed a similar patience to that of Joseph Moody's. Checkley wept almost continually, even when in the pulpit. He had lost nine of his twelve children before they reached maturity. Shortly after the last one died in 1752, he suffered a mental collapse. Checkley was pastor of the New South Church from the 1730s to the mid 1760s, when another minister was appointed to help him. He continued to live at the church until his death in 1769, tolerated by the congregation, to whom he used to deliver sermons in gibberish.[13]

Thomas Gilver, a distracted minister in Topsfield in the mid eighteenth century, was not as fortunate as some of his colleagues, perhaps because his madness took on a less benign form. His wife said his "distemper" came upon him while he was fasting and in rainy weather. The congregation was not sympathetic and charged him with giving reproachful and reviling speeches from the pulpit. This was probably harder to tolerate than Checkley's gibberish. Gilver finally refused to give any more services at all, whereupon the congregation petitioned the court to free them from this "intolerable burden," a request the court granted.[14] Gilver's refusal to preach was the last straw as far as his congregation was concerned; it caused them to abandon their remaining patience.

Another minister with bizarre habits, Joseph Belcher of Easton, Massachusetts, had the habit of "going to the church with his pockets full of sermons which he kept reading until dark," long after the congregation had left. Belcher served the congregation from 1731 to 1744 in this manner, until the church council finally voted to oust him. What precipitated the exhaustion of their goodwill is unknown. In revenge, he took all the church records and town records with him on his departure. When confronted by church members, he denied having these records, claiming that the Covenant did not exist and that, "if there was no Covenant there could be no Church, and if no Church, no Records." After this episode, Belcher took on the job of schoolmaster in Stoughton, a role he performed from 1747 to 1752. When his wife died in 1753, he apparently sank further into madness and fled the town after borrowing money and mortgaging his property, leaving his children behind. He was never heard from again.[15]

The most famous example of a distracted yet eminent colonist was James Otis, Jr., an important political figure in pre-Revolutionary Massachusetts.[16] Otis saw his public career end in "majestic ruins" in 1770, when, after a long pattern of irascible and bizarre behavior, he exploded into a "mad freak" and broke all the windows in the Boston Town Hall.[17] Another account has him "madly firing the guns out of his window" on that grim day. After this outburst, his friends "took charge and removed him to the country."[18] Otis began practicing law in Boston again a year later and was elected to the provincial assembly. There he relapsed: "he raved, jumped out of windows and was pitifully bewildered to find his clients seeking other assistance." As a distracted person, he was assigned a guardian by the judge of probate and removed from town forcibly to confinement in the country. Three years later Otis again reentered public life, this time in the thick of the pre-Revolutionary political turmoil. He relapsed again, was confined to his father's house in Barnstable, where he spent the war years (teaching school part of the time), and reappeared several times in public life whenever he temporarily regained his rationality. On these occasions his friends gave him important, responsible positions (such as moderator of the town meeting and advocate in a case before the court of Common Pleas), which he managed to handle for very brief periods of time. At other times he was seen to be "wandering the roads again," or "making himself a nuisance" at Harvard College.[19] Otis spent the last years of his life in the home of a Mr. Osgood in Andover, who kept several insane on his large farm.[20]

Well before that dramatic day in 1770, Otis had demonstrated the strange inconsistencies of behavior, violence, emotional outbursts, and "incessant talking" that were to characterize his latter years. Yet he was a highly influential and respectable member of the Boston pre-Revolutionary legal and political community. His madness did not carry a permanently disabling status. He maintained the respect of his colleagues and was welcomed back to political life whenever he could manage it.

While violent and threatening behaviors were promptly suppressed—witness Otis being removed to the country after his day of destruction—the evidence strongly suggests that Massachusetts residents were not unduly alarmed by less truculent kinds of madness. The response to the more benign forms was probably laced with a dose of fatalism. With both kinds of distraction there seems to have been an expectation that the mad would return to their senses, a belief that insanity was an episodic rather than a constant condition.

Those who did fall upon hard times while mad frequently returned to their previous status as soon as they recovered. Daniel Kirtland, who graduated from Yale in 1720, was dismissed by his church council in Connecticut shortly afterward on the grounds that he was insane. He later regained his sanity and was appointed minister of another church in Connecticut.[21] A young Harvard graduate, Abiel Leonard, had a "fit of distraction" in 1769 in which he went "raving mad." He later recovered and went on to become a leading minister, living out the rest of his life peacefully. During this episode, his friends sent for his mother, who stayed with him until he recovered. She summoned a physician who could do nothing but pronounce him "distracted" and leave.[22] Similarly, John Mascarene of the Harvard class of 1741 was insane for a time but recovered to live a prosperous, useful life.[23] Dummer Jewetts, another Harvard College graduate and a noted lawyer, was periodically deranged during the decade preceding the Revolution, although he continued to practice his profession. He figured prominently in the Revolution in spite of his distraction, but he finally jumped from a window to his death in 1788.[24] Jonathan How, a resident of Westborough, Massachusetts, was warned out of Boston as "crazy" in 1737. Later in the same year, apparently recovered enough to open a tavern, he was issued a liquor license by the Middlesex County Court.[25]

While this was the predominant reaction to madness, there is some indication that it could be a source of shame and embarrassment for a few. Cotton Mather, for instance, feared the exposure of what he thought was his wife's insanity and its impact on his reputation. In his diary in 1719 he wrote: "I have lived for near a Year in a continual Anguish of Expectation, that my poor wife by exposing her Madness, would bring a Ruin on my ministry. But now it is exposed, my Reputation is marvellously preserved among the People of God, and there is come such a general and violent blast upon her own head as I cannot but be greatly troubled by it."[26] Although Mather did not elaborate about the kind of opprobrium she suffered, clearly the damage done to his wife's reputation did not extend to his own. Yet he worried that it might, which suggests that insanity could be considered scandalous. Mather viewed his wife's madness as a distress given him by God to "quicken his obedience and finish his Repentance," and he "prayed for grace to behave myself well under my Distress." Yet he himself did not necessarily condemn the mad; in a later entry that year he noted that a "poor man, under grievous Distraction, must have my compassion expressed for him in all the ways I can think of."[27]

Lydia Mather's madness was cause for great distress for her husband, while other insane persons elicited his compassion. Since her insanity was characterized mostly by violent outbursts, described by Mather as "Satanic Possessions," this kind of distraction may have been a greater source of embarrassment than the milder forms, particularly for a minister.

The association of shame with madness is also evident later in the century in a letter Robert Treat Paine wrote in 1762 to a friend regarding the early signs of insanity of his friend, Abiel Leonard, who was to become raving mad seven years later. In discussing a day of prayer to be held by Leonard's friends on his behalf, Paine asked that the meeting be kept private and held at a private house. He explained that because of the "nature of this thing, one would desire it to be kept more secret."[28]

Yet all told, there are surprisingly few indications that madness was a matter for shame. Ministers by and large were able to escape disgrace when mad. Perhaps in these instances distraction could be viewed as test from God to the righteous, in which case feelings of empathy, not of condemnation, would be evoked. Yet even when madness became a matter of disgrace, there was little effort made to punish or restrain the insane who were not threatening others.

Some of the insane in colonial Massachusetts endured a far more difficult fate, however. While relatively few were confined, the severity of the treatment of those who were has fueled the argument that the colonists were cruel in their treatment of the mad.[29] One example of such mistreatment is offered by the case of Goodwife Witty of Braintree. The records show that in 1689 the town authorized payment to her brother Samuel Speare to build a house seven feet long and five feet wide near his own house for his insane sister's habitation.[30] The unfortunate Goodwife Witty never surfaced in the records again.

A search of town histories and records reveals three other examples of confinement of the insane in Massachusetts. Watertown officials arranged for the care of a "distracted child" in 1701. Five pounds per year was authorized out of the town budget to "maintain the child with sufficient meat, drink, washing, lodging, clothing (both wool and linen) in all respects as he had when he first came to said Whitney's . . . , provided said Child continue in his ordinary health and reason and be not disorderly in his carriage to said Whitney nor to said Whitney's wife."[31] The next year the town authorized another resident to keep the child. This time he was to be kept in a "little house . . . if he be distracted."[32] Here is a clue to the reason for confinement of the insane in the colonial period. The child may have been "disorderly" and may have exhibited violent or insulting behavior toward the first family who cared for him. It is likely that he was confined mostly when his behavior was extremely disruptive. John Swift, a minister in Framingham, also built separate quarters for his distracted wife in the 1740s.[33] No description of her behavior at the time has survived, although there is an earlier record in Middlesex County Court in 1720 of a John Swift and his wife bringing charges against Jonathan Maynard, a neighbor who had come to the Swift's house and held a gun on Mrs. Swift. He claimed she had come to his home in a "distracted" and "crazy state," threatening him many times. He said he would shoot her if she came again. Maynard pled "not guilty" and was fined by the court. If this is the same Mrs. Swift her husband may have locked her up to keep her from engaging in such "crazy" behavior.[34]

Israel Chauncey's story is an example of home confinement gone wrong. Chauncey, minister and graduate of Harvard College in 1724, settled in the western part of the state and tended a congregation in Berkshire County. He returned to his father's home sometime around 1727 when he became mad, and later was confined in a "small out-house," which burned down and incinerated him.[35] The newspaper account stated that "Chauncey of late was under a great Degree of Distraction, which obliged his Father to confine him in the out-house Building now consumed, where he used frequently in the Night Time to cry Fire in the most vehement Manner, without the least Occasion, which was the Reason why the Family took no Notice of his Cries when the Building was really on Fire."[36] If Chauncey's behavior was indicative of some earlier outbursts, his family may well have viewed him as unruly and felt the need to confine him. Or his disruptive behavior may have begun after he was confined. The reasons for his confinement and agony are lost to history.

Confinement was most likely to be the community's response to any violent behavior. Insofar as a mad person was seen to be running amuck, destroying person or property, he was controlled. Coolidge, for example, was confined in chains at one point in 1751 by the man paid for his care, because he became "disorderly." Toward the end of his days in 1763, he became "very much Disordered," and the town bought a lock for him and "thus put an end to his wanderings."[37] And although Otis's bizarre behavior was largely ignored, when he "raved and jumped from windows" in one of his frenzies, he was "carried off . . . in a post chaise, bound hand and foot."[38] When Henry Babcock was arrested and stripped of his command as a colonel of the Rhode Island militia in 1775, on charges of insanity, he was accused of being in a "lunatic frenzy."[39]

The violent mad constituted a direct threat to the well-being of others, and for this reason it was necessary to respond effectively to them.[40] The more benign forms of distraction, on the other hand, presented no challenge to the security of the townsfolk and therefore were not a matter of great concern. Part of the reason for this was the sense that little could be done to help the mad. But the most crucial factor seems to have been that colonial society had not yet found it important to insist on the more uniform standards of behavior that would underlie the response to most kinds of madness in later periods.

The evidence indicates that most of the insane in eighteenth-century Massachusetts were left alone if they did not become a financial burden to the community and if they did not present the threat of violence. The less privileged experienced a similar response to those who were more prominent. One such afflicted person was John Jubeart, a counterfeiter sentenced to death in 1769. Jubeart described his years of mental derangement in his preexecution confession. He was "thrown into a deep melancholy by the death of his wife" and became "unsettled and at times delirious." He was "haunted by uncomfortable ideas which he could only alleviate by continually moving from one place to another." He spent years wandering from place to place in an irrational, "distracted" state, occasionally stealing and working at odd jobs to support himself. He was left alone by the officials of the towns into which he wandered because he managed to support himself.[41]

In the smaller towns of Massachusetts, insane behavior may even have been viewed with some wry amusement. *Brampton Sketches*, a history of one such town (now called Hopkinton) was written in the late nineteenth century.[42] Though exact dates are not given, the author described several town residents from "the middle of the last century" who were considered to be insane. One "mad woman" roamed daily over the hills and fields of Brampton, happy and harmless. Surviving by means of begging, she was well liked in the town. Though this woman was financially dependent, she was apparently able to eke out a living by appealing informally to the generosity of the community.

Another "queer character" living in Hopkinton in the mid eighteenth century was Billy Buck, the "town Pauper," who lived in the almshouse. Billy's "insane" behavior included making insulting speeches, in high-flown language, which he delivered to everyone he met. His favorite audience, though, was the "waving stocks of corn in the field," which he addressed with "impassioned gestures."[43]

Brampton apparently had more than its share of distracted characters. Jack Downs, the "village jester," took particular delight in attaching a fish hook to a pin and lifting the wigs off the heads of fellow worshippers during Sunday service. He was also famous for throwing rotten apples at the minister's head during the sermon. Perhaps the most bizarre behavior in this eighteenth-century town was that of the five Smith brothers, who "held themselves aloof from the village folks and had their own ceremonies." The eldest brother, for instance, wore a hat with a band on it saying, "I am God." The others spent much time and effort attempting to convince other townspeople that he was indeed God. On Sundays, all the brothers would march around the meeting house seven times in stately procession. Another of their customs was never to turn back. If they had to return to the place whence they started, they would go any distance rather than turn back. According to this local historian, all these characters, though clearly distracted, were "tolerated and found amusing."[44]

In another town history, Charles Leonard, who lived "around the time of the Revolutionary War," is described as wandering around the streets of the town in "filthy clothes, deranged." He wore tattered garments and "sometimes frightened people." One example of this man's bizarre behavior was his "throwing the Bible into the fire after cutting it in two." He also talked gibberish and laughed in a "wild, insane manner." The townspeople generally left him alone and supported him out of the town coffers.[45]

In the *History of Winchester, Massachusetts*, a mad spinster member of the Thomas Belknap family is described as haunting the fields of the town at night in the 1760s. She appointed herself guardian of the gate that marked the entrance to the town: she stopped riders and questioned them, often attempting to refuse them entrance. Though the townsfolk viewed her as thoroughly distracted, they did nothing to interfere with her.[46] This story suggests an indifference in the face of bizarre behavior that later generations would have surely interrupted.

Madness certainly was not as threatening as witchcraft to the Massachusetts Bay colonists. Witches were seen as people with a great potential for doing harm; they were blamed for all kinds of things, personal and communitywide, that may have gone wrong in early New England.[47] Not so the mad. Rather than epitomizing potential harm or evil, the distracted residents of Massachusetts Bay Colony became a serious problem only when they actually engaged in harmful or destructive behavior. Perhaps this is one of the reasons why most were generally left to go their own way; they were not perceived as people who necessarily would cause harm, even though there certainly was evidence that some insane did in fact become violent. Although these were summarily dealt with through restraint or confinement, presumably any violent behavior would have invoked a similar response. The potential loss of control implicit in madness did not seem threatening to the Bay colonists.

Witches, on the other hand, while not irrational, directly assaulted the religious meanings fashioned by the colonists to order their reality. The challenge posed to the Puritan symbolic order by witchcraft was far more severe than that represented by madness, which was explained and thereby diffused by this same symbolic order. Insanity did not set off the deep stress points in colonial society that witchcraft did, which is another way of saying that the issues raised by madness were not as crucial in colonial Massachusetts as those provoked by witchcraft.[48] Witches harnessed the power of the supernatural to do harm; the distracted confronted the colonists with meaningless, potentially uncontrolled behavior. The reaction to madness suggests that issues of meaning and control were not electric ones in colonial Massachusetts.

The belief that madness could be cured through medical intervention was not widespread in eighteenth-century Massachusetts. Family and friends of the distracted rarely called on physicians to attend them; if anyone outside the immediate family was involved, it was likely to be the local minister, who offered the more widely accepted remedies of prayer and fasting. This lack of interest in medical remedies was not related to lack of information. The homeopathic suggestions of English physicians such as Nicholas Robinson, William Battie, and Nicholas Culpeper, including bleeding, purging, and emetics, were available in the colonies in the eighteenth century.[49] The practice of these humoral and other remedies in the effort to restore the insane to reason was not uncommon in England in this period.[50] Yet these were rarely offered to the distracted in colonial Massachusetts. One contributing factor may have been the relatively unsophisticated nature of medical practice in the colonies. The diffusion of medical practice in colonial America meant that ministers, women, and others whose primary role was not as medical practitioner were involved in the practice of domestic medicine. The knowledge of English remedies for insanity may have been limited among many of these uneducated practitioners. Yet clearly, members of the growing medical elite in the colonies were familiar with medical approaches to madness. In fact, insane patients were admitted to Pennsylvania Hospital in Philadelphia as early as 1752, although admittedly their treatment was more custodial than medical.[51]

In Massachusetts, however, there was little interest in providing medical treatment for the distracted during much of the eighteenth century. Similarly, there is no sign of the kind of astrological and quasi-magical practices that characterized Richard Napier's treatment of his distracted patients in England in the seventeenth century.[52] Instead, the residents of the Massachusetts Bay Colony, when called upon to minister to the insane, summoned their most powerful weapons—prayer and fasting. The response to many sorts of disaster, especially those involving a threat to community well-being, was to call for fasts and days of humiliation. These were especially common in times of smallpox epidemics.[53] The prayerful response to madness was not unique; it was related to the belief that the supernatural order was directly implicated in distraction, as it was in all things. The powerful religiousness of the Puritans is an important reason why the residents of the colony were slower to look to medical intervention in cases of distraction than were the residents of Pennsylvania.

Ministers in eighteenth-century Massachusetts were frequently called upon to lead the family and friends of the insane through a day of prayer and fasting. Samuel Sewall participated in these days arranged for his distracted friends.[54] Ebenezer Parkman in western Massachusetts provided this service for members of his congregation.[55] Of course, ministers were also expected to visit the distracted members of their congregation on a regular basis in order to pray for them. Both Mather and Parkman visited the distracted in their homes and led their families in prayer.[56] William Thompson's friends and minister prayed for him, as did John Warham's.[57] Samuel Chandler participated in several days of prayer for Joseph Moody.[58]

As late as 1762, a day of fasting and prayer was planned for Abiel Leonard by his friends. By this time medical advice apparently was beginning to be taken more seriously among the educated residents of the colony. Robert Treat Paine, in discussing the plans for this day, warned that other means of treatment might be more essential than prayer. "The greatest and most experienced physicians agree that strict regimen, a total confinement from all company—sometimes to a dark room, severe discipline and subjection to the degree of fear and some medicine" are the most effective ways of treating such a person." Paine's enthusiasm for the advice of medical men did not preclude him from participating in the day of prayer, though, for he knew that "this condition is caused by the Being that governs all" and "can only be treated fully by the Blessing of that being." Therefore, he had "no objection to the day of prayer." Yet prayer was not seen as likely to be the most efficacious means of help; it clearly had a secondary role. Paine felt strongly that Leonard should not be present for the day of prayer since he was "utterly incapable of joining in." Moreover, "the way he will want to be treated on such an occasion" with all his friends present is "directly opposite to the necessary method of his cure." He apparently thought that Leonard needed to be treated with coolness and detachment, something that everyone would find difficult.[59] Paine's letter indicates that medical treatment of distraction was beginning to be seen as helpful (although seven years later a physician summoned by Leonard's mother could do nothing for him). This new perception was related to the shift away from the supernatural order in the understanding of madness that was taking place at the same time in the colony.

When it became common for medical remedies to replace religious ones in Massachusetts is difficult to determine from the records. When Sewall and Mather mentioned going to the home of the distracted to pray, they did not refer to the presence of physicians or any medical efforts. Mather did not say that he called on any physician to help his own wife. Parkman apparently attended distracted members of his congregation without any medical help. In 1749 he sent for a doctor to help a woman who had "fits" while in his church. The doctor, however, declined to attend.[60]

One glimpse of how physicians attempted to help the insane can be found in a letter written by a Massachusetts resident in 1768. In it David Kingman noted that a "French doctor" was called to see a "distracted woman" in Braintree. The people in the town "flocked after him to such a degree that the House would not hold them all and they had to stand outside the windows to see him bleed her."[61] Perhaps the curiosity of the townsfolk was aroused because the sight of a physician ministering to a distracted person was unusual. Since bleeding was a common response to physical disease, it is unlikely that it alone would cause such a stir.

English medical practice emphasized the importance of bleeding as one of the heroic remedies that were thought to be helpful in physical as well as mental disorders. It was sometimes combined with the other heroic remedies of purging, blistering, and the administration of emetics. Based on the humoral theory of the Greeks, such remedies were thought to be akin to natural body responses and were used to keep the humoral system in balance.[62] The English physician William Battie urged that the insane be purged, bled, and evacuated. He was also convinced that they must be removed from all objects "that act upon the nerves" to a "different place." In addition, he felt that all "unruly appetites" of the insane should be checked and their bodies and places of residence be kept clean, while their minds were kept occupied.[63] Nicholas Robinson suggested fresh air and exercise on horseback as well as the more traditional remedies of purges and the administration of opium.[64] In the colonies, Cotton Mather suggested homelier folk remedies for distraction such as the administration of the "blood of an ass drawn from behind the ear." He also advised "riding with agreeable company, leeches, syrup, and drinking whey."[65]

Clearly, suggestions for treating the insane, no matter how fanciful, were not scarce in colonial Massachusetts. Several factors combined to make their use unlikely for the greater part of the colonial period. Unlike Pennsylvania, Massachusetts had no hospitals for the physically ill with the exception of shelters for smallpox victims on two islands in Boston harbor. The inchoate development of medical practice in Massachusetts no doubt was a deterrent to a systematic medical approach to insanity. Yet Tomes found that, while insane persons were admitted to Pennsylvania Hospital in the eighteenth century, only the "most dangerous and disruptive lunatics," not the nonviolent insane, were placed there. This suggests that the medical view of insanity was not necessarily dominant in that colony either.[66] In Massachusetts, madness was thought to be a supernatural as well as a natural phenomenon for much of the colonial period, in which case human intervention alone was unlikely to be considered effective. Furthermore, there really were no effective physical remedies at this time, notwithstanding the suggestions of English physicians. Then again, madness was not viewed as inevitably incapacitating, and certainly not permanently so. An unfortunate condition, to be sure, but not one that wiped out a person's responsibility to be a productive member of society. Since at least some distracted persons in the colony were able to continue to function in society, albeit marginally, the impulse to cure insanity was not a very powerful one. Finally, the fact that Massachusetts residents do not seem to have been particularly frightened of the nonviolent distracted in their midst is likely to have diminished their motivation to search for effective cures.

After the explanations of madness shifted from a religious to an ethical context and the biology of madness was emphasized, a keener interest in offering medical treatment to the distracted as well as in separating them from the larger population, appeared. But for much of the period before the Revolution, the insane lived alongside the sane, with little effort made to cure or confine them. There are exceptions to this pattern, a few cases where the insane were confined under brutal circumstances and no explanation can be teased from the records, but this was not the dominant pattern.

Of course, this muted reaction to insanity was not very helpful in alleviating the suffering of the distracted. In this sense, the reaction should be construed as indifferent rather than tolerant.

Certainly, the residents of Massachusetts Bay Colony cannot be described as tolerant, since other kinds of deviant behavior were strictly prohibited, especially those that treatened religious beliefs or social mores.[67] Madness, however, was not a crime; in fact it could be used as a defense against conviction in the eighteenth century.[68] The distracted residents of the colony were no doubt seen as irritating nuisances, but in general not as persons to be controlled, confined, or cured.

3   Non Compos Mentis in Colonial Massachusetts

Although many distracted residents of Massachusetts were able to live their lives as at least marginally productive members of the community, there were a number who had to depend on the care of others. The family had the clear responsibility to care for any insane members who could not care for themselves, just as it was the initial bulwark against any kind of catastrophe in the eighteenth century. Families were expected to "look after" distracted members, as suggested by the case of Abigail Somes in 1681, whose brother complained that he had been "forced to make it his whole employment to look after her."[1] In addition, family members who lost control of insane relatives left in their care were liable for damage done by their charge. Stephen Atherton of Milton, according to a privately published genealogy, for example, was fined by the town of Concord in 1708 for letting his distracted brother wander into that town and cause a great disturbance.[2]

While cases of private care of the insane are difficult to locate, evidence strongly suggests that family care was the dominant pattern. All of the distracted persons mentioned in the diaries of Parkman and Sewall were cared for in their own homes, as were all the people suffering from various forms of madness in Cotton Mather's accounts. The ministers who went mad in eighteenth-century Massachusetts lived with their families. Nathan Hale, graduate of Harvard in 1739, spend "most of his life" in a room of his father's house in Salem after he went mad. He died there in 1775.[3] In 1786 two Yale graduates, Charles Goodrich and Charles Chauncey, were taken in by their respective families when they went mad.[4] When the family was unable to provide for the insane, friends were sometimes willing to take them in. Joseph Moody spent many years in the home of a member of his congregation. John Adams, a minister who graduated from Harvard in 1721, went mad sometime in the early 1740s. His friends raised funds to keep him in Cambridge; otherwise the town would have insisted he leave, as he had no means of support.[5]

Later in the century private madhouses, which were operated as domestic businesses, appeared and were patronized by families who wished to pay others to care for their insane. Similar establishments served a considerable insane clientele in England in the eighteenth century, where the proprietors frequently advertised the efficacy of their treatment in order to attract clients.[6] In New England word of mouth was sufficient endorsement. James Otis was cared for in two different private asylums in Massachusetts when his madness overtook him. During his most violent period he lived at a home for distracted persons in Hull, owned by Captain Daniel Souther.[7] When he became less obstreperous, he was moved to a farm in Andover, where he peacefully ended his days.[8] For most colonists, however, there was little alternative to family care of the insane. No special provisions were made for any disabled groups at this time in Massachusetts. The sick were nursed in households, not hospitals. The only exception to this pattern was the case of the pauper insane, who were cared for by towns in the same way as were all indigent persons in the colony.

The legal basis for town responsibility for resident insane is found in a law passed by the General Court in 1678. It ordered selectmen in towns disturbed by "unruly Distracted persons" to "take care of all such persons that they do not Damnifie others," and also to "take Care and Order the Management of their Estates in the Times of their Distemperature, so as may be for the good of themselves and Families depending on them; and the Charge be Paid out of the estates of all such persons where it may be had, otherwise at the public charge of the town such persons belong unto."[9] This law assigned public responsibility for control of the mad in case of their causing disturbance or danger. In addition, it protected the rights of the insane by providing for guardianship of their property.

In 1694 the General Court specifically addressed the issue of the care of insane residents of the colony. In "An Act for the Relief of Idiots and Distracted persons," the court stated,

When any person . . . by the Providence of God shall fall into distraction and become *non compos mentis*, and no relations appear that will undertake the care of providing for them, or that stand in so near a degree as that by law they may be compelled thereto, in every such case the Selectmen or Overseers of the Poor of the town or peculiar where such person was born, or is by law an inhabitant, be and hereby are empowered and enjoined to take care, and make necessary effectual provisions for the relief, support and safety of such impotent or distracted persons, at the charge of the town or place whereof he or she of right belongs if the party has no estate of his or her own, the incomes whereof may be sufficient to defray the same.

This statute also empowered justices of the peace to dispose of the estates of distracted persons and use the proceeds to support their families. To defray the cost of town support, judges could order the insane person to "any proper work or service he or she may be capable to be employed in."[10]

The principles for official town response were established by these two laws. Normally the only time madness became an object of concern to town authorities was if the issue of financial dependence arose. Authorities were rarely called on to control a distracted person who had "damnified" others.[11] Towns had little to do with guardianship cases, which usually involved merely the legal sanction by the courts of an existing private arrangement. In cases of dispute, however, town selectmen made the determination of sanity.

When towns were forced to assume responsibility for their resident insane, they usually boarded them in homes of other town residents, who were compensated for their trouble. The same provisions were made for all other paupers in these towns.[12] Some towns were more willing than others to pay for board and care. Selectmen willingly paid for the care of Mary

Goose of Salem after her husband died in 1664.[13] The town of
Braintree paid for Abigail Neal's care from 1699 at least until
1707 but with considerable complaint. Before resigning themselves to ongoing support, the selectmen attempted to rid themselves of her by offering a neighbor twenty pounds to "clear the
town of her forever." The neighbor was not successful in this
charge, and in 1707 Abigail went to live out the rest of her days
as the only insane boarder of a man who kept a number of poor
and sick persons.[14] Haverhill town fathers paid for Lydia Smith's
keep for six years in the 1720s at the house of her neighbor,
until he finally reported that "her reason was restored" in
1728.[15]

Towns did what they legally could to reduce their expenditures for resident paupers. Watertown, as we have seen, boarded
out Samuel Coolidge for over twenty years, periodically trying
to exact repayment by insisting that he teach school. The selectmen of Groton petitioned the court in 1737 for permission to
sell the estate of a townsman named Barrow, who had "fallen
into distraction by the Grace and Providence of God" and became non compos mentis. They complained that they had been
"obliged to provide for his support at the expense of the town."[16]
In a case at the end of the seventeenth century, Concord town
fathers sold one distracted resident into bondage to a farmer in
Charlestown. "Tobe," who apparently had no chance to protest
his banishment from Concord, was probably a slave; he had
gone mad while serving a Concord family.[17]

Occasionally, boarding the insane could be dangerous. In Groton an insane man who was kept as a boarder by a humane sher-
iff (at town expense) in the 1770s, turned on his benefactor and
murdered him.[18] Another mad town charge, Samuel Frost, was
kept by one family or another in Worcester County for almost
twenty years, roaming through the countryside of western Massachusetts from the 1760s on. In 1783 he finally killed the last
man he was boarded with and was subsequently hanged for his
crime.[19]

While the towns of the colony, however begrudgingly, provided for the care of their own pauper insane, they took special
pains to rid themselves of distracted strangers. Measures to con-

trol the nonresident insane were largely a reaction to their status as strangers, rather than to their madness. Warning out was the legal means by which towns ensured that they would not become responsible for indigent strangers. It did not necessarily mean that a person was physically escorted out of town; rather, it served as notice of financial nonresponsibility on the town's part.[20] Some insane who were warned out were already financially dependent, but many others were only "likely to become a charge."[21]

Sometimes towns engaged in long contests with insane strangers in their midst in their efforts to stave off financial dependency. In 1750, Atherton Clark, Harvard College graduate, was warned out of Hopkinton (and asked to leave) on the grounds that he was "so far *non compos mentis* that he was likely to squander away what remained of his estate." Clark enlisted the aid of his friends to fight the town action, but it was through his marriage to a Hopkinton woman that he really won the battle and was allowed to stay. Seven years later, however, he was forced to return to his hometown of Newton by the Hopkinton selectmen on the grounds that he had "squandered away Great Part of his Substance in the most Romantic manner."[22]

Some towns were so eager to rid themselves of insane strangers that they often forcibly returned them to their hometowns. The records of Middlesex General Sessions Court for the early part of the century show several instances of persons reimbursed for "carrying a distracted person from Cambridge" to their town of origin.[23]

Not every town in the Province was so adamant about banishing the distracted strangers. In 1769 a distracted woman came into Townshend "in most distressed circumstances in most severe weather." The overseers thought that "humanity required care should be taken to prevent her from perishing." Anna Valkins was therefore taken into a home in Townshend and provided with food, shelter, and clothing. The town did petition the General Court for relief, since she was not a resident. The court, however, ordered the overseers to continue to "provide her with the necessaries and conveniences of life" while attempting to discover her town of residence. It suggested that the overseers advertise in the Boston and Worcester newspapers to find her family or friends.[24]

The town fathers of the largest town in the Province were particularly eager to rid themselves of distracted strangers. Unlike other towns in Massachusetts, Boston kept its pauper insane in the town almshouse, along with other paupers, for much of the eighteenth century.[25] The town was home to eleven thousand souls by 1720, and the boarding out system was impracticable. When it was not possible to return the nonresident insane to their towns of origin, Boston selectmen would put them in the almshouse, at the same time seeking reimbursement from the town of residence until the unwelcome visitor could be returned home.[26] When the town of origin was unknown, selectmen disposed of the insane stranger as economically as possible. Michael Carney, for instance, fell into a cistern in 1767, was "distracted," and "could not tell from whence he came." In this case selectmen sent Carney to the almshouse.[27] More often, they put the distracted strangers in the bridewell or jail, where they were supported more economically at town expense.[28]

Great pains were taken to remove these troublesome strangers from Boston in the mid eighteenth century. In one case in 1762, selectmen even paid the passage to Guernsey for one insane resident of the town almshouse who was a native of that distant place.[29] In 1767 the town fathers sent a constable to ask the brother-in-law of Joseph Norcross of Brookline, a "distracted person," to come and get him from the almshouse and take him back to Brookline.[30] A strong note to the overseers of Ipswich accompanied Edward Eveleth, who was in turn accompanied by a constable in 1765. The Boston overseers sternly warned that Eveleth was "disordered in his senses," and that "Persons of his turn of Mind being disposed to wander, you should make sure he doesn't return to us or we'll make a charge to your town."[31]

Selectmen even denied payment of board to a Mrs. Pines, who came to the town meeting in 1749 asking to be reimbursed for her care of Widow Pexlen, a stranger to Boston. Mrs. Pexlen, a woman of "very Poor and Disordered Mind," had come to her house several months earlier and had never left. The town selectmen voted that "Mrs. Pines should be satisfied at the charge of the Province for entertaining the said Mrs. Pexlen, until she can be otherwise provided for.[32] The selectmens' reluctance was not based solely on financial reasons, since towns could be reimbursed by the provincial government for the care of nonresident insane. Yet the town rarely assumed that responsibility, probably because of a distaste for encouraging other nonresidents to move into their towns and ask for help.

Some nonresidents of higher social status were treated with more dignity and generosity. Such was the case with the distracted Mr. Bowen of Woodstock, who in the 1770s frequently visited his brother, a prominent minister in Boston, causing the "inhabitants of the town uneasiness and distress." On one of those occasions, the selectmen wrote to the overseers of Woodstock that "we have not taken with him the legal and usual method to remove strangers, as we are compassionate his circumstances." However, they added, "this is the second time we have contrived to send him home in a more private and easy manner," and they asked the Woodstock overseers to take measures to keep Bowen in Woodstock.[33]

Selectmen had a difficult time ridding the town of Sarah Hartshorn, who was warned out as a distracted pauper in 1768 but returned in the 1770s to Boston, where her name appeared on the list of almshouse residents, along with the description "crazy." In 1771 she was released and went to her sister's home. On the day of her release, the overseers sought to ensure her permanent removal, ordering the keeper of the almshouse "to deliver the things belonging to Sarah Hartshorn, disordered in mind, to her sister, who now has agreed to care for her and she is not to return while her sister is alive."[34]

Boston officials were having problems coping with the number of distracted residents in the town in the mid eighteenth century. In 1739 the town established a workhouse where some insane paupers were sent.[35] In a 1751 report the overseers of the poor complained that the workhouse was not self-supporting because of the number of "distracted, helpless and infirm people there."[36] It was during this time that Watertown officials failed in their attempt to have Coolidge admitted to the Boston workhouse. There apparently were a significant number of insane paupers in the Boston almshouse as early as 1729, when the selectmen called a town meeting to consider, among other things, "making some addition to the Almshouse for keeping distracted persons separate from the Poor."[37] Selectmen brought up the subject again in 1746, when they considered a motion of the overseers of the poor "that some proper House may be provided for Distracted Persons."[38] In 1745 they had considered purchasing Bridewell House for a "madhouse."[39] A few months later a committee was appointed to look into the purchase of a "proper house for distracted persons," but apparently the matter was soon dropped.[40]

In 1764 Thomas Hancock left the town a bequest of six hundred pounds for "Erecting a House for the reception of such unhappy Persons as it shall please God in His Providence to deprive of their reason." Selectmen resolved "to determine what steps shall be taken in order to comply 'with the conditions of the bequest.'"[41] Again the matter was dropped, but it surfaced in 1766, when a resolution was passed at a town meeting voting to "open a subscription to raise money for Building and Endowing a Bedlam for the insane."[42] In spite of all this interest, a separate facility for the mad was not built in Massachusetts until the nineteenth century. Until then insane paupers lived alongside sane ones in the town almshouse.[43]

One reason for the uneasiness expressed at this arrangement may have been related to the fact that Boston's almshouse was filled to capacity in the 1760s as a result of a severe economic depression.[44] Perhaps the selectmen there saw the removal of the insane paupers as a way of relieving the overcrowding. But even before this, in the 1740s and 1750s, Boston was undergoing some important changes and dislocations. Poverty began increasing in the town in the late 1730s; by the 1740s, one in four townsfolk had too few assets to pay taxes.[45] In the 1750s Bostonians suffered a smallpox epidemic, serious economic problems as a result of King George's War, and an increased number of poor. During this period, wealth stratification in the town continued to increase. The growing number of persons from neighboring towns who were warned out of Boston in the mid eighteenth century suggests that there was a relatively high rate of mobility in and around the town.[46] All these changes meant that Boston was undergoing severe dislocations in the mid eighteenth century; these ruptures in an older way of life are likely to have had an impact on the Bostonians' reaction to the insane. Increased population in the town, growing numbers of poor there, and economic instability were all related to the problematic status of the distracted paupers in the town.

The provincial government, while technically responsible for distracted paupers with indeterminate residences, in practice had very little to do with the insane in the colony. The only exception to this laissez-faire attitude (which extended to other potential social problems as well) was the case of guardianship arrangements for mad persons with property. In guardianship cases the courts of the Province either appointed guardians or approved already existing arrangements. In addition, the courts alone could revoke a guardianship. These laws were based on the fear that the insane would squander or dispose of their property unwisely and so end up a town charge. Very few guardianship cases appeared in the colony before the 1736 law specifying the procedures for determining mental incompetence.[47] Under its provisions the selectmen of each town were authorized to determine the sanity of the suspected distracted person, but the method to be used was not specified. It is clear, though, that the judgment of insanity was based solely on the perceptions of the selectmen; no physicians were involved. These officials "discoursed" with the suspected madmen and attempted to determine whether they were "wanting of reason."[48]

The kind of issue that the selectmen raised in the determination of insanity can be inferred from the case of one distracted resident of Medfield by the name of Benjamin Hall. In 1770, Hall appealed his guardianship status on the grounds that he was now compos mentis. The Appeals Court for the Province asked the selectmen of Medfield, who had found Hall to be non compos mentis, if they had "ever seen him at a tavern" or known him to "spend money unnecessarily," or "ever heard him make a bargain" unwisely. After each selectman answered no to these questions, the court called upon the Boston selectmen, who were familiar with Hall, to testify as to their opinion of the fairness of his guardianship status. The records show that they responded that "Mr. Hall was a Gentleman" and that they "imagined he was capable of conducting his own affairs." The guardianship was revoked.[49] For men, at least, the proper management of business affairs was crucial to a judgment of sanity.[50] Court records indicate that the guardianship status was always revoked when the person in question managed to argue his case as far as the Appeals Court.[51] In another, earlier case of appeal (1760), Samuel Lothrup petitioned the judge of the Quarterly Courts of Suffolk County to end his guardianship status as he was "worse for being under guardianship." Selectmen paid Lothrup another visit and he was determined to be compos mentis, and guardianship was revoked.[52]

Guardianship, then, was not irreversible. Atherton Clark was in and out of guardianship and successfully petitioned the courts to have it removed on several occasions.[53] James Otis also dispensed with his guardian shortly after he was assigned one. The guardian himself joined in that request and asked the court to "discharge him from the trust" because "James was now restored to his right mind."[54]

The numbers of distracted persons referred to Probate Court for guardianship petitions were relatively low before the Revolution. Between 1733 (the date of the first guardianship case in the records) and 1776, the mental competence of sixteen men and ten women was investigated by the Boston selectmen.[55] In each case the person in question was found to be non compos mentis. After being notified of the decision by selectmen, the Probate Court then named a relative or friend, usually the one who had requested the action in the first place, to serve as the guardian. The guardian was directed to "take care as well of the person as of the estate, both real and personal of the said idiot or distracted persons, and to make a true and perfect inventory of the said estate." Guardians were further enjoined to manage the estate of the insane "frugally and without waste and destruction and to provide for the insane and his family out of the income of the estate." In some cases, the property of the insane person was sold for his support. Guardians were to be given "a reasonable allowance for their charges and trouble," which was to be paid out of the estate. The guardian in return had to give a bond to the judge of probate to ensure his honest management of the estate.[56] In 1764 a standardized form appeared for binding the guardians, an indication that the practice had become fairly widespread.

The case of Henry Dove in 1746 is probably typical. Boston selectmen visited Dove and reported that "at times he has lucid intervals, yet at other times he is so wild and ungovernable that we are of the opinion that he is in no way capable of managing his own affairs." William Haislup, pinmaker, was appointed to be his guardian. After this, disputes between Haislup and Dove led the probate judge to appoint three men to settle the controversy, which revolved around the issue of how much Haislup was to receive for his services. Dove won his case for a lower payment to Haislup and was eventually released from guardianship.[57] Like others under guardianship, Dove was rational at times. It is clear that persons assigned guardians were not presumed to be permanently incapable of handling their own affairs.

Massachusetts residents provided for distracted paupers in the same manner as they did for sane paupers. Whether in board and care arrangements or almshouses, those insane residents whose family or friends could not care for them enjoyed or suffered the same treatment as other dependent townsfolk. Their status as paupers was far more important in determining their fate than was their madness. In general, the financial dependence of the insane was a greater concern than their insane behavior. The guardianship laws were designed primarily to ensure that the insane did not become financially dependent; the great care taken to warn out distracted strangers suggests a related fear of long-term financial incapacity.

While the conceptions of madness in mid-eighteenth-century Massachusetts were moving in the direction of individual responsibility, the reaction to the insane in the Province continued to be one of relative indifference until the decades following the Revolution. The decision of Boston selectmen to put pauper insane in the town almshouse in the eighteenth century did not reflect a greater anxiety about madness; instead, it was related to the need for more institutionalized means of providing for all paupers in the town. Structural changes, such as increasing economic dependence on the part of certain segments of the population, an increase in population, and an accompanying growing complexity of organizational structures, led Boston to formalize its response to all paupers earlier than many other towns in the state. Glimmerings of another reaction to the insane were first suggested by the growing disquiet of the town fathers there at having the sane and insane paupers living side by side, an anxiety not expressed elsewhere. Yet even in Boston this discomfort did not lead to a change in the care of the pauper insane, who continued to live alongside the sane in the almshouse and workhouse until the end of the century.

A paucity of financial and institutional resources in colonial Massachusetts did not encourage the erection of a special building for insane paupers. Yet this is not the most important reason for the decision not to separate them from the rest of the paupers, for, when this separation did occur at the end of the eighteenth century, insane paupers were confined in separate parts of the same almshouses in which they had previously lived. Other distracted residents were confined in already existing town jails. The absence of special institutions was not the key factor in their treatment, just as lack of medical knowledge was not the most significant reason for the very limited efforts to cure them. The most important determinant shaping the response to the insane in eighteenth-century Massachusetts lay in the meaning that madness had for its residents.

The system of beliefs, or symbolic order, shared by many of the residents of this colony to a great extent shielded them from one of the distressing aspects of madness—the apparently meaningless nature of mad behavior. This anomalous quality can threaten to unveil the relativities of accepted ways of thinking and acting. The power of the Puritan symbolic order made such a challenge unlikely and thereby reduced the threat of madness. This is not to say that the Puritan metaphysics did not cause its own deep anxieties around issues of sin, repentance, and salvation. But these people were surer than were later generations of the certainty of their own reality. Their relatively unified and coherent worldview served as a hedge against the anxiety that meaningless behavior may cause. In colonial Massachusetts, those who seemed unable to join that world, who seemed lost in their own private reality, did not present a threat but rather prompted feelings of pity or irritation.

Madness poses another threat to the sane, insofar as the insane seem to be out of control. The anxiety conveyed by the uncontrolled behavior of the mad is not limited to violent behavior. Talking gibberish, wandering, wearing a handkerchief over one's face—all these signal a breakdown of self-control. While the Bay colonists reacted swiftly to those insane who were actually violent, they could apparently tolerate a high degree of uncontrolled behavior so long as it was not violent. The reasons for this can be found in the structure of material life in the towns of colonial Massachusetts. Life there was shaped by a series of external controls, which served to reduce the need for individual self-control. The small size, the patterns of intense social interaction, the complex kinship networks, the persistence of generations in the towns, the legally sanctioned methods of surveillance, and the commitment to communitarian values all formed a system of external controls that caught the individual in an intricate net of personal and public expectations.[58] Life was lived in a highly personal context. These townsfolk were extremely sensitive to the opinions of others; shame may have been a more important sanction for deviant behavior than guilt.[59] Town life imposed such a strong set of external controls that an individual's lack of self-control (as long as violence was not involved) was not crucial.

Furthermore, individual decision making was not strongly valued in many areas of life. Insofar as deference and consensus characterized the political culture, the role of individual political choice was deemphasized.[60] The Bay colonists' economic relationships were often embedded in family, patriarchal, and neighborhood relations. Their own economic choices were limited by these relationships, by the lack of currency in most of the colony, and by the consequent need to barter and exchange on the local level; by the subsistence nature of much of the agricultural production; and by the low growth rate of the colonial economy. All these features of the economy, along with the relative economic equality enjoyed by many of its residents, tended to minimize individual competition and striving.[61] There was far less emphasis on individual economic behavior or decision making than there was to be in the nineteenth century.

Most residents of Massachusetts Bay Colony concerned themselves largely with what was going on in their own and nearby communities. Townsfolk were absorbed in a much smaller world than we are. They did not view themselves so much as isolated individuals, but rather as part of a local community, a community where there may have been a good deal of dissension and periodic strife, the normal quota of discontent and irritation, but a community nonetheless.[62]

In such communities the individual's capacity for rational, independent action and therefore for internal control was not paramount; the ability to forge one's own reality was not crucial. The lack of self-control implicit in madness posed little threat because the need for individual responsibility, decisions, and functioning was not critical. The distracted resident with his or her incomprehensible, annoying, and even occasionally violent behavior could not tear this textured and intricately woven world. The insane could move in and out of this reality, accepted when they could perform their duties in some limited capacity, supported if absolutely necessary, warned out if they were strangers, restrained when they were violent, and otherwise left more or less alone. Distracted strangers would pose a special problem in these towns, for they would not be caught in the same web of expectations, social constraints, familiar patterns of deference, and face-to-face knowledge as were town residents. Their madness was potentially more threatening. For this reason, as well as for their potential financial dependence, they were removed from the towns.

Of course, not all towns fitted this description; Springfield and Boston showed only some of these features, as individual striving and acquisitiveness were more important features of life there. Yet even in these towns, economic relationships were largely embedded in personal contexts.[63] In Boston, selectmen continued to be responsible for surveillance of town residents and strangers up to the Revolution.[64] Yet, because of the population growth of the town and other economic and social dislocations endured by Bostonians in the eighteenth century, some of the mechanisms of external control did not survive. Insanity clearly was a problem there earlier than in other Massachusetts towns, which was the reason why, after 1730, town fathers periodically considered separating the distracted paupers from the others. Yet even in Boston this separation was not accomplished. James Otis wandered in and out of provincial politics in Boston with apparent impunity; paupers continued to live alongside their insane comrades in the Boston almshouses. Some characteristics found in the smaller communities of the colony survived in Boston, and no doubt in Springfield. Perhaps the continuing belief of most Bostonians in a deeply felt supernatural order continued to defuse the potential threat of madness. In any case, Boston's response to the insane was different in 1760 from what it was to be in 1820.

The more affluent, educated members of society who were mad elicited a similar reaction to those who were at the bottom of the economic ladder; there seemed to be little class distinction in the reaction to the insane in eighteenth-century Massachusetts. The "great confinement" of the insane that characterized the early modern period in Europe did not take place in colonial New England, although the movement had clearly begun in Pennsylvania in the eighteenth century. The reaction to the insane in eighteenth-century New England more closely resembled the seventeenth-century world of MacDonald's *Mystical Bedlam*, where the distracted were cared for largely by their families and generally not confined. Yet Puritan New England, especially in the eighteenth century, did share many of the features of the pre-modern world that Foucault and Rosen described as being responsible for the separation of the insane from the sane in Europe, as well as those underlying the asylum-building movement that began in earnest in England in the eighteenth century.[65] In colonial New England the rational elements of the social order did not displace the power of the community to absorb the irrational. Though far from a feudal society, colonial New England replicated the personal context in which life had been lived in earlier times. In addition, the vividness of the Puritan religious imagination, elaborating on the mysteries of the devil, sin, and other imponderables of the supernatural order, provided a foil for the intricacies of this carefully drawn society, a foil the insane did not need to offer. All told, the reaction to madness in colonial Massachusetts was far different from what was to follow.

4　The Medical Face of Madness

The period after the American Revolution was a watershed in the history of insanity in Massachusetts. During this period a medicalization of the understanding of madness took place, as the religious context in which insanity had been elaborated for much of the eighteenth century disappeared and was replaced by a wholly naturalistic view, one in which human biology and personal ethics were joined to create a new understanding of madness. This new approach was eventually to result in the emergence of the mental hospital to confine and treat the insane; by 1833 two hospitals, one public and one private, would be established in the state. The transformation of insanity into an essentially medical problem was the result of the confluence of several wider changes, including the waning of the supernatural explanations evident since the middle of the eighteenth century; the increasing systematization of medicine and professionalization of medical practitioners in Massachusetts; the growing influence of the first American medical colleges in Philadelphia and New York; and European and English speculations about the nature and causes of insanity. The new view of madness liberated the insane from the fatalism of the older supernatural understanding at the same time as it placed the responsibility for insanity squarely on their shoulders.

The new, naturalistic views of madness left little room for the speculations of ministers. If God and the devil were no longer active participants in the drama, ministers had little role in its explanation. Instead, physicians increasingly took up the challenge of explaining madness and treating the insane. An important reason for this was that the inchoate nature of medical practice in eighteenth-century Massachusetts began to be replaced by a more systematic and more self-conscious effort to organize the medical profession after the Revolution. The increased demand for medical care during the Revolutionary War served as a catalyst for the new emphasis on the professionalization of medicine in the state. The appearance of the first medical societies there in the 1780s also was part of the quest for social improvement that characterized these early, heady days of the Republic.[1] The Massachusetts Medical Society, the most important of these groups, initially embodied these new Republican ideals by not insisting on monopoly to practice medicine for its members; instead, for the first thirty years of its existence, members focused on public education. Those engaged in the quasi-amateur medical practices that flourished in colonial times were welcome to participate. In 1790 the society began publishing the first medical journal to appear in Massachusetts, *Medical Papers*. Its offerings were far from arcane; its major goal was to popularize medical and scientific information.[2] In this climate the medical ideas about insanity were likely to be widely disseminated.

In 1782 the first medical school in New England was established at Harvard College by John Warren, who had been a surgeon at the army hospital in Boston during the Revolution.[3] With the founding of Harvard Medical School, another important step had been taken in establishing the hegemony of the professionally trained physician in matters of health and disease. However, the authority of physicians trained in medical school did not immediately supplant the practice of medicine by those trained under the older apprentice system. In fact, by 1840 only one-third of physicians practicing in New England had been trained in medical school; the rest had learned their medicine under the older tutorial method.[4] Furthermore, since the first hospital in the state was not opened until 1821, medical training was limited in its effectiveness.[5] In spite of these obstacles, the professionalization of medicine in Massachusetts, especially in Boston, was far greater in 1803 than it had been in 1760.[6] The cultural influence of medicine, therefore, was more profound than it had been in the colonial period, and the medical version of madness was bound to gain increasing legitimacy as a consequence.

Massachusetts physicians like John Warren who were interested in improving medical practice in the state looked to the already established medical schools in New York and Philadelphia both as models and as sources of medical knowledge. By the late eighteenth century a medical elite, trained either at Edinburgh Hospital, Scotland, or the Pennsylvania Hospital, existed in the major urban areas of the country.[7] The medical college at Philadelphia was a particularly important influence on these physicians and therefore on American medical practice in general. The first medical students graduated from the College of Philadelphia, later to become the University of Pennsylvania, in 1768.[8] With a medical school and a full-scale hospital (which also admitted insane patients), Philadelphia clearly eclipsed Boston as the seat of medical expertise. This dominance continued into the nineteenth century, as no other state could boast of an equally rigorous training of its physicians. Warren consulted with Benjamin Rush, one of Pennsylvania Hospital's leading lights, about his plans to establish a medical school at Harvard.[9] Physicians trained at Pennsylvania Hospital were more interested in theory building than their counterparts elsewhere (especially in Massachusetts) and they were more likely to have had some education in European medical schools. Their publications were widely read (especially the dissertations written by graduating medical students) and can be taken as an indication of where American medical thought was moving in this period.[10] In addition, many New England physicians were trained at Pennsylvania Hospital.[11] All told, the influence of the Philadelphia medical establishment on medical practice elsewhere was profound. This would have been particularly true in Massachusetts, where physicians were struggling to establish themselves as professionals with special training and expertise.

None of these efforts to create a more scientific professional medical practice led to systematic speculations about the nature of insanity among physicians in Massachusetts. No serious medical writing on madness was published by physicians in the state in the decades following the Revolution. Those interested in the medical views of insanity had to look elsewhere: to publications from the medical schools in Pennsylvania and New York and to European, particularly English, writings.[12] These sources provided the context that would shape the understanding of madness among physicians and eventually among laypersons in Massachusetts.

European speculations about madness in the latter part of the eighteenth century had begun to emphasize a strong connection between the mind and body, in an effort that united the once distinct fields of psychology and medicine. Passions, especially excess passions, were thought to be the conduit through which the mind operated on the body to cause illness as well as abnormal mental functioning. Well-regulated passions were therefore crucial to the maintenance of health.[13] The belief that excess passions were responsible for many forms of insanity had been present in English medical speculations since the sixteenth century; it was to be an increasingly important theme in the late eighteenth and early nineteenth centuries.[14]

The role of the passions in American writing about insanity in this period was, if anything, even more significant. For Americans, focusing on the role of the passions continued an important emphasis on the moral dimension of madness, an emphasis that might have been lost with the waning of the supernatural explanation. The increased emphasis on the role of excess passions was also related to the impact of the Enlightenment in the new Republic. An emphasis on balance, order, and harmony borrowed from the Greeks was central to those writers who were part of what has been called the moderate Enlightenment. Moderation itself was thought to be the key to the good life and its absence to result in a whole range of problems, madness being one of the most dramatic.[15]

Three medical dissertations written by graduates of the medical schools in Pennsylvania and New York toward the end of the eighteenth century represent the first systematic treatment of madness in America since Cotton Mather's *The Angel of Bethesda*. These dissertations, by Edward Cutbush (1794), Henry Rose (1794), and Alexander Anderson (1796),[16] indicate the eagerness with which American physicians seized on the theme of passions when writing about insanity.

All three authors indicted excesses of various sorts as responsible for insanity. Mental excesses such as "fixing one's mind too strongly or too long on an object" and "intense study" were mentioned and bring to mind the earlier opinion that "too much study" had caused David Trumble's madness. Far more important (and interesting) to these authors, however, were excesses of sensuality, or excess passions. These new physicians warned that "immoderate terror, joy, fear, lust and passionate love" were directly responsible for the onset of insanity. Edward Cutbush, graduate of the University of Pennsylvania medical school in 1794, offered the most elaborate version of how excess passions could disrupt the mind. He thought that "sudden, habitual or violent passions are accompanied by a vibration which produces a slight impression on the brain." Continued over time, reasoned Cutbush, this produced an "habitual motion in the brain which will eventually usurp reason." [17]

These authors did not use the term *distraction* but instead referred to the more scientific categories of *mania* and *melancholy*. Mania was thought to be uncontrollable or furious madness where behavior was violent, frenzied, boisterous, or delusional; whereas melancholy was characterized by withdrawn, morose, and dejected behavior. Distraction had been relegated to the category of folk description, and indeed it would still be used occasionally by laypersons in Massachusetts in the early nineteenth century. Medicine demanded a more exact and more vivid description of insanity, especially of mania, which was directly connected with the most excessive emotions (especially jealousy, rage, and lust). [18] It was clear in these writings that insanity was a dangerous and even treacherous state that resulted from a failure of self-control. All three dissertations carried implied warnings to readers to avoid the loss of moderation that would lead to madness.

Another Pennsylvania Hospital medical student, Joseph Parrish, writing in 1805, listed the usual passions—love, envy, jealousy, fear, anger, and grief—as causes of insanity. The antidote "under all circumstances was fear," since "madmen are generally cowardly." In a suggestion reminiscent of Cotton Mather, Parrish recommended virtue, "the regulating principle given man by the Creator to help control his will," as the way to prevent madness.[19] Writing in the same year, William Gibbons, who was also studying medicine in Philadelphia, described hypochondriasis as a "peculiar state of the mind wherein the patient is very attentive to his health." He thought the condition was manifested both in mental, obsessive symptoms and in physical symptoms that centered in the stomach region. Gibbons thought that both passions and intense study could cause hypochondriasis, but he believed the most likely cause was another form of sensual excess that was to play an important role in the ideas about madness in early nineteenth century America, "the vice of masturbation." Gibbons was convinced that this relationship was virtually self-evident, for "when we consider the remarkable connections between the intellectual and genital functions, we are not surprised to find disease in the latter to have a great effect on the mind."[20]

While these authors were clearly influenced by English writing on madness, they also represented the culmination of the transformation of the conceptions of insanity from a supernatural context to an ethical one, a shift that began in Massachusetts earlier in the eighteenth century. The axiomatic connection between excesses, especially of passions, and derangement formed the basis of this ethical conception, in which insanity was seen as the direct and natural result of personal moral failure. The moral aspect of insanity was the dominant note struck by these dissertations, far overshadowing speculation about its biological side. While religious lessons about God, the devil, and sin were no longer drawn, these newer conceptions resulted in another set of moral imperatives: excesses of passion and sensuality could lead to madness. The flexibility implicit in the supernatural view was gone; now every insane person was presumed to have erred in some way and thereby courted madness. Insanity had come under human control, in its prevention, if not in its cure. Its meaning was now inextricably linked to the normative demands of a new social order.

These medical efforts to understand madness were likely to have been read by physicians struggling to restore the insane to rationality, especially those undergoing formal medical training or reading the new medical journals. Medical dissertations were important sources of knowledge for practicing physicians, and the significance of these writings lies not in the careers of their authors but in their influence on their readers. One indication that these ideas about madness were circulated in Massachusetts is found in the journal of a prominent physician in Salem. Writing in 1810, Edward Holyoke worried about the importance of moderation and self-control. He warned himself to avoid "excesses of every kind," especially "violence and impetuosity, inordinate desires, ambitious vices and grand projects." Such are "rocks on which the happiness of thousands has been shipwrecked," he fretted. Holyoke ended his self-exhortation by adding that these self-indulgences can "lead to becoming insane." He was much concerned that his "inordinate desires and passions" would lead him into madness.[21] In 1798 a layman in Massachusetts also linked unruly passions to insanity. A father, begging pardon for his son who was condemned to prison for theft, wrote the governor that his son was "shattered in his brain" because he had "suffered his passions to rule over his head."[22]

Of course, the change in ideas about madness did not overtake all medical practitioners at once. Those who did not give passions a primary role were likely to become more sympathetic to those who had gone mad. In 1802, John Vaughan, a physician in Vermont, described an entire family that had been afflicted by madness, an event so unusual that he could only ascribe it to an "infectious mania." Since he acknowledged that "witchcraft and conjuration" could no longer serve as explanations, and since no bodily disease preceded the mania, Vaughan concluded that the children became mad from a "sympathetic orgasm" inspired by the sight of the madness of the mother. The "mind, the nervous system and the blood vessels" all interacted to produce the condition of mania, as each was "subjected to a participation in the morbid affections of the other."[23] While Vaughan's theory of how all these elements worked together was typically vague, he demonstrated the prevailing faith that the mental and physical sides of human nature were somehow related.

The importance of excess passions to the discussion of madness in the early nineteenth century made the task of accounting for insanity in the virtuous more difficult. Daniel Sanders, president of the University of Vermont, took on this challenge in 1805, when he discussed the case of a young woman whom he had known as an exemplary member of the church yet who had been insane for seven years. Sanders called on an earlier generation's explanation when he declared that such calamities are one of the "mysteries of Providence, which we cannot fathom." Yet Sanders was also a man of the nineteenth century, for he made a point of reminding his listeners that reason can be abused by man, especially through intemperance.[24] Like masturbation, the excessive use of alcohol was beginning to be given a significant role as a precipitator of madness. Both behaviors seemed to be the dreadful result of loss of self-control, now also crucial to the maintenance of sanity. Any compromise of self-control was a likely target in these speculations about causes of madness.

None of these early medical observers had offered a systematic explanation of the somatic aspects of insanity although all had assumed that human biology was implicated in its occurrence. The famous Philadelphia physician Benjamin Rush made the first and most elaborate attempt to link the somatic and ethical dimensions of insanity in this country. Rush practiced medicine at Pennsylvania Hospital from the mid 1770s until his death in 1813. There he developed a holistic theory of disease that he was eager to apply to insanity. While Robinson and other English physicians writing on madness had argued that irregular actions of the nervous system were the prime cause of irregularities of the brain and finally of the mind, Rush believed that the vascular system was the seat of all illness, including insanity. He borrowed from these earlier theories of irregular motions but moved from the nervous system to the blood vessels. In 1812 he wrote that insanity was "seated primarily in the blood vessels of the brain and it depends on the same kind of morbid and irregular actions that constitute other arterial diseases." Rush is further distinguished by being one of the first American authors to describe madness as a disease. It was, he thought, a "kind of chronic fever; which affects the part of the brain which is the seat of the mind." Although hypertension was the somatic cause of insanity, Rush joined other Republican physicians like Cutbush and Anderson in emphasizing the role of mental or emotional excess, such as "inordinate sexual desires and gratifications, intense study, frequent and rapid transition of the mind from one subject to another, avarice, joy, terror, grief, and of course, intemperance," as causes of hypertension. Rush was convinced that madness had increased in the United States since 1790 because of "an increase in avarice and ambition," which could also presumably cause the excitement that leads to hypertension. He also worried that "different religions and different tenets of the same religion are more or less calculated to induce a predisposition to madness." In an interesting inversion of contemporary speculations, Rush thought that wealth increased the risk of madness, as the "poor do not have the time to worry about the things that make the rich insane."[25]

Earlier in his career Rush had engaged in some metaphysical speculations about madness that suggest the difficulties inherent in attempting to locate the seat of insanity. He decided that since it was at least partly a moral phenomenon, it must be located in the spiritual as well as the biological side of human nature. Therefore, he thought, madness could affect both the will and the reason, since the will was thought to be the seat of the moral faculty. The notion that the will was affected by madness was central to the belief that failure of willpower could lead to the condition. Realizing that he might have sounded too much of a materialist in suggesting that spiritual faculties are subject to somatic disorders, Rush hastened to add that this relationship did not mean that the soul was not immortal, but only that it might not be immaterial.[26]

However bewildering Rush's metaphysics may have been, he offered the most complex explanation of madness in America until the Jacksonian period, when superintendents of the newly established asylums began writing extensively on insanity. Yet

Rush's contributions did not stand the test of time. Whereas he was the leading expert on insanity in his own time, by the 1840s he had lost all credibility in the medical profession.[27]

One of the main reasons for Rush's eventual eclipse in American medicine was the influence of the Frenchman Philippe Pinel. Pinel also believed that moral faculties were implicated in madness; in fact, in his work with mental patients in Paris, he noticed that some showed no intellectual derangement but still behaved in violent, excessive ways. For these patients he created the category *manie sans délire*, or moral insanity, a concept Rush had introduced to American medicine in 1786.[28] Pinel's interest in moral insanity was linked to his conviction that the passions were responsible for madness. Since he believed emotional excess to be the most frequent cause of insanity, he also believed that manipulation of the patients' emotions through manipulation of their environment and other psychological factors was the way to help them.[29] While the legend of his freeing the insane at Bicêtre from chains in one dramatic gesture has been dismissed, Pinel did contribute significantly to humane care of the insane. While working at Bicêtre and at another hospital, La Salpêtrière, he found that "insanity was curable in many instances by mildness of treatment and attention to the state of the mind exclusively."[30] This suggestion was a revolutionary one in post-Revolutionary France, where the insane had been treated with heroic remedies such as bleeding and purging or had been brutally confined in the belief that they were little more than animals. Pinel believed that most insanity was a functional, not an organic disorder and could be treated by moral methods, or what he called *traitement moral.*[31]

Pinel revolutionized the study of insanity in another way. He was committed to the inductive method of understanding madness and recorded daily observations about the behavior of his patients. In his belief that observations came before theory, he established the rationale for the case history of the mental patient (a practice still important in contemporary mental hospitals). As a careful observer of the behavior of the insane, he brought a more scientific and presumably more dispassionate attitude to their treatment, thereby encouraging more humane methods.[32]

Pinel's major interest was not in ferreting out the causes of madness but in its treatment. He left it to his student Esquirol to elaborate on the role of passions in madness and other human misfortune.[33] Essential to the treatment of the insane, Pinel believed, was the asylum, which he viewed therapeutically rather than punitively. He believed that in the asylum the insane could be restored to reason through kindness, regular routines, and work. He was convinced that these psychological or moral techniques were far more effective than drugs or other somatic remedies (such as bleeding), which, he felt, should be used only occasionally.[34]

Pinel's major work, *Treatise on Insanity*, though published in France in 1801, was not available in English until 1806. His greatest impact in America lay in his *traitement moral*, which became both the rationale and the foundation of the movement to build asylums in early nineteenth-century America. In addition, his interest in detailed observation moved the discussion of insanity away from the effort to find a unitary cause, an effort to which Rush had devoted a great deal of energy.[35] In this way Pinel's influence eventually served to revise Rush's influence on American medicine completely. In another sense, Pinel served to corroborate the growing conviction of American physicians that excess passions were responsible for many cases of insanity.

The relationship between psychological factors and the somatic processes remained mysterious in Pinel's work, just as it was in American medical thought. Yet this was a necessary connection for physicians to make, for without it there would have been little reason for them to be involved in the treatment of insanity. Insofar as insanity involved passion, moral faculties, and failures of control, its treatment did not demand any medical expertise. The success of the effort to unite the biological and ethical aspects of madness was crucial to its medicalization.[36] Pinel had made little attempt to bridge the gap between psychology and somaticism; in fact, he paid scant attention to medical treatment of insanity. American physicians, however, were still committed to these older medical remedies in the early nineteenth century. Rush, most important of the early figures, advocated older, heroic remedies such as bleeding and purging, measures Pinel eschewed. Yet in his optimism about the possibilities for cure, Rush was similar to Pinel and may have been influenced by him. Equally interested in human behavior and biology, it was Rush who represented the Republican synthesis of the somatic and the psychological in the understanding of madness.[37]

A man astride both the old and the new worlds of medicine, Rush also suggests the ambiguity at the heart of the new medical interest in madness in this country. The optimistic belief that the insane could be cured was linked to a more negative conviction that their condition was brought on by their personal failings. Rush combined a highly moralistic attitude with a humanitarian one. In this sense, he exemplified most clearly the tension between control and treatment that would be at the heart of the Jacksonian asylum.

Rush was very influential in his own time, in both his writings and his teaching at Pennsylvania Hospital. He also had a hand in the creation of Harvard Medical School, whose founder John Warren, corresponded frequently with the Pennsylvania physician and sought his advice.[38] Since Massachusetts physicians wrote very little on medical matters in this period, those interested in insanity are likely to have been familiar with his work. Rush's advice about somatic treatment may have seemed especially appealing to physicians in the preasylum period, before Pinel's ideas about moral treatment became important there.

While Pinel's advocacy of moral treatment laid the groundwork for the humane treatment of the insane in this country, the most influential figure for the early asylum builders in the 1820s was William Tuke, a Quaker merchant, who operated an asylum for the insane in England known as the Retreat. Tuke's views on insanity were widely known in medical circles in this country, largely through the work of American Quakers, who established Friends' Asylum, based on Tuke's model, in Frankford, Pennsylvania in 1813.[39] In addition, several physicians who were in-

fluential in the creation of the first asylums in this country visited
the Retreat and based their conviction about the curability of
insanity on their understanding of Tuke's program.[40] In 1813,
his grandson, Samuel Tuke, published *The Description of the Retreat Near York for Insane Persons of the Society of Friends.* which
quickly became the most important source of information about
moral treatment. In it Tuke asserted that "insane persons generally possess a degree of control over their wayward propensi-
ties."[41] This belief, not widely articulated in the first wave of
American medical speculations about madness, became the basis
for an increasing optimism about its cure. Not clear at the time
was the way that this conviction could also be used to justify the
punitive treatment of those refusing to control themselves.

While Tuke ignored the somatic side of madness, in America
his optimistic views resulted in a broader acceptance of the idea
that insanity was a disease. The belief that madness resulted
from a breakdown in natural law, both physical and moral, was
one way in which the biological and ethical aspects of madness
could be united. The emphasis on both immorality and disease
meant that the prevention of madness and the restoration of
reason were within human control. The way in which the disease
model could serve to encourage humanitarian sentiment is suggested by a circular letter written in 1810 by two Boston physicians, John Warren and James Jackson. They called for the establishment of a "hospital for the reception of lunatics and other
sick persons"; madness was a "disease of the mind," and even
the "virtuous and industrious are liable to become objects of
public charity" in its wake. Clearly, an emphasis on the immoral
qualities of the insane would be unwise in soliciting funds for an
asylum, but the negative consequences of ignoring madness
could be emphasized. In this way the two physicians introduced
the rationale for the medicalization of madness that was to form
an important part of the argument for the establishment of asylums in the coming years: "when those who are unfortunate in
this respect are left without proper care, a calamity, which might
have been transient, is prolonged through life."[42] The notion
that insanity could be cured if treatment was begun soon after

its first appearance would be a recurring theme among reformers, who argued that it was a disease whose victims deserved a hospital for their treatment.

American physicians struggled to achieve a synthesis of the ideas of disease, moral failings, and moral treatment. Theodoric Beck, who had been strongly influenced by Tuke, wrote a medical dissertation in 1811 calling for a humanitarian program of treatment for the insane and basing his appeal on Tuke's argument that the insane could learn self-control. Along with his interest in curing the insane, he had an equal interest in reminding his readers that ill-regulated passions led to madness, especially to mania. Beck repeated the list of failings and intellectual excesses catalogued by physicians fifteen years earlier: avarice or intoxication, intense study, excess passions, and even political contests. Presumably the insane could relearn the self-control they had given up. While Beck gave little attention to the physical aspects of madness, he did believe that the brains of the insane were inflamed, an inflammation presumably related to their lack of self-control.[43]

On the other hand, the belief that madness was a disease could lead to a rejection of psychological forms of treatment. In a review of Beck's work, one anonymous author claimed that Beck was premature to recommend so confidently a program of largely mental treatment for the "disease" of insanity. He warned, "We have not yet arrived at those satisfactory conclusions of the peculiar character and seat of this disease which are necessary to insure a judicious and successful practice."[44] This author was one of the few to be concerned about the apparent discrepancy that existed between moral and traditional medical treatment.

One Massachusetts physician added a new twist to the discussion of madness in 1817 by suggesting that it had different causes in women and men. George Parkman thought that women were driven to insanity most often by jealousy, irresolution, and religious enthusiasm; while men were likely to become mad from impatience or petulance. Whereas most other American physicians considered the brain to be the physical seat of madness, Parkman thought that the digestive organs were the source of insanity.[45]

Rush, Pinel, and Tuke all were influential in the formative years of asylum building in this country, yet in many ways they represented opposing responses to madness. The first, epitomized by Rush, emphasized the conviction that it was a disease brought on by moral failings. Accompanying this emphasis was a strong reliance on somatic treatment, much of which could be very strenuous in nature. The second, introduced by Pinel and Tuke, focused far less on the causes and instead stressed the curability of madness through nonmedical, moral treatment. This approach embodied a high degree of respect for the insane based on the belief that they possessed innate capacities for self-control, given the proper environment. Both these approaches were combined in the minds of the early asylum builders in this country, with mixed results for the insane confined there.

The medicalization of madness was achieved slowly, not without some resistance and confusion on the part of laypersons. If medical experts could not agree on its exact nature, the general public could be expected to be confused about exactly what kind of disease madness was. In Massachusetts this confusion led to a disinclination on the part of state and local officials to accept medical opinions about insanity. Members of the Superior Court of Massachusetts, for example, were not persuaded by medical testimony offered about the insanity of defendants. In 1812 the court ruled that insanity could not be offered as a defense in a slander case, because the "equivocal nature and appearance of the disorder" made it impossible to determine its existence.[46] The court chastised the physicians testifying on behalf of the defense for presenting *opinions* on insanity as opposed to facts, and it ruled that their failure to present such facts disqualified them as expert witnesses. As late as 1831 the same court refused to rule on a case of insanity, saying that "insanity is sometimes hard to detect. It is sometimes difficult to determine what constitutes insanity and to distinguish between that and general weakening of understanding. The boundary between them may be narrow."[47]

Similarly, in 1829 a Haverhill man murdered a neighbor in a particularly gruesome manner and claimed insanity as a defense. The overseers of the poor and other townsfolk refused to believe him, in spite of a physician's testimony, for they assumed he was lying to escape punishment. Insanity, the overseers argued, "was impossible to prove and easy to simulate."[48]

Early in the nineteenth century, medical opinion was not viewed as constituting expert testimony in legal cases involving insanity in Massachusetts. The Superior Court of the state was always convinced that it could make a far better estimate of a person's rationality than could a physician. Furthermore, the court was more likely to take the word of a person's friends or even the testimony of the distracted themselves over the word of physicians, family, or even town officials, who could be suspected of having self-serving motives. Generally, the court was very reluctant to assume that a person was mad without unequivocal evidence, which always meant a personal interview with the defendant. Even the testimony of guardians was discounted.[49] In the case of Benjamin Chase, the court overturned a guardianship decision made by another judge in 1817. Chase appealed the decision, claiming that he was not non compos mentis and that the unannounced visit of Boston selectmen to his house for the purpose of determining his sanity had taken him by surprise. After interviewing him, the court agreed and revoked Chase's guardianship status, noting that he had "exposed himself to the view of the judge and proven by his own conduct and actions the falsity of the charge."[50] In two other cases in the same period, the court protected defendants accused by family members of being mad. In both instances the court ignored medical opinion and based its ruling of sanity on personal interviews with the defendants, declaring them sane.[51]

While courts may have been reluctant to declare persons legally insane, once such a designation was made, either formally through court procedures, or informally by town selectmen, those so designated suffered a constriction of their civil rights. Towns in this period began questioning the right of the insane to make legal settlements, on the basis that a "lunatic has no civil rights."[52] There was also some question as to whether an insane person was able to enter into a marriage contract or inherit an estate.[53] None of these issues had been raised before the Revolution, as distracted persons in that period had enjoyed all the rights of sane townsfolk, unless placed in guardianship, in which case they could not manage their own estates. But this deprivation of rights occurred only after a formal hearing. A change in the reaction to the insane in the state in this period was becoming evident. The designation of insanity began to be tied to a more constricted status. This new perception was clearly a negative one, which may account for some of the reluctance on the part of the Supreme Court to give formal legal approval of the designation *insane.*

In spite of a continuing reluctance to accept testimony of physicians as experts on insanity, in 1825 the Superior Court did begin referring to madness as a "disease." Up to this date, judges and other court officials had referred to it as "that most calamitous visitation from Providence."[54] Less exalted townsfolk were likely to call their insane neighbors *deranged, crazy,* and *lunatic* in the early nineteenth century.[55] *Lunatic* seems to have been reserved for the most serious and dangerous.[56] The term *distracted* appears only occasionally in the records in the nineteenth century. Like medical men, laypersons seem to have required a more rigorous vocabulary of madness.

There is some muted indication that a highly negative image of the insane, accompanying the shift in lexicon, was gaining credibility among ordinary townfolk. One public-spirited citizen of Salem wrote a letter in 1819 to the overseers of the poor in that town asking that a workhouse be built where the "deranged" and the "idle and vicious" poor "may be compelled to labour." This letter offers evidence of how the disparate elements in the new conceptions of insanity could be loosely linked together in some peoples' minds. He argued that these paupers "have brought themselves to this necessity first by illness, from this by an easy process of vice of every description and then to wretchedness."[57] In Danvers, the overseers wrote in 1818 that "the deranged cannot be pitied, for they bring on their own misery."[58] Boston's *Independent Chronicle*" demonstrated a far less sympathetic attitude than the Boston physicians who had solicited funds for an asylum in 1810, and warned its readers in 1817 that if an asylum were to be built in Boston, residents would be exposed to a "malignant distemper."[59] The phrase *malignant distemper* suggests that the notion that madness was a disease did not necessarily lead to a tolerant attitude.

The belief that insanity was a disease was a double-edged sword; it could carry a negative connotation (depending on why the condition appeared), or it could fuel the conviction that the insane could be treated and eventually cured. In this way the medical view of madness provided the means by which rationality could be restored. The evolution of the efforts to establish places of cure was based in large part on this deepening conviction that madness was a disease, even though the first formal efforts to treat the insane in asylums in the 1820s and 1830s were based on the premises of moral treatment, a nonmedical approach.

One of the most influential figures in the asylum movement, Amariah Brigham, illustrates the importance of the disease model to these early reformers. He insisted that insanity was a "corporal disease, located in the brain" and sounded the hopeful note of the reformer when he wrote: "Just views respecting the disease now more generally prevail than formerly. It is no longer regarded as a disgrace, or as a disease resulting from some criminal offense. It is now considered a physical disorder, a disease of the brain, and one which can be as readily cured as a disease of the body."[60] Brigham did not completely ignore the passions in his speculations about madness; he was convinced that "too strong excitement of the feelings" may cause an "unnatural amount of blood to flow to the head and increase the size and power of the brain." The excitement itself he blamed on the "peculiarly intellectual character of the present age, the high mental excitement which pervades all classes of society," especially the "strife for wealth, office, political distinction and party success."[61]

As David Rothman pointed out, Brigham and other early asylum builders were concerned with the flux and stresses threatening the precarious stability of Jacksonian society. Many of them turned increasingly to the Jacksonian social structure in

their search for the causes of madness.[62] Brigham's views are
indicative of a wider shift away from an indictment of personal
moral excess to a concern with Jacksonian society. Presumably
the vicissitudes of the social order (especially the economic
temptations) seduced individuals from the path of moderation
and self-control, leading them into those excesses that cause
madness.[63] The opening up of the causes of madness to include
social forces did not exclude the theme of self-control, but it did
lend a more humanitarian tone to the discussion. Individuals
alone were not to blame; perhaps few could be expected to resist
the blandishments of Jacksonian society. This softening of the
rhetoric was related to a new optimism about the potential of
the new asylums to cure the insane. It led some physicians who
worked in these asylums to attempt to revise the negative attitudes articulated earlier in the century.

The most important medical authority on insanity in Massachusetts in this period was Samuel Woodward, superintendent
of the first public asylum in the state, which opened in 1833. At
Worcester State Lunatic Hospital, Woodward had ample opportunity to observe insane patients; his ideas about madness
tended to emphasize the ethical aspects more than the social
ones. He was convinced that a great deal of madness was caused
by masturbation and intemperance. In 1835 he wrote, "No cause
is more influential in producing Insanity, and, in a special manner, perpetuating the disease, than Masturbation." Many insane
in this asylum indulged in "daily, almost hourly recurrences of
the practice," which was the "most deplorable, hopeless, disgusting fatuity." When insanity was caused by masturbation, it
was also incurable, Woodward believed, since the vice was almost
impossible to give up.[64] Masturbation was second only to intemperance as the most frequent cause of insanity, according to
Woodward.[65] In his reports to the Massachusetts legislature, issued in his capacity as asylum superintendent, he speculated extensively about the nature of insanity. Like his fellow superintendent Brigham, he believed it to be a "disease of the physical
system, ensuing from a derangement of the functions of the
brain and nerves."[66] Like his predecessor Rush, Woodward
seemed ambivalent about the insane. On the one hand they were

victims of a disease; on the other hand, if they brought on the disease through contemptible practices, they were instigators of their own misery.

Woodward was one of the first Americans to distinguish between curable and incurable insanity. The latter he thought to be a kind of chronic insanity, where "confirmed habit, or organization of the brain may establish the wanderings of intellect or blot it out forever."[67] Like others in his day, he was convinced that only recent cases of insanity were susceptible to cure; therefore he frequently emphasized the importance of early treatment and hospitalization.[68]

Woodward also occasionally agreed with Brigham that social conditions, especially economic ones, could cause insanity, although that was not his main emphasis. In 1837 he noted: "During the last year, there have occurred many instances of insanity from the depression of business and the disastrous results of speculation. The radical difficulty consists in the spirit which impels to hazardous adventure, and the want of that discipline of mind which will buoy it above the vicissitudes of fortune."[69] Like Brigham, he thought that women were particularly susceptible to madness caused by religious excitement.[70]

Woodward's experience at Worcester led him to revise and refine his classification of various types of madness. He was especially interested in what he called "periodic insanity," in which the patient was intermittently lucid, sometimes for long periods, only to lapse back into madness. Woodward was fascinated and puzzled by this kind of behavior since, according to medical opinion, madness was a more or less permanent condition, which could be reversed only through exceptional care and attention. He therefore could not explain periodic insanity; he found it mysterious, "one of those unaccountable circumstances of disease, which is hidden from human scrutiny."[71] He would have been baffled by the behavior of James Otis in pre-Revolutionary America, a clear example of what he called periodic insanity. The idea that madness was an intermittent phenomenon had been commonly accepted in Massachusetts in the eighteenth century; by Woodward's time this possibility was seen as a strange anomaly.

Woodward was also impressed with the lucidity of some maniacs at the asylum. In 1837 he wrote: "If by mania be understood only that form of insanity which is attended by an equal disorder of all the faculties of the mind—then, indeed, there are few cases of mania. The most violent and chaotic state of the mind if often attended by a lucid action of some one or more of the faculties, the recollection of persons, events, and circumstances which is often quite surprising."[72] The ability of many of his patients to control their behavior when he reasoned with them was something Woodward did not expect. To explain this he borrowed the concept of moral insanity from Pinel and Rush. According to Woodward, moral insanity did not involve delusions or hallucinations but instead was a "disease of passion and propensity." He had found a way of explaining why many of his patients at times appeared as lucid as he did.[73] The concept of moral insanity was a necessary concomitant of the conviction that insanity was a disease. Like the idea of periodic insanity, it solved the dilemma posed by the rationality of those considered insane, for if some were lucid, even occasionally, how could their brains be diseased? Both concepts were ways of explaining the sometime sanity of the insane, thus preserving the integrity of the disease model.

Woodward is a central figure in the history of insanity in Massachusetts, indeed in the entire country. In his emphasis on personal vice as a cause of madness, his ideas are directly linked to the earlier theories of Cutbush and Rush, who indicted the failures of individual self-control. As a Jacksonian asylum superintendent, he also advocated the newer theories that looked to the vagaries of the social order to explain insanity. In his insistence that masturbation and intemperance were primary causes, Woodward was not typical of his fellow superintendents, who were more interested in engaging in a broader critique of the social order than in condemning personal excesses.[74] Yet in his belief that insanity was a disease that could be cured if treated early, he laid the philosophical foundation for future asylum building in the state, an effort that was to meet with considerable success.

Did the insistence of physicians like Woodward that insanity was a disease result in a more tolerant attitude toward the insane in the state in the Jacksonian period? According to Luther Bell, superintendent of McLean Asylum, the first private asylum in Massachusetts, it did. Bell, who was sure that "insanity was a disease," felt that this understanding was far more beneficial to the insane than the older belief that madness was the sign of an "inscrutable visitation from God." He was happy to report that "the public is seeing that the alienation of the mind from disease brings no disgrace to the sufferer."[75]

The trustees of Worcester State Lunatic Hospital were not nearly as optimistic about the acceptance of the insane under the new medical rubric. In 1838 they wrote:

Not only is insanity regarded by the community at large as one of the greatest afflictions to which our nature is liable, but it is looked upon by some as a malady which brings disgrace as well as suffering. Instances have come to the knowledge of the Trustees, where a family has resorted to various devices, for a length of time, to conceal the insanity of one of its members; supposing that if the fact were known, it would affix a reproachful stigma upon the character of the unfortunate sufferer.

Although decrying the practice of concealing the insane and keeping them from medical attention, the trustees could understand the reason for this shame, for "the causes of insanity are various, . . . some are voluntary, others involuntary; . . . some of them are as free from the slightest suspicion of wrong or dishonor as any epidemic can be, while other cases are wholly referable to the previous fault or crime of the sufferers themselves." How was one to tell who should be blamed for this madness and who not? The trustees advised that "those upon whom the disease has been entailed by their own ancestors, or who suffer under it from causes beyond their own control, will be regarded with deep and genuine pity; while such as are the direct authors of their own melancholy fate will be regarded— with pity it is true, but not unmingled with condemnation."[76]

The understanding of insanity had been transformed in the state since the colonial period, with ambiguous results for the insane. Some people may have been eager to bring family and friends for treatment, but others clearly were reluctant to expose their connection with the insane. While the conviction that madness was a disease may have liberated some insane from their suffering, for others it could not soften the negative attitudes that had developed. In fact, the notion that madness was a disease may have exacerbated this new sense that it was a fearful disorder, for the concept of disease carried with it the idea of contagion, an inference that may have heightened anxiety.

Yet this newer version of the disease model had the potential for a more humanitarian response, as Bell commented. The blanket condemnation of the insane as persons unable to master themselves and their passions that had characterized medical writing earlier in the century was replaced by a more flexible causal scheme. Those who became mad because of their wickedness or weakness were condemned (as well as pitied); whereas those who were innocently robbed of their reason because of stresses in the Jacksonian social order or because of hereditary factors were hapless victims to be treated with compassion and understanding. The potential humanity of the disease model is suggested by the 1838 report of the board of trustees of Worcester State Lunatic Hospital.

Formerly the common idea was that insanity was an affection of mind, not a disease of the body, produced by direct visitation from Heaven, instead of being the consequence of some departure from the organic laws to which our nature is subject, which laws men can discover and obey. It was further the common belief that the victims of this visitation of Heaven must continue to suffer its unknown and inexhaustible agonies, until rescued from them by another direct interposition of omnipotent power, . . . instead of supposing it to be a malady, curable by such restorative influences, as have been graciously placed within our own control, and even susceptible of being prevented beforehand.

In case anyone wondered about the nature of madness, the trustees reminded them.

Insanity is a physical disease, . . . it has its origin in certain natural causes, being induced by a violation of some of the organic laws upon which mental functions depend; . . . these causes are not mysterious and inscrutable in any peculiar sense, . . . they are capable of being understood, like the causes which bring on consumption or the gout; that insanity is a curable disease . . . that the means of effecting its cure have been graciously put into our hands.[77]

Just as the supernatural conceptions of madness in the colonial period allowed the holy man to be pitied and the sinner to be judged, so too by the 1830s the conceptions of madness embodied a moral perspective that supported another set of cultural sanctions for human behavior. In the colonial period, the meaning of insanity had been refracted through the moral imperatives of Massachusetts society. The explanation of why people became insane had been framed to encourage commitment to the supernatural beliefs that were an important part of colonial social order. After the Revolution, the moral content of madness remained, but in a secularized context, for the phenomenon of madness continued to serve as an object lesson that reinforced the dominant cultural values.

Intemperance and sexuality had each taken on new significance in New England in the early nineteenth century.[78] The concern for private sexual behavior suggests how important self-control was now thought to be. Anxiety about intemperance and masturbation rested on the perception that these behaviors led to a dissolving of self, an undoing that also could lead to madness. Both the excesses that were thought to bring on madness and the phenomenon itself suggested that control of the self had been abandoned. Passion was an enemy in a society that valued control highly, for it could sweep away the orderly internal structures that regulated behavior. Even worry about increasing avarice, ambition, and the proliferation of religions was tied to a fear that these social forces would undermine self-control.

The Enlightenment emphasis on reason as the crowning glory of human gifts also colored madness with more significance than had been the case earlier. Insanity threatened, if not directly assaulted, reason and was now an unwelcome state. The positive side of this was the accompanying belief that human reason could understand and ultimately manipulate the natural world; this suggested that insanity, like all other things in the natural order, could be brought under human control.[79] The trustees of

Worcester State Lunatic Hospital boasted that insanity was an "agency whose action can be put aside in most cases by adopting certain precautions; or can even be repelled, when expending its force upon us, by the application of certain known remedies."[80] This new instrumental view, the notion that loss of reason could be avoided and even reversed, was the most revolutionary note struck by the writings on madness in the 1830s.

After the Revolution madness was entirely shorn of its supernatural meaning at the same time as it took on a greater significance when self-control and reason become more important. Because human moral agency was assumed, the responsibility for insanity fell squarely on human shoulders.[81] One result of this new understanding was that the unwelcome appearance of madness could lead to a negative reaction to the insane. On the other hand, the medicalization of madness carried with it an optimism about the ability to reverse its course, thereby offering the possibility of a more humane response. Both reactions would appear in Massachusetts after the Revolution.

5 Dangerous to Go at Large

The treatment of the insane began to be transformed in Massachusetts in the years following the American Revolution. Accompanying the new understanding of madness as a natural phenomenon caused by personal behavior and moral failings, there was a new interest in the state in confining the insane in jails and almshouses. The movement to separate the insane from other members of society was spearheaded not by physicians but by laypersons: public officials, townsfolk, and families of the insane.[1]

The early efforts to confine and segregate the insane were not related to the asylum movement and did not necessarily depend on the new medical understanding of madness. Yet the fact that insanity was no longer linked to the supernatural order, but instead to personal excesses and vices no doubt informed the more punitive response that developed in the state. The movement to separate the insane from the rest of the society resulted in their confinement in structures that had existed before the Revolution. Those who viewed them as persons who had forsaken self-control may have seen these structures as the means by which control would be restored.

In the post-Revolutionary period, some towns in Massachusetts began to segregate insane paupers from other paupers in local almshouses. Other towns began incarcerating the insane in local jails, and it became more and more common for families and friends to confine them. Boston provides the clearest example of the progressive isolation of the insane in the late eighteenth and early nineteenth centuries. The town had supported its pauper insane in the almshouse throughout much of the eighteenth century, but in 1789 the insane paupers were sent out of the Boston almshouse. That year the overseers of the poor released a Mr. Mahoney from the almshouse on the grounds that he was "in a state of insanity and therefore an unfit subject for the almshouse." In the same year two insane almshouse residents were sent to Deer Island in Boston Harbor, to be cared for by Andrew Tukesbury, who was paid eight shillings a week by the town for his trouble.[2]

The insane were aided outside the almshouse in private homes from 1789 until sometime around 1805, when evidence indicates that they began filtering back there. Then in 1807 the overseers of the poor authorized the erection of a suitable wooden house at the northeast corner of the yard "for the maniaks." In 1809 the overseers voted to pay the "keeper of the maniac house" two dollars a month.[3] Apparently the maniac house was not big enough for all the pauper insane in the town, because in 1811 a committee was formed to "consider the subject of a subscription to build another maniac house." While this new structure was not built then, by 1813 there were eighteen insane paupers living in a "wooden house at the Northeast corner of the [almshouse] yard," which presumably qualified as a maniac house.[4] It is significant that the structure was referred to as a maniac house, which suggests that the condition of mania, thought to be the most violent and unpredictable form of insanity, had become emblematic of every manifestation of the disorder. Presumably all insane paupers in the town, including those exhibiting less dramatic kinds of insane behavior, were kept there.

In 1814 John Gorham, the physician for the Boston almshouse, described the condition of the insane paupers confined in this separate maniac house. They were kept in a "small house containing a range of cells, warmed by a Pollock stove." Gorham noted that the "establishment is exceedingly deficient in method and conveniences." Two of the inhabitants were "turbulent and almost ungovernable" and were confined in "straight waistcoats," but some that Gorham treated were only "periodically" insane; others in the maniac house were calm and not violent, surely not "maniacs." Yet all were apparently locked in their cells for most of the day.[5] These insane clearly were viewed as potentially dangerous, or at least their presence was viewed as highly disagreeable, since even those who were quiet were kept in cells. Some also were kept in the bridewell, the town jail, in the early years of the nineteenth century.[6]

Confinement of the insane had come in the wake of a 1796 Massachusetts law authorizing local authorities to commit the "furiously mad or those who were dangerous to the peace and safety of the good people" to houses of correction and jails. Three years earlier, Connecticut had passed a similar law.[7] The purpose of these laws was to confine men like Mary Gifford's husband, who was sentenced to a public whipping for an unknown crime in 1792. Mary wrote the governor of Massachusetts pleading for a pardon for her husband on the grounds that he was "so frequently bereft of his reason his going at large is almost always dangerous and the danger will be enhanced by the ignominious public punishment he is to suffer." Instead, she requested that he be sentenced to three years' labor in prison, claiming that "his confinement would be safer for the family." The governor granted her request, and the legislature obliged her and others like her with the 1796 legislation.[8]

This legislation does not seem to have been inspired by a dramatic change in the forms that madness was taking in the state. James Otis's violent behavior twenty years earlier had not inspired similar efforts at long-term confinement. The majority of those confined in the Boston maniac house do not appear to have been violent; and if they were violent when they were confined, they were not released when they calmed down. In Gloucester a man who ran into the street "almost naked and delirious" in 1808 was "taken by force" and confined in a local house for an unspecified amount of time, a measure not likely to have been taken with such vehemence fifty years earlier.[9] The 1796 law was used to confine not only those who were furiously mad but also those whose madness was quieter. This pattern of confining the nonviolent was to become increasingly important in the state in the early decades of the nineteenth century. Nor does there seem to have been a growth in the number of insane.[10] Instead, insane behavior itself had become a significant issue.

The changes in the reaction to the insane in the state did not take place all at once. Around the turn of the century there still were some affluent insane folk who moved freely around their communities. Timothy Dexter, a wealthy member of Newbury society who died in 1806, was considered the town eccentric. Much of his behavior was clearly mad (and his neighbors recognized it as such), but his wealth and social standing in the town protected him from disgrace. Only when his behavior became dangerous (as it did one day when he fired a pistol at a curious onlooker) did the town lock him up.[11] In Fitchburg, members of the First Congregational Church allowed their minister, John Payson, to continue in his duties despite his "demented and decomposed" state. At a town meeting in 1792, residents voted to allow Payson to preach part-time and continued to support him until his death. In Plymouth, John Porter, who became "raving distracted" while a student at Harvard in 1767, practiced law between intermittent spells of madness. He died in 1799, a respected citizen. Payson and Porter were among the last of the insane in the state to live out their lives with little interference. They were cared for by family members during their bad times, as were other members of affluent families in the smaller towns of New England at the turn of the century.[12]

Although these informal patterns of care probably persisted in some of these towns well into the early nineteenth century, in more populated areas the new mechanisms of control were seized upon as soon as they were created. Like Boston, Cambridge made special provisions for its insane residents at the end of the eighteenth century and began to incarcerate them in the town jail soon after the passage of the 1796 law. Town fathers continued this practice until the opening of Worcester State Lunatic Hospital in 1833.[13]

I have studied in depth the reaction to the insane in three towns in early Republican Massachusetts. These towns, Danvers, Salem, and Concord varied in population size and social and economic organization.[14] Until the opening of Worcester State Lunatic Hospital, local officials had to devise whatever means they could to control and care for the mad. The patterns of response in these towns were likely to have been approximated by similar towns in the state.

Danvers was an inland community of farmers and small manufacturers. With an essentially homogeneous population and limited population growth, in the post-Revolutionary period the town had not yet felt the social and economic dislocations that would accompany the significant growth of shoe manufacturing in the 1820s and 1830s. The vast majority of the work force was self-sufficient, and the town's poor relief was necessary only for those widows and children unable to support themselves.[15] Board and care were a sufficient method of caring for the town poor in the eighteenth century. Insane paupers were cared for in one private house in the town, along with other sick paupers. After 1797 the four insane paupers were confined apart from the others in one room in that house. In 1803 the first almshouse in Danvers opened its door to town paupers; the insane were confined separately there, in one room.[16]

The story of Ruth Parsons suggests the concern of Danvers officials to limit the towns's expenditures for insane paupers. In 1801 this unfortunate woman, described as "deranged in mind," was boarded out by the town with a local family. In 1803 she was one of two insane paupers confined in a separate room in the new almshouse. Overseers then began a long campaign to find another town to claim her as a legal resident. When this failed, they wrote to her mother in Salem. Her mother's reply indicates how few options existed for the care of the mad among the poorer townsfolk.

I took care of her in Cape Ann as long as I was able, she grew so bad last fall and winter that I was under the necessity to obtain help from that town. Toward spring she got better and I sent her into the country by Mr. Ewins hoping she would still get better. I moved last spring to Portland and had news lately that she is much worse. I was obliged to come up and find she must be delivered to your care as she is a poor miserable creature. I hope you will do well by her and wish you will be rewarded for your kindness hereafter.[17]

Mr. Ewins probably operated a private madhouse similar to the two where James Otis had stayed in the 1770s.[18] The overseers were unsuccessful in their efforts to remove Ruth Parsons, who was confined along with two other insane persons in a small room in the Danvers almshouse until her death in 1806.[19]

Archelaus Putnam, an apothecary from Danvers, suffered a brief period of madness in 1809. Since he was not a pauper, his account of his experiences suggests how the insane who were not town charges may have fared. The first alarm of madness came in 1807, when the apothecary wrote in his diary, "All is darkness, discouraging—all is hopeless, am losing ground," and then, "I feel most seriously alarmed that the adverse state of my circumstances will bring on such a melancholic state of mind as will end in insanity." Putnam's words were prophetic, for he sneaked out of his house in the middle of that same night, stole a ferryboat, and crossed the Merrimac River alone. On the other side he became involved in several fights with persons whom he had alarmed with his cries. As he described it later in his diary, he was "crazy" and in a "deranged state of mind." Some friends came for him and returned him to Danvers, where "chains were put on my legs and I was kept in confinement in a boarded up chamber for 19 or 20 days. Here I experienced indescribable torments occasioned by the cold. I was lashed for a number of nights to my bedstead on a bed filled with shavings and hand-cuffed. . . . But though lashed hands and feet and body with chains and ropes, yet I always found some method to clean my-self up in the course of the night." After a few weeks he was released from the chamber and, although now calm, was kept in the house in leg chains. Putnam then managed to escape to a neighboring farm. There he was caught, sent back to his family, and confined again by leg chains in his mother's chamber for over three weeks. Finally he was put under the care of a Dr. Kittredge in Andover. After months of rest (during which he was allowed "no reading or intense thought") he was "restored to rational health by the kind care of a Mrs. Bridges," with whom he stayed during the time he was under the physician's care. Kittredge did not care for the insane in his own home, as Ewins did, but boarded them with others in the town and visited them daily.[20]

Putnam's initial treatment was rather harsh, much like that of a prisoner. According to his account, he continued to be restrained after he had regained the use of his reason. Yet, while he was in Andover, he was afforded far more sympathetic care, evidence of a humanitarian response to the insane that existed alongside the impulse to confine them and would become increasingly important in the state in the 1820s and 1830s. Putnam returned to his hometown, as far as we can tell none the worse for his brief foray into madness. He was still able to enjoy a return to sanity and respectability, a pleasure that may not have been possible in later decades. The stories of Putnam and the insane at the almshouse suggest that at least some Danvers residents had come to look on the mad as persons needing close supervision and confinement.

Salem, the largest of the three towns, was bustling with fishing and commercial activity during this period. It was probably the wealthiest town in the country in per capita income in 1800. Some of the richest families in America lived there, along with a sizable number of poor and unskilled laborers, a mixture that resulted in a highly stratified society, with a great deal of commercial activity and growth.[21]

Salem built its first almshouse in 1719, considerably earlier than Danvers. Here some insane residents were housed, alongside their more rational fellow paupers, while others were boarded out.[22] By 1815 the complexity of life in Salem demanded other solutions. In that year a new almshouse was built, this time with a special section for the mad, who were kept there in cells. In the first years of its operation, eight "deranged" persons were kept in the almshouse cells.[23]

Significantly, not all the insane confined in the Salem almshouse were paupers; in fact, in 1815 only one was so described. The rest were confined for their behavior, not their financial status. One such person was the deranged James Snow, whose neighbors in 1815 complained to the overseers that he "menaced with threats in a most shameful manner." What was Snow's offense? According to his neighbors, his "language was intended to corrupt the morals of our children." These neighborly folk signed a petition demanding that he be committed to the almshouse. "We consider ourselves not perfectly safe while the saide

Snow is at liberty," they necessarily declared, in order that he might meet the criterion of the 1796 law. Although he was not a pauper, Snow was kept in one of the cells in the insane wing for over eight months under the provisions of that law, which had turned some local almshouses into jails for the mad.[24] In his case, menacing language had brought him under the rubric of the "furiously mad." In spite of the severity of the punishment meted out to Snow, Salem town officials were genuinely concerned with the accommodations that he and others would have to endure while in the almshouse. In a letter in 1816, one overseer asked another, "Are the cells for the insane such as humanity requires?"[25]

Salem confined only its own residents in its almshouse; other paupers were sent back to their towns of origin. Throughout the 1820s the town continued to exercise its prerogative under the 1796 law; in fact, the overseers regularly made payments to residents who took on the no doubt rather unpleasant task of rounding up the insane in the town and delivering them to the almshouse.[26] Salem had found it necessary earlier than the smaller towns in the state to make systematic arrangements for confining the mad. It was more like Boston, and its treatment of the insane was very similar.

Concord, the seat of the Revolution, was the smallest of the three towns. Nevertheless, it had become a prosperous agricultural community by the turn of the century, and its merchants had used the town's natural geographic advantage to develop an important center of trade.[27] Concord by and large still resembled the small towns of mid eighteenth-century Massachusetts more than either Danvers or Salem did, and for that reason its efforts to control the mad were less rigorous.

Concord boarded out all town paupers in the last years of the eighteenth century. Between 1784 and 1800, seven insane residents were cared for in the homes of their neighbors. One of them, "Crazy Joel Hosmer," was boarded out in the summers, since his madness came on him only at that time. The rest of the year he lived with his family and tended his farm. More severe measures were taken with another mad resident, Peter Smith, who was committed to the town jail in 1796, apparently for displaying a threatening form of madness. The town constable found him "dangerous to go at large."[28] What this actually meant is impossible to determine; it may have been anything from insulting language to violent behavior that made Smith's freedom unacceptable to local officials.

On the whole, Concord overseers took their responsibility to provide for their insane neighbors very seriously. In 1804 the overseers there received an irate letter from their Boston counterparts complaining about one of Concord's residents. "I have this day been desired to inform the Overseers of the Poor of Concord that there is a woman by the name of Wheeler who says she belongs to Concord who has for a considerable time been strolling about in town thinly cloathed and much deranged and has no means of subsistence but the charity of individuals . . . and we desire the Overseers to send for her as soon as possible." The Concord overseers brought Mary Wheeler back to town and boarded her out until she died in 1812. In another case in 1811, they paid a father to bring back his "deranged" son from another town and care for him.

While town officials in Concord toyed with the idea of building an almshouse, until 1828 paupers were boarded out. Perhaps the more bucolic atmosphere of Concord did not encourage madness, for there were few pauper insane there from 1800 to 1820.[29] Those few who did appear were boarded out with other paupers. Sometimes such boarders caused a great deal of trouble, as is suggested by a letter from one angry woman in 1820, who demanded payment for "boarding and nursing Alexander Hamilton and for damage done to my bed, bedding and windows when insane."

Around 1820 there was a change in Concord's response to the mad. The earlier provisions the town had made for its insane residents began to seem more troublesome, and it was becoming reluctant to board them out in the local community. In 1824 the Boston overseers wrote asking for the removal of Rebecca Barron and her daughter, Nancy, from the town. Unfortunately they added the caveat that the daughter, "being insane," was a great expense. Concord overseers seem to have ignored this request, for six months later another letter from Boston arrived written in an even more urgent tone, stating that Nancy was now in a "violent deranged state" and must be removed immediately, otherwise she would be brought to Concord. The overseers still did not bring her home. In 1827 Rebecca herself started pleading with the Concord overseers for money to return to Concord. Interestingly, she described her daughter as "sick," not as deranged. The distraught woman enlisted the aid of a Boston physician who testified to Nancy's "derangement of mind" in a letter to the overseers. Concord continued to ignore these pleas for assistance. Finally the physician wrote again, reporting that, as Nancy had become so "outrageously insane as to disturb the peace of the neighborhood and even to induce in some the fear of their lives, something must be done immediately or officers of the city must be applied to." Nancy then disappeared from the records.

What was the source of Concord's reluctance? Although the overseers surely were not eager to take on the financial burden represented by Nancy, they did retrieve other, noninsane paupers from neighboring towns in 1827.[30] A clue is offered in a donation given by town residents toward the building of McLean Asylum for the Insane in 1818. Concord officials, the only ones in Massachusetts to make a separate donation to the insane asylum, described it as "the place for lunatics."[31] In that year the town was supporting three "lunatics" in private homes. It seems Concordians were becoming eager to rid themselves of their insane neighbors and reluctant to support any more.

A negative feeling about the presence of the mad was becoming increasingly evident in other towns in the state. In 1812, Westminster officials locked up Thomas Ball, a Concord resident who had become insane while visiting that town. Town officials recorded that his imprisonment was "just punishment in such cases."[32] Similarly, in Haverhill a man from a neighboring town was put in the town jail in 1810 "forever on account of his insane behavior."[33] The towns of Lynn and Newburyport also confined insane residents in cells or in small rooms in separate sections of their almshouses during the 1820s.[34] One local official directly expressed the anxiety that was developing about the insane. An overseer from Sudbury wrote to state officials in 1824 asking for help in sending one insane resident of the town to jail. His insanity was a "loathsome disease," claimed the official, which made it necessary to confine him to the Ipswich jail in order to remove him from East Sudbury. Since East Sudbury did not have an almshouse in 1824, the clearly unacceptable alternative would have been to board him out with a local family.[35] The overseers' remarks again suggest that the understanding of madness as a disease did not necessarily soften the response to the insane.

In the western areas of the state, the town of Deerfield was confining its insane residents in irons by 1820. John Wilson, who boarded all the paupers in Deerfield, kept one of his insane charges in a cage from 1820 to 1831, when she was removed to the house of correction in Greenfield. Accompanying her was a letter he wrote to the jail-keeper. "I had kept her chained or in a cage for a long time before, there was no diminution of her malady, but it seems to be increasing." Deerfield sent any "lunatic paupers, considered to be dangerous" to the house of corrections in Greenfield after 1824.[36] In Greenfield, a "deranged Daniel Wells" was kept in a straitjacket in the town jail from 1820 to 1824, when he was sent to McLean Asylum.[37]

Even Concord officials drastically altered their treatment of the insane in the 1830s. By then the reluctance to keep the mad in the town had hardened into a policy of repressive confinement. Beginning in 1830, insane residents were kept in the new town almshouse in cages. Five were incarcerated there in 1830, out of a total almshouse population of twenty-one.[38]

The stringent treatment of the insane in Concord was also characteristic of Danvers in this period. In 1825 the overseers there committed Asa Richardson to the town jail as "an insane and dangerous person in society." The records do not indicate what form Richardson's madness took, but some suggestion of how narrowly the boundaries of sanity were being drawn is offered by the town's reaction to James Daily. In 1829 the Danvers overseers were informed that Daily, a Danvers resident, had taken up lodging in a barn in Ipswich and "appeared to be partially deranged." The Danvers overseers "thought it improper that such a person should go at large," so they ordered that he be sent to the county receptacle in Ipswich, which served as a jail for the surrounding towns. They then wrote to Daily's father, asking what he wished done. "Did he want him returned to the almshouse?" The senior Daily did not want to become involved in any arrangements for his son "but preferred having him remain where he is." In other words, he preferred to leave his son in jail rather than have him housed at the town almshouse or care for him at home. Daily's derangement consisted of his belief that someone was trying to murder him; consequently he hid from everyone. He clearly was not a threat to the community; he was not "furiously mad"; nevertheless he was jailed.[39]

In the years immediately preceding the opening of the first public asylum in the state, the insane often fared poorly at the hands of public officials. A town committee investigating the situation of those insane confined in the Salem almshouse in 1832 reported that there were twenty insane residents exposed to public view. They were kept in cells and "recent complaints have arisen from this circumstance." One "poor maniac has been shamefully abused . . . and kept destitute of proper clothing to protect him from the severity of the weather and nothing has been done to make his situation more comfortable," the committee complained. Suggesting that the accommodations Salem offered its insane residents were hardly unique, the committee claimed that although the conditions at the almshouse were unsuitable, they were "not inferior to the conditions found in similar institutions, if we may judge from the fact that repeated applications have been made to us from other towns in the county for admission of this class of sufferers."[40]

It is impossible to determine from the records whether any or all of these confined persons were paupers. But given Salem's earlier record of locking up nonpauper insane, it is probable that at least some of them were not. It is clear that many nonpauper insane were confined all over the state in this period, as allowed by the 1796 law. Richardson was not a pauper; in fact, he had a father who presumably could have supported him. None of the evidence from the outlying towns of Deerfield and Greenfield suggests that the insane confined there in the 1820s were paupers. Insanity had bestowed a new status on the residents of the state, a status conferred independently of financial means.

The movement in the state to confine the insane appeared in some places earlier than in others. In 1810, Salem residents had treated their insane neighbors very differently than had the residents of Danvers and Concord. But by 1830 provisions for the treatment of the pauper insane in all three towns were very similar. Salem, the most densely populated and complex of the three, had found it necessary to provide stringent measures of control earlier than the two smaller ones. Yet by 1830 all three had established punishing forms of confinement as their official response to the insane.

The change in the reaction to madness that began at the end of the eighteenth century had overtaken much of the state by the late 1820s. In 1829 a committee of the Massachusetts legislature asked the towns to report on the "lunatics and furiously mad" in their midst.[41] One hundred twelve towns reported a total of 289 "lunatic persons." Of these, two-thirds were confined in almshouses, private homes, or jails. Thirty-eight of those confined were in chains. This report suggests that the movement to confine the mad was relatively recent. Three-fourths of those confined had been so less than eight years, and over half for less than three years.

The stories of confinement might well have been appalling to those who read them. One man in Groton had been chained in his father's house since 1812. Another sixty-three-year-old man from Chelsea had been confined for thirty years in a room without a fire. A man in Marlborough had been confined for ten years in a "small building erected for confining him."

This report offers strong evidence that the criteria for confinement had widened considerably since the 1796 law. Twenty-one lunatics were under lock and key for "wandering or strolling about." Solomon Griswold was confined in the Springfield jail for over eight years for "outrageous language, breaking windows and threatening much mischief." A woman from Leominster had been confined in the county house at Worcester for two years for "throwing stones at the dwelling house and breaking glass." Significantly, of those chained, over half were de-

scribed as "deranged but not furiously mad." While Malden reported only two insane people in the town, the overseers there
informed the committee that they nevertheless had erected "a
separate building for the special purpose of containing persons
that are lunatic and furiously mad."

In the largest town in the state, the problem of what to do
with the insane was becoming increasingly serious in the 1820s.
In the Boston almshouse, now called the house of industry, from
thirty-five to forty insane paupers were confined in cells in a
separate structure at any one time.[42] A committee visiting the
facility in 1833, just before the opening of the Worcester State
Lunatic Hospital reported that the almshouse looked like "an
asylum for the insane." Most of the inmates were locked in small
strong rooms, with three insane in each room. These inmates
were let out once a day to exercise in a small yard.[43] The director
of the house of industry pleaded many times with the town fathers and the state legislature to enlarge this space, arguing that
the yard was so small that only three inmates could stand in it
at one time.[44]

It was in the jails of the state that the insane suffered the most
terribly. Since the 1796 legislation, local authorities had been
committing the mad, without trial and without formal commitment proceedings, to these jails, where they could languish for
years with little or no possibility of release. In 1827 the Boston
Prison Discipline Society, a charitable organization with prison
reform as its main goal, published a now famous report exposing the inhumane treatment of the insane in prisons across the
state. The reformers who visited jails found that thirty "lunatics"
were imprisoned in deplorable conditions. The founder of the
society, the Reverend Louis Dwight, described the conditions
suffered by the insane; this celebrated description is unequaled
in its terrible vividness.

One was found in apartment in which he had been nine years. He had
a wreath of rags round his body, and another round his neck. This was
all his clothing. He had no bed, chair or bench. Two or three rough
planks were strewed about the room, a heap of filthy straw, like the nest
of swine, was in the corner. He had built a bird's nest of mud in the iron
grate of his den. Connected with his wretched apartment was a dark

dungeon, having no orifice for the admission of light, heat or air, except the iron door, about 24 feet square. . . . The wretched lunatic was indulging some delusive expectations of being soon released from this wretched abode.

Women were treated no better.

The female was lying on a heap of straw, under a broken window. The snow, in a severe storm, was beating through the window, and lay upon the straw around her withered body, which was partially covered with a few filthy and tattered garments.[45]

A similar investigation of prisons in the state was carried out in the same year by a committee of the legislature, which reported that the insane everywhere were more wretchedly treated than the other prisoners. They had the dirtiest quarters, with the least light and warmth. They were poorly clothed and ill fed. The injustice of the treatment struck these legislators powerfully.

Many of them have never been accused or charged with any crime, and have remained many years in the most wretched condition. Less attention is paid to their cleanliness and comfort than to the wild beasts in their cages, which are kept for show. Some of these miserable beings have been confined for twenty years or more, and seem to have been left to wallow in their own filth. In visiting the various prisons where they are found we have found no exceptions.[46]

These reports were crucial in fueling the ire of reformers in the state, who were working to establish a public asylum for the insane.[47] Horrified visitors to jails were viewing the results of the 1796 legislation empowering authorities to confine the furiously mad. Many insane persons who fitted that description are likely to have been confined in the jails; the reports indicate that some had been held there since the early years of the century. But some who were not "furiously mad" were probably also living out their lives in these jails. Certainly a great number of insane confined in local almshouses were not dangerous. Those confined in jails early in the nineteenth century may have been more dangerous than those in local almshouses in the 1820s, as the first wave of confinements was likely to have swept up the insane with the most antisocial and threatening behavior. The evidence indicates that an increasingly wider range of behavior was cause for confinement in the almshouses in the 1820s and early 1830s. It is clear that by this time violent and nonviolent insane alike were routinely confined by local officials and by some families, who preferred to put their relatives in jails and almshouses than to care for them at home.

Before the opening of Worcester State Lunatic Hospital in 1833, this policy of confinement was not linked to efforts at cure. Neither was it moderated by the earlier ministerial concern about the spiritual lessons implicit in madness. Physicians had not yet established themselves as the group able to take public responsibility for insanity; ministers had declined in authority in the state since the Revolution. Insanity, however, was an increasing problem. In the absence of other alternatives, public officials moved to fill the gap and control the insane as best they could. The new beliefs about the nature of madness that suggested personal responsibility for the maintenance of sanity, insofar as they were known, would have provided a rationale for confinement. If the insane had indeed brought on their condition because of excesses and lack of self-control, these controls would be provided by others, in expedient, if not necessarily humane ways. Before reformers and physicians established the public asylum to confine and treat the insane, Massachusetts towns had found ways to reduce their threat.

6 The Place for Lunatics

While the public response to the insane in early nineteenth-century Massachusetts developed largely independently of the medical view of madness, another movement to cure the insane, directly linked to these medical views, was slowly gaining in importance. A tension existed between the need to confine the insane, in order to protect the public from the potential danger they represented, and a more benevolent reform impulse to treat them and restore them to reason. This tension was resolved when the asylum came to be viewed as the most humane solution to the problem. Well before asylums were established in the Northeast, however, the medical profession there had developed a heightened interest in the insane, partly based on the newer theories of madness. While much of this interest seemed to center on efforts to explain it, there was also an increased attention to the possibility of cure. The increasing emphasis on the biology of madness was reflected in a growing tendency to rely on medical treatment, some of which was very strenuous. Both reactions to the insane, the need to confine them and the desire to cure them, were essentially new; together they reveal how significant an issue madness had become in the state.

Early medical treatment of the insane was not necessarily more humane than lay measures confining them in public facilities. One Massachusetts physician, Edward Holyoke, described his efforts to cure one patient in the 1780s. Holyoke was treating a "Captain Jos. T. who grew disordered in his reason" upon meeting with difficulties, which left him with a "difficulty in uttering himself and an evident want of recollection." Though the captain was apparently only mildly disturbed and not violent, Holyoke commenced a course of treatment that put his patient in a ferocious mood. He first purged and "blooded him," then began giving him opium. The day after the treatment began, the captain "grew more disordered in his understanding than ever." The physician increased the dosage of medicine, continued to bleed his patient and purge him though without visible effects. Still the medicine was increased until he was taking six grains three times a day. During the course of the treatment, the captain was sometimes quiet, but "his distraction" continued. When Holyoke visited him a "fortnight later," he found his "understanding in no respect mended"; he alternately raved and was calm. After three months of this regimen, the captain was as disturbed as when this treatment commenced.[1] Holyoke was prescribing the standard medical remedies of his day for madness, omitting only the blistering of the scalp to cause eruptions.

Other physicians were even sterner in their suggestions for cure. The English physician George Wallis, in a medical text published in this country, advocated psychological remedies such as scaring the madman and forcing him to engage in constant and hard labor. "Mad people," claimed Wallis, " are always cowardly and can be awed by the look of a very expressive countenance." He also urged that bleeding, purging, and blistering the head all be used freely.[2]

Edward Cutbush and Henry Rose also urged the use of fear and coercion. Cutbush suggested "throwing them into the sea until they nearly drown." He also advocated compressing the arteries in the neck, though he warned the reader that he had received a severe blow from a patient when he tried this. In a irritated postscript to these instructions. Cutbush complained that the relatives often do not allow these methods to be employed.[3] Alexander Anderson was convinced that shaming the patient was the best cure for insanity, although he also thought "plunging the patient into cold water" could be useful.[4]

Another physician, John Vaughan, described how he attempted unsuccessfully to treat a maniac in 1802 by applying "cold water to the head for 36 hours, without any effect but an occasional shuddering sensation." With the same case he also "attempted a revulsion of excitement by the application of blisters to the scalp, hands and feet, but with no success."[5] Taking a similar tack, a physician writing in 1801 claimed that he had cured five cases of madness with water. "After a failure of the most approved medicines and practice, the application of cold water to the head, persevered in for many days, performed the cure." His particular technique was to wind a handkerchief around the head of the insane person and keep it wet until it produced a "shivering fit." After ministering in this fashion to one patient for thirty to fifty hours, "sobbing and sighing came on, which have hitherto proved the criterion of the incipient return of rational ideas."[6] William Gibbons, an early expert on hypochondriasis, suggested the use of a series of electric shocks as a cure for madness.[7]

While some of these heroic remedies were the same ones called upon to treat physical illness, the more painful were thought to be especially useful in treating madness, since it was believed they distracted the insane from their mental preoccupations. In addition, painful and drastic measures were considered helpful in subduing the patient's will, a necessary step in cases where willfulness and lack of self-control had caused the condition.[8]

Benjamin Rush's treatment of the insane at Pennsylvania Hospital was typical of this period. Rush was very interested in bleeding, which made eminent sense to him since he believed that madness was caused by vascular tension. He also blistered and purged his patients, put them in straitjackets and restraining chairs (which he called "Tranquillizers"), starved them, gave them shower baths, and dunked them in water. He sometimes threatened them with death—especially by drowning. He called this measure the "fear of death." Rush referred to all these measures as punishment, not as treatment, since they were used primarily to subdue unruly patients. Of course, since to subdue the wildness of mania was part of the process of cure, this distinction was really not a crucial one. Rush also thought that solitary confinement, "keeping them erect to tire them out," fasting, cold water, and digitalis might be useful with some insane patients. Others responded better to ridicule and humiliation, he found. These measures were not idiosyncratic to Rush; in fact, many had been used by English physicians in the previous century.[9] Rush was unique in this country, however, in the wide range of vigorous techniques he urged and in the vehemence with which he did so.

In spite of the punitive nature of his treatment, Rush also demonstrated strong humanitarian feelings for the insane in his care. He suggested first trying kindness and using the other remedies only when kindness failed (as it apparently did frequently with him). His "mental therapy" as he called it, involved his frank talk with the patients about their fears. Rush was optimistic that medical science would find a way to cure the mad. In 1812 he wrote with great sentiment:

After the history that has been given of the distress, despair and voluntary death, which are induced by that partial derangement ... I should lay down my pen, and bedew my paper with my tear, did I not know that the science of medicine has furnished a remedy for it, and that hundreds are now alive, and happy, who were once afflicted with it. Blessed science! Which thus extends its friendly empire, not only over the evils of the bodies, but over those of the minds, of the children of man![10]

Rush was clearly not a cruel man; the punishing nature of some of his treatment was directly related to his beliefs about the nature and causes of madness. If it was brought on by excesses of mind or body, then the imposition of strict measures to counteract this lack of control were necessary. Rush's underlying belief that madness resulted in part from personal failings and weakness was shared with many other physicians in his day and may have contributed to the severity of his treatment. Insofar as he assumed that the insane could control themselves if they wished (one of Tuke's main arguments), Rush would also believe that harsh treatment would force them to take hold of themselves.

That Rush was not unique in his approach to treating the insane is clear from the remedies used by John Gorham at the Boston almshouse in the early nineteenth century. Dr. Gorham bled, blistered, and purged his insane patients daily. One pauper who received these treatments unwillingly "became exceedingly turbulent and almost ungovernable" afterward. The physician was puzzled at the negative effect of his attempts to cure the man and finally put him in a "straight waistcoat." Gorham's usual response to insane paupers was to give them doses of opium, but this could also be counterproductive with already excited patients. This same unruly pauper became stronger after a dose of opium and would not sleep, so the physician increased the dosage daily until he began sleeping all day and "appeared in a state nearly approaching to the comatose." Gorham marveled that the patient "seemed to have exchanged the state of active mania only for the quietude of idiotism."[11] He was surprised at the stuporous effect that accompanied the administration of heavy doses of opium, but some later physicians working at lunatic asylums would make wide use of this drug—and its sedative effects—in order to control the overcrowded patient population.

Among the private madhouses operated by physicians in Massachusetts in the early nineteenth century, one seemed to specialize in harsher remedies. In a later account, Isaac Ray described the establishment of a Dr. Willard.

The main idea was to break the patient's will and make him learn that he had a master; to teach him that there was a mind and physical strength there all superior to his own. That was the principal object to be kept in view, and it was to be gained at any risk. If fair means would not do, other means should; if strong words or curses would not answer then resort was had to the knock-down arguments. This was thought to be the proper way; no secret was made of it, and the friends of patients understood it perfectly well.

One method of treatment was

the process of submersion, and the idea was . . . that if the patient was nearly drowned and then brought to life, he would take a fresh start, leaving his disease behind. Dr. Willard had a tank prepared on the premises, into which the patient, enclosed in a coffin-like box pierced with holes, was lowered by means of a well-sweep. He was kept there under water until bubbles of air cease to rise, then was taken out, rubbed and revived. What success followed this process I never knew. Of the fact itself I have no doubt, for I was told of it by those two gentlemen who had witnessed it themselves.[12]

On the other hand, Ray described another private establishment, in Andover, offering more humane methods. The proprietor, Thomas Kittredge, began treating the insane in the 1790s and acquired a reputation for having a special expertise. He usually cared for ten to twelve insane persons at a time.[13] His methods of firm kindness were continued after his death by his son, Joseph Kittredge. Ray described the establishment in glowing terms.

They never received their patients in their own homes, but made arrangements for boarding them in two or three private families. These families were presided over by strong, fearless, capable and good natured women, most of whom had husbands, and the patients were under little restraint, though subject to constant supervision. They do not appear to have belonged to the most violent classes, as there do not seem to have been any strong rooms in which to confine them.[14]

While Ray presumed that there were no strong rooms because there were no violent lunatics, it is also possible that Kittredge found other ways to calm his patients. Archelaus Putnam was taken to Kittredge's in leg chains in a state of fury and was restored to tranquility and reason by the family who boarded him.

Kittredge's judicious treatment of his charges resembled the program of moral treatment developed by Pinel and Tuke. While Kittredge was unlikely to have been influenced by either man, both Pinel's and Tuke's ideas were crucial to the asylum movement in Massachusetts. The initial efforts in New England to open an asylum based on principles of moral treatment were made by the Massachusetts physician George Parkman, who had studied with Pinel. Parkman had also read Samuel Tuke's description of the York Retreat, in which he argued that it was necessary to remove the insane from their own families to a quieter place.[15] In 1814 Parkman published a description of a proposed asylum to be built in Boston based on Tuke's model.[16] While he did not realize his dream of founding a significant asylum for the insane in the state, he continued to be eager to suggest cures, such as treating the insane to douches, placing them on a rotary swing, and putting them in a boat with ropes, to stimulate "the calm and passiveness of seasickness."[17]

The principles of moral treatment as outlined by Tuke did not include any of Parkman's suggested contraptions but emphasized psychological methods, the most important of which was a gentle, respectful attitude toward the insane in the asylum. Tuke eschewed medical remedies; instead, like Pinel, he believed that the insane could relearn self-control through proper environmental cues, especially participation in work and religious services as well as the judicious application of the "principle of fear."[18] In the latter recommendation, Tuke resembled Rush and others who used strong measures. Yet on the whole, Tuke's ideas eclipsed those of Rush, for his main emphasis was on the more humane features of moral treatment, which were to be both the rationale and the foundation for the movement to build asylums for the insane in this country in the 1820s and 1830s.[19]

The first asylum established in New England was designed to be a faithful replica of Tuke's Retreat. McLean Asylum in Massachusetts, funded largely by private subscriptions raised by Boston's elite, opened its doors to the first insane patients in 1818.[20] The founding of McLean Asylum was part of a larger movement to found a hospital for the sick in the city. John Warren was one of the key figures in the drive to raise funds for the first hospital in the state, known as Massachusetts General Hospital. While the charter for this hospital and some monies had been given by the state government, both the hospital and the asylum were essentially private enterprises. In keeping with the movement to separate the insane from the rest of the population, the trustees of the hospital decided early on to house the insane outside Boston in a separate facility.

Most of the insane who came to McLean Asylum in the early years came from the homes of their families, where many had been confined in very unpleasant circumstances.[21] In the main, McLean Asylum served the wealthiest insane. While provisions for poorer patients were included in the original plan, only a few were treated there each year.[22]

Rufus Wyman, the first superintendent of the asylum, had been strongly influenced by the practices at Tuke's Retreat, and his main goal was to "divert the mind from unpleasant subjects of thought."[23] McLean Asylum, along with Friends' Asylum in Pennsylvania and the Hartford Retreat in Connecticut, were important early models of moral treatment and influenced both physicians and reformers in their ideas about treatment of the insane.[24] At McLean's the most cherished hopes of the advocates of moral treatment were realized. In the first years the residents spent their time playing chess and backgammon, working in the garden, sawing wood, or exercising their creative talents through music or writing. Attendants were chosen with great care; many of them were former schoolteachers. The patients could and did bring their own servants with them. Wyman visited each patient daily and often took them on excursions into Boston.[25] In 1825 Wyman described the physical surroundings that the insane enjoyed at McLean. "Each family is also provided with dining and work rooms, a separate airing court and has access to it by separate stairs, that the members of different families may not mix together. The courts are so arranged that patients in an improved state of mind will not see those who are in a worse condition."[26]

The opening of McLean Asylum was significant for two reasons: it marked the acceptance and legitimation of the disease model of insanity on the part of Boston's elite, and it represented the first reform efforts in the state to help the insane. Although this asylum was founded on the precepts of moral treatment, more strenuous and even punitive approaches were evident there from the beginning. Strong rooms, muffs, chair and bed straps, and even manacles were used to restrain patients in the 1820s.[27] Drugs, especially laudanum, were administered; in fact, patients who requested discharge were often administered extra dosages of drugs.[28] Those who demanded release in more vehement ways were locked in strong rooms.[29] At McLean's, moral treatment had not eliminated the more rigorous treatment of insanity but had merely softened it.

McLean Asylum could serve the needs of only a small number of the wealthier insane residents of the state. Throughout the

1820s the majority of the mad still languished in jails, alms-houses, and private homes, sometimes neglected, sometimes treated harshly. Reports about the condition of the insane in these places began to proliferate in the late 1820s, as we have seen. Perhaps inevitably, the reform movement that had begun privately became a matter of public concern in the 1830s, when prominent Massachusetts reformers Horace Mann and Louis Dwight spearheaded a drive to open a public asylum for the insane in the state. The desire of reformers to reduce the sufferings of the insane was by this time inextricably tied to the now dominant belief of the medical profession that insanity was a disease and that the insane therefore belonged in a hospital under the care of a physician. At the same time, Mann and others concerned with the plight of the insane were convinced that moral treatment, basically a nonmedical approach, offered the best, if not the only hope for the recovery of lunatics. The apparent inconsistency of offering a nonmedical therapeutic in an essentially medical setting did not trouble these early reformers, since they believed that a hospital was the only place the insane could receive humane care. They had accepted the medical view that these disparate assumptions concerning the disease model and the usefulness of psychological treatment were reconcilable, and they did not concern themselves with the way in which this reconciliation was achieved.

In a report to the legislature in 1830, Mann claimed that there were at least 500 insane in the state lacking suitable accommodations. As chairman of a legislative committee appointed to study the problem, he recommended that Massachusetts establish a state lunatic hospital for 120 "furiously mad" residents.[30] He argued that at this hospital a system of humane treatment would "supersede a system in which fetters, whips, confinement, starvation and suffocation in water almost to drowning," were the "standard remedies" for madness.[31] Furthermore, Mann argued, 50 percent of the insane were curable, if given proper therapy.[32]

Mann's optimism was put to the test at the opening of Worcester State Lunatic Hospital in 1833. The first public mental hospital in the state received more than one-half of its 164 patients from jails, almshouses, and houses of correction.[33] The confrontation with these often long-confined insane horrified Samuel Woodward as well as the trustees of the hospital, because all concerned believed that only recent cases of insanity were curable. The trustees' report in 1834 was the beginning of a long series of complaints about the "incurables and chronics" sent to Worcester.

Another obstacle to success has existed in the peculiar character and condition of the patients sent to the Hospital. Other institutions, both in Europe and America, which have exhibited the most remarkable proportion of cures, have discriminated in their admissions, receiving the more hopeful cases only. The inmates at Worcester have been a more select class than were ever before assembled together; but unfortunately for success in regard to cures, it has been a selection of the most deplorable cases in the whole community. Of the one hundred and sixty four individuals received . . . about one-third of the whole number had suffered confinement for periods varying from ten to thirty-two years.[34]

Many of these first admissions did have an air of hopelessness about them. In 1832 the director of the Boston house of industry (formerly the almshouse) had written Mann to ask when the new hospital would be open. He complained that, of his 500 inmates, "50 are more or less insane and about half may be described as furiously mad and requiring constant confinement in closed dormitories. . . . In a majority of cases no hope of complete restoration to sanity exists."[35] According to the original mandate of the state legislature, all of the insane confined at the Boston house of industry would have been sent to Worcester. Compounding the difficulty, in 1833 the legislature passed a law authorizing the courts henceforth to commit all furiously mad residents of Massachusetts to the new state lunatic asylum.[36] To legislators, this law made eminent sense. Since these dangerous lunatics were to be confined anyway, humanity dictated that they should be put in a place where they could be cured, rather than in jails and almshouses. Of course, their confinement at Worcester would also serve to remove them a good distance from the sane population of the state.

In spite of the difficulties of overcrowding and too many "incurables," the trustees' reports for the first six years are sprinkled with miraculous accounts of raving lunatics turning into docile, well-behaved inmates. In 1833 they wrote:

Not less than one hundred of those brought to the Hospital seemed to regard human beings as enemies, and their first impulse was to assail them with open or disguised force. Now there are not more than twelve who offer violence. Of forty persons who formerly divested themselves of clothing, even in the most inclement seasons of the year, only eight do it now. Through all the galleries, there is far less susceptibility to excitement, more quietude, more civility and kindness exercised towards each other. The wailings of the despondent and the ravings of the frantic are dispelled.[37]

The successes of the early years of Worcester can no doubt be attributed to the regimen of moral treatment practiced by Samuel Woodward and the rest of the staff there. The superintendent was a strong advocate of this therapy, but he also believed that the standard somatic remedies, such as bleeding, purging, emetics, and blistering, should be employed for good measure. He frequently administered heavy doses of narcotics and other drugs.[38] Woodward believed medical treatment was necessary to "control the range of symptoms and to bring the patient within the range of moral influences."[39] Labor, as well as participation in religious and social activities, was strongly encouraged, if not mandated. Most patients worked either on a farm attached to the hospital or within the asylum itself. Woodward was very involved with patients, visiting many every day and recording frequent, sometimes daily entries about each one.[40]

Calm, orderly, and cooperative behavior was the most important sign of cure. Means of controlling the patients were more strenuous than those used at McLean Asylum: strong rooms, restraints, drugs (especially laudanum and opium), and blistering were all used more frequently at Worcester. Woodward bled uncooperative patients, while the superintendents at McLean Asylum did not.[41] The most serious offense apparently was to request (especially to demand) discharge. Such requests were generally ignored in the 1830s and, if vehement enough, were answered with narcotics.[42]

While Woodward was calm and fatherly with many patients, he disliked those who had become insane because of their moral flaws. One man whose intemperance was thought to have caused his insanity moved Woodward to write in the case record: "The moral principle is deranged with this man. He does not adhere to the truth in the least degree. He is disgusting."[43]

Woodward reserved his greatest disdain for those patients who masturbated. A male inmate committed in 1837 practiced this habit incessantly, according to Woodward. His mind was "dull and torpid as a consequence and his health run down." Although the patient was "calm and pleasant," Woodward could not help despising him. "He is a miserable man," he wrote two months later, when he released him, in a "miserable imbecile condition."[44] Woodward had a tendency to use the strongest remedies for patients who, he believed, caused their own insanity by their distasteful habits. It was not uncommon for him to blister these patients, bleed them, and give them frequent doses of narcotics.[45] In this sense Woodward was linked to the medical tradition of Rush and Cutbush rather than to moral treatment. As was the case at McLean Asylum, the more benign methods of moral treatment did not seem sufficient at Worcester. Patients were regularly locked in the strong rooms for uncooperative behavior.[46] Woodward's conviction that stresses in the Jacksonian social order were responsible for some cases of insanity may have contributed to the gentleness and humanity of his treatment of many of his patients, but he was not as sympathetic to those with obvious vices. More importantly, as the asylum became increasingly crowded with incurables, his beliefs about causes would be less significant in informing his treatment. Control of the patient population would necessarily become the greater priority.

Whatever the methods of restoring the insane to reason, the process was apparently often successful in the early years, if we are to believe the case histories the trustees recounted in their reports. One man had been

28 years in prison—seven years he had not felt the influence of fire, and many nights he had not lain down for fear of freezing. He had not been shaved for 28 years, and he had been provoked and excited by the introduction of hundreds, to see the exhibitions of his raving. He is now, and has been, comfortable in health, well clad, keeps his bed and room remarkably clean, and, although very insane on certain sub-

jects, is most of the time pleasant, compassionate and entirely harmless and docile. He shaves himself twice a week—sits at table with sixteen others—takes his meals—walks about the village and over the fields with an attendant to accompany him, and enjoys himself as well as his illusions will permit.[47]

These patients and many others like them described in the reports and records were no longer furiously mad.[48] Yet even though they were harmless, they continued to be confined at Worcester. The patients who more or less conformed to the standards of the hospital but who were still considered irrational were known as incurables. The trustees thought these patients required "but little medical treatment, no nursing and no selection of diet, all they require is good substantial food and comfortable apartments."[49] In other words, incurables required custodial rather than moral treatment. In spite of their acknowledged inability to treat these patients, the trustees and the superintendent of the hospital wished to build separate facilities for them; they did not want to release them. The desire to keep the incurables in the hospital is a sign of the new significance attached to all forms of madness in the society. Even the mad who presented no threat to others and who could not benefit from any therapeutic regime were seen as persons who should be confined.[50]

The opening of Worcester had a significant impact on the operation of the McLean Asylum. In 1837, Luther Bell, then superintendent of McLean, wrote of his gratitude that Worcester was taking all the pauper lunatics as patients, since this "relieved the wards of those who could not be brought in consociation with the body of our boarders who are from middle and upper classes of society, without detracting from the highest practical comfort of each. To the polished and cultivated it is due as much to separate them from the coarse and the degraded, as to administer to them in other respects."[51] As a consequence of the increasing homogeneity of the patient population, McLean became even more resortlike than it had been. Most of the patients expected to be treated with a high degree of deference. The wealthier refused to speak to those of lower social standing.[52]

Thomas Lee, superintendent of McLean from 1834 to 1836, described the elegant style of life there.

> We meet them as friends and brothers; we cultivate their affections. . . . In doing this, we consult their tastes, feelings, their former habits and pursuits. Games of all kinds, chess, checkers, backgammon, ninepins, quoits, battledores, graces, reading, writing, walks, rides and field sports, are some of their occupations. We invite the quiet and convalescent into our family, seat them at our tables and give weekly parties for their amusement and benefit. On such occasions, we engage in and participate with them in marching and dancing. We assemble them every evening for family worship, which consists in reading a chapter from the Bible and singing two hymns and a prayer.[53]

Even so, stronger methods of control continued to be necessary. Bell used opium freely on his patients, according to his journal. He found it "very difficult" to abandon its use once he had started to administer it. The patients given opium were the "old and helpless cases." In 1836 a separate building known as "the Lodge" was built to confine violent patients in strong rooms.[54]

While conditions at McLean's were far more luxurious than those at Worcester, there were still elements of coercion for some of those placed there. In 1833, Robert Fuller published a pamphlet protesting his experiences at McLean, where he claimed he was held for sixty-five days against his will, although fully rational. Fuller wrote that he was seized and then taken to McLean in chains, put in a room alone, and stripped of his possessions and clothes. He claimed that he rarely saw a doctor and was detained in that room for weeks despite his demands for release.[55]

The authenticity of Fuller's account has been questioned; it may well be one of several sensationalized accounts of insane asylums written at that time by patients who did not understand the purpose of the treatment; therefore it may be problematic to take it completely at face value.[56] However, several of Fuller's contentions are verified by the records. Troublesome and uncooperative patients were put in strong rooms and stripped of their clothing.[57] Patients could be brought to McLean on the basis of a certificate that stated that they were insane. While the process of investigating sanity was a rather thorough one, there was no commitment law establishing a judicial procedure for prospective patients of this asylum.[58] Regardless of how exaggerated Fuller's account of McLean Asylum may have been, it is conceivable that a rational person could have had a similar experience there. As with Worcester, the humaneness of McLean's treatment was for the cooperative, not the recalcitrant. Fuller thought that the very existence of such asylums was bound to lead to a broader definition of madness.

If the number of inmates of that Institution is a true index of the number of insane, the increase of this disease since its establishment leads to melancholy reflections. Insanity was once a rare occurrence; the community did not feel the want of such an asylum, and but few were considered the proper subjects of such a place. Insanity is no longer rare: the Asylum is open to receive all, whom any persons may think the proper subjects. Mere suspicion or malice is enough to fix on anyone the charge of insanity. Witches were never convicted with less testimony than the insane are now. An Asylum, prepared for the insane alone, is made the common receptacle of the sick, insane, idiotic and suspicious.[59]

Fuller was correct about the growing number of persons sent to McLean. Figures from the annual reports indicate that 103 persons were admitted in 1833 as compared with 44 in 1820.[60]

In spite of the difficulties these asylums faced and the punitive nature of some of their treatments, those who were discharged as cured from Worcester State Lunatic Hospital and McLean Asylum in the 1830s had learned a number of important things: to labor productively, to control those personal habits that were considered dangerous or distasteful, and to interact with others in an acceptable way. They had successfully rehearsed for life in the society outside the walls of the asylum.

While there were clear differences between the elegant treatment the wealthy received at McLean's and the homelier program at Worcester, both institutions represented serious attempts to develop programs based on the principles of moral treatment. A humanitarianism and optimism characterized the early years of these institutions, as their founders were convinced that much madness was curable. If a cure meant that a released inmate could function according to the expectations of the wider society, then many were cured.

Most of the insane in Massachusetts, however, did not benefit from all the enthusiasm and optimism. Instead, greater numbers of them continued to be confined in jails and almshouses in the 1830s.[61] The pressure of overcrowding at Worcester forced a shift in policy in the state. In 1836 the legislature required every county with a house of correction to have a "suitable and convenient apartment or receptacle for idiots and lunatics or insane persons not furiously mad."[62] Under this law some could be discharged from Worcester and returned to the same local institutions from which they had recently been liberated. Although only three counties ever opened such receptacles for the insane, the legislation seemed to signal a shift away from the recent medicalization of madness.[63] In reality this return of the insane to town jails and almshouses was a sign of the now accepted need to confine all the insane.

By the end of the decade, the hospital was returning incurables to local facilities at a rapid rate. In the report for 1838 the trustees lamented the fact that out of "painful necessity" they had been forced to return to the jails and houses of correction of the respective counties whence they came, a large number of the inmates, in order to make room for the more ferocious, committed by the courts." They decried the necessity of removing quieter patients for the more violent," who have brought their insanity upon themselves by their own misconduct or crimes."[64] The connection between moral failures and violent madness seems to have become axiomatic in the trustees' minds.

Some insane were shuffled back and forth between almshouses and the lunatic hospital during the 1830s. In addition, more and more who either had been discharged or could not gain admittance to Worcester were accumulating during the same period in Boston. There pauper lunatics released from Worcester languished in the house of industry. By the close of the decade, there was a growing sense that the house of industry was not the place for lunatics. As more and more pauper insane were returned there from Worcester, the city began to consider ways to care for their increasing number. In 1839 the solution was achieved with the opening of the Boston Lunatic Hospital. This facility quickly became a purely custodial institution, designed to take the pauper incurables who were residents of Boston out of the increasingly crowded Worcester State Lunatic Hospital.[65] With the opening of Boston Lunatic Hospital, an era had ended in the state. Viewed as a custodial institution almost from its inception, this asylum represented a turning away from moral treatment and the belief that all insanity could be cured—the belief that had inspired reformers like Mann and Dwight to work for the establishment of Worcester State Lunatic Hospital. It signaled instead the final acceptance of the profound change in the relationship of the insane to the rest of Massachusetts society—a change that was first evident after the Revolution. Whether or not the mad could be cured, they had to be confined.[66]

While the dominant trend in the decades immediately following the Revolution was to isolate the mad from the rest of Massachusetts society, by the 1830s a tension was evident between those who wished to cure the insane and those who merely wished to confine them in the most expedient manner. The first group consisted largely of reformers who insisted that only a lunatic hospital could provide humane care and treatment; the second group was represented by town officials who wished to save money and keep local insane in the almshouse rather than send them to Worcester. All concerned parties, however, shared a common assumption that the insane could not and should not live alongside the rest of the population. They were no longer thought to be "fit to go at large."[67] Even moral treatment, through which the insane were to be resocialized into the socially constructed meanings and commonly accepted behaviors of the society, had a steely side to it. A process of reeducation, it also provided a mechanism of social control. Moral treatment helped the mad learn or relearn self-control, necessary because the environment outside the asylum was structured in such a way that self-control was essential. In the final analysis this therapy provided a laboratory atmosphere where the skills necessary to function in Jacksonian society were learned.[68]

In spite of the cultural sanctions and normative elements inherent in moral treatment, it was a humane therapy. It presumed an innate goodness in the insane (how else could they respond to gentleness and kindness?). Yet Woodward did not necessarily view all the insane as innately good, since he felt that they often were responsible for their own condition. Furthermore, the assumption that insane patients could control themselves, first argued by Pinel and Tuke, could also be the basis for punishment for those who did not. Restraint, confinement, and harsher medical treatments akin to those suggested by Rush and Cutbush could be used for those who would not demonstrate this control. Beyond the issue of personal reformation, the need to bring order to the asylum sometimes demanded stricter measures of control than would be possible under complete adherence to the principles of moral treatment.

Those charged with the care of the insane often exhibited both humanitarian and negative attitudes toward them. Woodward believed that madness was sometimes a matter of disgrace, even as he thought it a pitiful condition that ought to be interrupted. In spite of his occasional lapses into righteousness about the behavior of his patients, Woodward must be counted as a genuine reformer in his belief that the insane should not be subject to purely custodial confinement in jails and almshouses, but instead deserved a chance to be cured at the state hospital. By the time he welcomed the first patients to Worcester, the post-Revolutionary hope that the insane could be cured had developed into a strong faith among medical and lay reformers in Massachusetts. If Woodward was sometimes discouraged over the number of what he called incurables at Worcester, he never lost faith that, under the proper conditions, the care offered could redeem many of the patients sent there. Given the miserable condition of a number of insane in the state prior to the opening of Worcester, it must have been easy for these reformers to assume they could do better. Even those insane who were not mistreated were receiving little or no medical treatment; by the 1830s this was tantamount to neglect. Whatever decline eventually overtook the asylum at Worcester, the motives of its founders were clearly humanitarian.

As soon as Worcester State Lunatic Hospital was built in 1833, it began to suffer from overcrowding.[69] McLean Asylum also faced increasing numbers of applicants and patients in the 1820s and 1830s. The proliferation of insane at these asylums and at local jails and almshouses suggests that their number was steadily increasing in the 1830s. It is difficult to determine whether this was a real increase or rather an apparent one caused by a growing tendency to assume that various sorts of eccentric or deviant behavior were signs of madness. At least part of the increase seems to have been related to a broader conception of insanity. This is suggested by the cases of two women who were confined in McLean Asylum in the 1820s because they confessed to despising their husbands. They were believed to be mad by those who treated them, and the women themselves shared this view. The superintendent thought they suffered from the moral insanity discussed by Rush and Woodward, wherein rationality was intact but the moral sense was disordered.[70] This type of madness could cover a multitude of deviant and unwanted behaviors. It was clear, madness in any form had become a serious problem in the state. Whereas in 1796 the legislature was concerned with protecting the public from the furiously mad, by 1835 the withdrawn, passive, and harmless insane were confined at Worcester, as well as at local almshouses and jails.[71] Reformers themselves could have contributed to the broadened definition of insanity by alerting the public to the problems of the insane. The concept of madness became a widely available symbolic construction to explain a broad number of unacceptable and disturbing behaviors. In the same way, the creation of an institution specifically for the mad clearly influenced the perception of madness and the ideas of what should be done about it. Families may well have been more likely to place insane members in an asylum than in a local jail or almshouse. The existence of a state lunatic asylum was likely to encourage its use, whether or not there was a rise in the actual incidence of madness.[72]

Insanity had a very different meaning for the nineteenth-century residents of Massachusetts than it had for the colonial generation. Madness now seemed to be a more or less permanent state. The ability of the insane in colonial times to move in and out of rationality and to be accepted back into the community when they were rational did not exist in the same measure in the Jacksonian period. Insanity had become fused with identity. This fusion was becoming permanent, as the chance for the insane to return to their former lives and roles was becoming more and more limited. Although some of the Worcester inmates were apparently restored to rationality early in the hospital's history, most of those sent there in the ensuing years remained insane, at least as far as the hospital caretakers and the wider society were concerned. Most Worcester patients who were released after these first few years were returned to local facilities as insane persons. Woodward's ideas about periodic insanity meant only that he recognized that some insane had periods of rationality, but as far as he was concerned they continued to be mad. To be labeled insane was now permanently disabling; the physical separation of the insane had been accompanied by a moral one. Furthermore, while the intervention of the physician might restore the rationality of some, very few reclaimed their own sanity. By contrast, in the colonial period, recoveries that did occur seemed to be spontaneous and self-generated.

In 1833, with the opening of the Worcester State Lunatic Hospital, the transformation in the reaction to madness in Massachusetts was complete. Madness had been recognized as a social problem for which public funds should be specifically allocated, whether in the state lunatic hospitals or in local jails and almshouses. Public officials had made confinement of the insane, under medical or nonmedical auspices, the accepted solution. In some cases it was unclear which solution was actually more humane; for instance, was a patient at Boston Lunatic Hospital or one confined in a strong room at Worcester better off than an insane pauper in an almshouse in a small town? One thing was clear: insanity was a public issue in a way that it had not been before the Revolution. But more significantly, it was a threat to the people of the Commonwealth in a way that it had not been to the citizens of the colony.

The change in the reaction to the insane was tied to a broader matrix of changes in post-Revolutionary Massachusetts society. The economic and social changes first evident in Boston in the middle of the eighteenth century began to overtake the smaller towns of the state after the Revolution. Population in the colony increased considerably in the latter half of the eighteenth century.[73] Partly as a consequence of this population growth, Massachusetts was becoming increasingly urban after 1790.[74] Persistence rates began declining in this period and showed a dramatic drop after 1800.[75] Accompanying the increased geographic migration was an increased number of transients in the towns of the state. These strangers were likely to be poor and so were unwelcome on two counts in the New England town in the latter part of the eighteenth century. The older means of keeping poor strangers out were no longer adequate under conditions of dramatically increased mobility, and new measures had to be devised.[76] Where urbanization occurred, it resulted in the rise of a more cosmopolitan outlook, which increasingly replaced the older parochial mind-set of the colonial town.[77]

A decline in deference accompanied the growth of political democracy in Massachusetts after the Revolution; as a consequence political office holding was more widely distributed and the range of choices for voters increased. The demand made by Republican government for independent, rational political actors became the main catalyst for the change to an atomistic conception of government.[78] An increase in the number of voluntary associations after the Revolution likewise increased the number of social choices and made the patterns of association of many citizens far more complex than they had been; multiple association patterns that were more individualistic began to become more characteristic of the residents of this state.[79]

A significant shift away from values of community and consensus and toward those of individualism and striving took place at the town level in the decades after the Revolution. Community life was becoming increasingly fragmented, and opposing interests now became legitimized as the norm, replacing the earlier ideal of communitarianism.[80] While some of the emphasis on individualism was related to the demographic and political transformations taking place, another source of this energy was based on the new economic realities facing the Massachusetts citizen after the Revolution. A growth in wealth stratification in the period immediately preceding the Revolution led to an increasing number of poor and unskilled workers, some of whom became part of the numbers of transients going from town to town looking for work.[81]

Additional transformations of the economy were taking place in the hinterlands of the state. In much of Massachusetts production had been locally oriented throughout a good deal of the eighteenth century. Beginning in the middle of the century, agricultural production in the outlying towns, as well as production in Boston, was becoming more market oriented, and a widespread system of decentralized markets became evident by the end of the century. The growth of the commodity market and the appearance of a number of propertyless, unattached men provided the infrastructure necessary to the development of a strong manufacturing sector in the state in the early nineteenth century.[82] These economic changes, like the political ones, made greater demands for individual decision making and independent economic functioning than had existed in pre-Revolutionary Massachusetts.

At the same time as social, political, and economic choices were multiplying, so too were religious ones. A proliferation of religious sects that had occurred after the Great Awakening was given greater impetus by the disestablishment of Congregationalism in the Massachusetts state constitution of 1780. The growth of religious diversity in the state meant that personal choice was increasingly important in the practice of religion. Competition for church members encouraged individuals to choose among various theologies.[83]

It can be argued, then, that the American Revolution was a kind of watershed in the history of Massachusetts. In the decades following independence, the world probably looked quite different than it had in the colonial period.[84] A far more complex world had succeeded the colonial one. These changes had dislodged many from the the external constraints that had limited the range of individual choice and decision making earlier. In the economic, social, and political arenas of daily life, a new reality confronted a great many residents: new responsibilities for economic survival inherent in the participation in a market economy and a growing wage labor market;[85] an increased emphasis on rationality and individual decision making in the political sphere; an increasingly complex set of interactions with others, who were less likely to be family members and long-standing neighbors, more likely to be strangers or semistrangers. The residents of the Bay State were less likely to live out their lives among intimates, and the strangers who replaced those intimates were more likely to be competitive and striving themselves. Individualism assaulted the values of community, consensus, and harmony that were still dominant, at least on a symbolic level, in the colonial period. This transformation in values is likely to have had a significant impact in unleashing individual energy and ambition. An expectation of wider associations, broader involvement in the political and economic spheres, and a readiness for movement and change meant that individuals had to develop a strong measure of internal control, for they could no longer depend on the external controls embedded in community life before the Revolution.

It is not surprising that the transformation experienced by the residents of the Commonwealth would have a significant impact on their reaction to the insane. Madness threatened internal control; in fact it seemed directly to oppose it. With increased demands for individual responsibility and decision making in many crucial areas of life, irrationality could no longer be safely ignored. The explosion of energy and the multiplication of structures that overtook Massachusetts after the Revolution left little room for insane behavior; new opportunities brought heightened demands for self-control and rationality. Not only the violent but also the harmless insane needed to be confined, because even they represented potential loss of control. This possibility was no longer acceptable. At the same time, these changes may have contributed to a real increase in the rate of insanity in the state and so exacerbated the problem presented by insane behavior. The growing numbers of poor, transient, and unattached males in the towns no doubt also increased the anxiety about madness, for their existence itself represented a potential threat, and they would be even more frightening if some were also insane. These complexities were evident in Salem sooner than in Danvers and Concord and were the main reason why Salem confined its insane earlier than the other two towns. In this sense the nineteenth century came to Salem sooner.

The absorbing and relatively unified system of symbolic meanings constructed by the Massachusetts colonists to explain their reality had undergone significant transformation in the Revolutionary period. The multiplication of religious sects and the rise of rationalism increased individual choice in the matter of religion at the same time as it threatened to expose the relativity of any one system of beliefs. The price of diversity in matters of meaning was uncertainty, and this uncertainty threatened to become anxiety in the face of the meaningless behavior of the mad. The grasp that the colonists had on their reality was loosened in the face of competing explanations. As a result, madness threatened to expose the fictive and relative nature of the symbolic order as it could not have done earlier. The private world of meanings of the insane was now a source of uneasiness, since the coherent symbolic order of the Puritan no longer served as a hedge against it.

In addition, the certainty of the supernatural explanation of madness had been able to disarm its threat, a service the more equivocal medical explanation was not yet able to perform. The new disputes about the nature and causes of madness characteristic of medical thought in the first part of the nineteenth century may have left those who heard them puzzled about the meaning of insanity and therefore more vulnerable to its implicit threat.

It can be argued that the rise of the asylum and the growing medical interest in the mad were related on the one hand to the Enlightenment and Revolution-inspired sense of efficacy with regard to all problems in the natural order, including disease, and on the other hand to the increased financial resources in the public and private sectors of the Northeastern economy in the early nineteenth century. All these factors were important to the success of the reform movement to build asylums for the insane. But the first interest shown in the insane was not a humanitarian one and had little to do with the asylum; rather, it was based on a new anxiety about their presence. This anxiety, which appeared in Massachusetts after the Revolution, was not related to a heightened awareness of the plight of the insane, nor to an increase in public and private resources available for their care. Instead, it was linked to significant changes in the social order that demanded, first and foremost, that the insane be removed from the larger society. The residents of Jacksonian Massachusetts were not the first generation to find the presence of the insane a problem; in fact, they sought to rescue the mad from the largely benighted reaction of their post-Revolutionary predecessors.[86] By 1840 a reform impulse that sought to release the insane from the conditions imposed on them after the Revolution had resulted in the widespread acceptance of the mental hospital as the best way to help them, at the same time confining them. The Jacksonian asylum represented the synthesis of the humane and fearful responses to the insane in Massachusetts. During the early years at Worcester State Lunatic Hospital, the tradition of Pinel and Tuke merged with that of Rush and Cutbush, and within its walls the medicalization of madness was complete. Yet many insane in the state who were confined in jails, almshouses, and private homes would not experience their condition as a medical problem until more lunatic hospitals were built. It would be only a matter of time before the public asylum became the sole solution to the problem of insanity, and the desire to cure the insane would be completely fused with the stronger need to confine them.

Epilogue

In 1840 there were three hospitals for the insane in Massachusetts; in 1870 there were six.[1] By this time, the mental hospital had been accepted as the only legitimate solution to the problem of insanity. In 1854 the second state mental hospital was opened at Taunton at a time when conditions at Worcester had deteriorated severely.[2] Yet there was little dissent among the policymakers about the need for more hospitals; in fact, reports on worsening conditions typically led to a call for another hospital.[3]

The reification of the medical view of madness was accomplished not because of any breakthrough in medical knowledge, but because its acceptance and the need for the hospitalization of the insane that followed from it were, on the surface, more humane solutions than confinement in places where no cure was pretended. Within the asylum various mixtures of moral treatment and custodial care were practiced. As the two public hospitals in the state began to receive more immigrant and pauper insane (mostly Irish) after 1840, the superintendents increasingly turned to somatic explanations of insanity. Organic lesions of the brain, ill-health, and irritation of the brain were all part of the new rubric of "physical causes" adjudged more and more frequently as prime movers in madness.[4] George Chandler, Woodward's successor at Worcester State Lunatic Hospital, wrote in the 1850 superintendent's report that "insanity, whether of physical or mental origin, is accompanied by some organic lesion of some part of the system. It is, in most cases, the result of physical disease."[5]

As Norman Dain has pointed out, most superintendents of

American lunatic hospitals in the nineteenth century shared a conviction that, whatever its remote causes, insanity was ultimately a disease of the brain.[6] In Massachusetts those who worked with pauper and foreign insane were increasingly likely to cite biological factors as primary. As these groups began to dominate the public asylums, interest in social causes would die out, leaving the more purely somatic explanations unaccompanied by precipitating factors.

Hereditary factors also played an increasingly important role in the speculations of medical superintendents in Massachusetts after 1840. While heredity had been mentioned as a cause of madness since the beginning of the century, it had always been considered one of several contributory factors. After 1840 it began to be mentioned more prominently as a cause; more significantly, it also began to be linked to incurability.[7] While heredity had not always been associated with a pessimistic view about curability, after the 1840s hereditarian thought became functional in explaining the failures of the reform effort in lunatic hospitals.[8]

The attenuation of the reform effort in state hospitals in Massachusetts was largely due to factors over which the staff had little control. As Worcester and Boston Lunatic Hospital began to fill up with paupers and immigrants, conditions there became far less conducive to moral treatment. Overcrowding, understaffing, underfunding, and an apparent increase in chronic patients all served to reduce the efficacy of these asylums in the 1840s.[9] Somatic and hereditary causes at this time seemed to preclude effective intervention, and therefore they were summoned more frequently by superintendents in public systems in Massachusetts and later by their colleagues around the country facing similar difficulties.[10]

Under these conditions, it was perhaps natural that more and more patients in these hospitals were thought to be incurable. In 1845, when over half the patients at Boston Lunatic Hospital were Irish immigrants, Stedman declared that the vast majority were "incurable and would stay there until they die."[11] The trustees of Worcester complained in 1851 that there were too many incurables and too many foreigners at the asylum.[12] As early as

1848 they worried that "the increase of foreigners is an evil the more to be regretted, because there is reason to fear that it may be, still further, an increase of *incurables*. The number of foreigners, mostly Irish, admitted the past year is sixty, being one fourth of the whole number admitted. . . . Their misery, their ignorance, and their jealousy stand in the way of their improvement at the Hospital."[13]

Moral treatment was not effective in a situation of extreme overcrowding, and it was even less so when cultural differences precluded adequate communication and trust between the patients and the staff. Without a common cultural background, the effort to resocialize the insane into the dominant cultural beliefs of work, religion, and sociability was unlikely to succeed. Asylum superintendents in this period (including all those in Massachusetts) were white Protestants with rural backgrounds.[14] When these men were faced with a large population of pauper and foreign insane who did not respond to the cultural sanctions implicit in moral treatment, they quite logically dismissed them as incurable. The belief that madness was largely hereditary and somatic reinforced their doubt about the possibility of cure in another way, for if madness was no longer thought to be a matter of moral choice, it was unlikely to be reversed by the personal reformation that moral treatment offered. If the will was no longer implicated in madness, willpower was unlikely to reverse its course.

One leading expert on insanity, Edward Jarvis, prepared a report for the Massachusetts legislature in 1855 on the problems of insanity in the state. He found that: "Among those whom the world calls poor, there is less vital force, a lower tone of life, more ill health, more weakness, more early death, a diminished longevity. There is also less self-respect, ambition, hope, and more idiocy, and insanity, and more crime, than among the independent." Jarvis pointed out that the source of all these difficulties lay in the physical constitutions of the poor, for they had "imperfectly organized brains and feeble mental constitutions."[15] In another context four years earlier, Jarvis had called insanity "part of the price we pay for civilization," citing "more uncertain and hazardous employments . . . more means and provocations for sensual indulgence" as some of the precipitators.[16] However, the social causes were not used to explain the insanity of the poor or the Irish. For them another set of explanations, far less hopeful, was offered.[17] Yet it was just these poor and immigrant insane who were to fill the public mental hospital in the nineteenth century, moving superintendents to explain insanity from a somatic and hereditarian perspective and thereby promoting and justifying the custodial treatment found there. By the 1850s whatever humanitarian benefits had accrued from conceptualizing madness as a disease were considerably diminished. In fact, after the Civil War the somatic view seemed to lead to a dead end in treatment.[18]

For all these reasons conditions at Worcester took a decided turn for the worse in the 1850s. Mechanical contrivances were used to restrain some inmates. The trustees were outraged to find that "seclusion of an insane person is a dainty substitute for fettering his hands or feet, or both, the fetters being of leather instead of iron."[19] All the cells for the furiously mad were occupied, some of them "unfit for the above dumb beasts." There was no room for the patients to exercise. The trustees were concerned that "the great want of stimulus to action is a serious evil, and one not easily remedied. Many of the insane are inclined to stand or sit about our wards listlessly, dreaming over their insane fantasies."[20]

At Boston Lunatic Hospital the situation was even worse, for this asylum began to take in a great number of immigrants almost as soon as it opened. Furthermore, the financial resources given Worcester were not available. In 1848 the board of visitors of the hospital wrote that if the inmates (as they were called) "were not mad when they came to the hospital, they soon would become mad" there.[21] In 1850 these same hospital officials declared, "This is to a great extent a receptacle." The inmates (many of them Irish) were spending all day "standing in the halls staring into space, with nothing to do," in the absence of "nearly all amusements and employment."[22]

Conditions were quite different at the only private hospital for the insane, McLean Asylum, after 1840. The accommodations there were "as good as any hotel in the Country," according to superintendent Luther Bell. Most of the patients lived in private apartments. The goal of the staff was to provide patients "with every comfort and every luxury to which they have been accustomed at home."[23] While narcotics were administered and some restraints used, on the whole the atmosphere was far more restful and pleasant and the staff more attentive than at the public asylums. In 1855, Bell claimed that little had changed at McLean since its opening and that moral treatment was still being practiced successfully there.[24] He did not share the growing hopelessness about the curability of insanity found among the superintendents of the public hospitals in the state, largely because the conditions in his hospital did not force him to.[25]

Confinement was an enduring theme in the state after 1840. Although the number of insane in all three hospitals in Massachusetts continued to increase in the 1840s and 1850s, many insane were still confined in jails and almshouses during this period.[26] Some of them were paupers kept in local arrangements by town officials reluctant to pay the cost of public asylum care; others were incurables sent out of the hospitals back to local care. In 1843 the trustees at Worcester declared that more lunatics were confined in the prisons of the state than before the hospital was built.[27] The condition of the jailed insane, some former Worcester patients, was often degrading according to a census of pauper insane in jails and almshouses in the state.[28] The insane also continued to be confined in local almshouses after 1840. The legislature found in this 1843 census that 540 insane and idiot paupers were supported in 235 towns: 361 in almshouses and 179 in private homes. Of these, 60 were confined in cages or strong rooms, 15 in chains.[29]

The descriptions of the mad in restraint echo the stories found in the 1829 census that had been a strong impetus for the founding of the first public asylum in Massachusetts. George Webster of Salisbury, aged 37, had been insane for eighteen years. He was confined in a private house for fifteen years, then put in the receptable at Ipswich for ten months. Upon his release from that institution, he was sent to Pepperell to a private home for ten weeks. In 1843 he was in the Salisbury almshouse, where he was confined in a straitjacket in a strong room with no fire. In Buckland one insane pauper "has not been allowed any exercise for a number of years; never has been taken out of his cage, but a few times since first confined." One man was kept in two rooms for fifteen years, going from one to the other only so that they could be cleaned. The town of Sterling had built a small building for its insane, where they confined one mad person in a strong room. A woman in Newburyport, Elizabeth Petton, aged 51, was confined alone in a strong room in a straitjacket for over five years. And in Concord, Nancy Barrons reappeared, having finally been returned to her hometown. She was now confined to a cage at night, "with slots about six inches apart," although she is "allowed to go at large during the day."[30]

On the other hand, the almshouse keepers sometimes took pride in reporting that their charges were doing better than they had at Worcester. In Amherst, Maria Bartlett was one such case. The keeper wrote, "The case of Miss Bartlett at the Hospital was a very bad one, necessary to be confined often, considered by Woodward to be a hopeless case, and that she would never be any better, but after a few months residence at the Almshouse she improved very much, now perfectly harmless, content, and happy—able to perform light work." A man in Westhampton was returned from Worcester and placed in a "private family in our town where under kind treatment and medical aid he soon began to mend and may now perhaps be called well again." In Chelsea, Ruth Brintal, who had been mad for eighteen years, was sent to a private family after her release from Worcester. At the hospital she had been confined to a strong room, but in Chelsea "the family has perfect control over her and she is likely to come and go as she pleases." When asked if he ever called a physician to minister to the insane in his care, this almshouse keeper responded, "There is no physician for the mind," suggesting that the medical view of madness had not yet been universally accepted among officials in the state.[31]

The number of insane in Massachusetts outside the asylums increased every year.[32] As legislative committees ferreted out the mad in local arrangements, and as the asylum superintendents complained about the overcrowding, the reform effort received renewed momentum. Having achieved the opening of Worcester in the 1830s, reform-minded citizens were faced with the realization that this hospital had been only the beginning. The insane were still confined in jails and almshouses or cared for by families ignorant of the medical nature of madness. To these reformers, any insane who were not in a hospital were victims of society's neglect or, worse, cruelty. Yet some of those in local almshouses were apparently faring better than they had at Worcester. Others lived in these places in relative peace, according to the 1843 census. Ironically, the State Lunatic Hospital and the local almshouse in some cases had exchanged places in terms of offering the most humane care.

Even as the specter of incurability was beginning to loom over the public asylum, the reformers seemed to derive their greatest energies for a campaign to open another mental hospital. The idea of the mental hospital had become firmly embedded in the minds of leading reformers by the 1840s and 1850s as the only means through which rehabilitation could be achieved. This was largely because, unlike the superintendents at the public asylums, they believed that all insane persons were victims of a curable disease.[33] Although reformers understood that conditions at Worcester were not ideal, this only encouraged them to pressure for the erection of more asylums. Still believing in the efficacy of moral treatment and the medical treatment of insanity, they had implicit faith that the medical profession would solve the problem of madness if given enough resources.[34]

By 1850 men and women in Massachusetts were confined for insane behavior that would have received far less attention in the colonial period, nor was this behavior included under the rubric of the 1796 law authorizing confinement of the furiously mad.[35] The trend of confining the harmless insane that appeared early in the century had become accepted policy. In addition, this confinement had been linked to a medicalization of madness. While not all insane were confined in mental hospitals in the 1850s, this was clearly the solution of choice for most informed citizens (the almshouse keeper notwithstanding). The power of the idea that most insane needed hospitalization is suggested by Jarvis's claim in 1855 that, out of 2,632 insane in the state, 2,018 were incurable; yet he thought that most of these, except for some who could stay in local almshouses, should be hospitalized for the protection of society.[36] The mental hospital was now frankly seen as the place to confine insane persons, regardless of whether they could be cured there.[37]

The resolution of the problem of insanity in Massachusetts was not unique to that state. The custodial mental hospital was the dominant solution all over the country until the middle of the twentieth century. By 1875 there were over sixty public mental hospitals in the United States. In 1976, thirteen years after the federal government inaugurated a policy of deinstitutionalization and a reduction in the number of state mental hospitals through the Community Mental Health Centers Act, there were three hundred public mental hospitals in the country.[38]

At the same time as the public mental hospital was legitimized as the place to confine (and possibly cure) the insane, another, private system of care was developing alongside it. This private system offered treatment similar to that characteristic of McLean Asylum for more affluent insane. The growth of private psychiatric practice in this country since 1950 is directly linked to the privatization of mental health care first exemplified by McLean Asylum. The concept of mental health itself is a social construction that has been reified and serves to legitimate private treatment, as it offers various therapies to those who can afford to pursue mental health as an increasingly scarce and elusive goal.

The history of insanity in Massachusetts is significantly linked to the broader history of madness in American society. The mad were removed from society everywhere in the country during the nineteenth century. In fact, Massachusetts lagged behind two other colonies, Virginia and Pennsylvania, in providing special structures to house the insane in the eighteenth century. Before the Revolution, both Pennsylvania Hospital and Eastern State Lunatic Hospital in Williamsburg offered the insane very strenuous treatments, or none at all; the staffs were unenlightened by the humanitarianism of Pinel and Tuke.[39] In the wake of their influence, and in the acme of moral treatment movements in this country, both hospitals reformed their practices and designed genuinely therapeutic programs. They each in turn experienced a similar decline into custodialism after the Civil War.

The difference in these three places is not in substance so much as in timing. In all three the tension governing the relationship between the sane and the insane resulted in the gradual expulsion of the mad beyond the boundaries of the social order. This tension was felt later in Massachusetts than in other places because the nature of town life there combined with the relatively monolithic symbolic order to defuse temporarily the anxiety that madness sets off. The residents of Massachusetts ultimately accomplished what was begun earlier in Virginia and Pennsylvania and would eventually take place all over the country: the separation of the insane from the rest of us. Historians such as Foucault, Rosen, Rothman, and Grob may disagree about the timing of this separation as well as about its causes, but their histories and this one make the same point: at some stage in the development of what we call modern society, madness became unacceptable.[40]

In this country, once this separation was achieved through a potentially humanitarian means—the public mental hospital—reformers and lawmakers dismissed the problem of insanity from their minds. When another generation of reformers and lawmakers decided to look again at the insane in the 1960s, the custodial public mental hospital was no longer viewed as a viable solution, and the mentally ill (as they were now known) were returned to the community. Yet our communities cannot accept and absorb them, any more than could Salem, Massachusetts in 1820. The insane live in conditions that are often no better and sometimes worse than those inside the mental hospital; sometimes homeless, often exploited, they are shunned by the rest of us. We have yet to find a humanitarian solution to the problem they continue to represent.

Notes

Introduction *(pages 1–11)*

1. Gerald Grob suggested that the increasing complexity of Massachusetts society and the increased availability of public financial resources led to a more bureaucratic response to insanity and the establishment of the public asylum in the state in 1833. See Grob, *The State and The Mentally Ill* (Chapel Hill, N.C., 1966), and *Mental Institutions in America—Social Policy to 1875* (New York, 1973). Albert Deutsch pointed to the rise of medical science, especially its humanitarian aspects, as responsible for the emergence of mental hospitals in the nineteenth century. See Deutsch, *The Mentally Ill in America* (New York, 1946). Michel Foucault and David Rothman have suggested variations of the social control theme. See Foucault, *Madness and Civilization: A History of Insanity in the Age of Reason,* trans. Richard Howard (New York, 1965); Rothman, *The Discovery of the Asylum* (Boston, 1971).

2. For a particularly trenchant criticism of Foucault's history of madness, see Laurence Stone's review "Madness," *New York Review of Books,* 29 (16 December 1982): 128–36. Stone commented that Foucault "has set the agenda for the last fifteen years of research."

3. (New York, 1967), p. 154.

4. Ibid., pp. 158, 161–65.

5. (London, 1963).

6. (Cambridge, 1981).

7. (New York, 1982).

8. Ibid., pp. 30–35.

9. Ibid., p. 43.

10. (New Brunswick, N.J., 1964.)

11. (Cambridge, 1984.)

12. See *A Generous Confidence,* especially pp. 22–27.

13. Tomes argued that the motives for sending the insane to Pennsylvania Hospital were the same in the eighteenth and nineteenth centuries: to confine them and to cure them. Yet her book has as its major focus the rise and fall of moral treatment, which she viewed as a new departure in the treatment of the insane in the nineteenth century.

14. See Peter L. Berger and Thomas Luckman, *The Social Construction*

of Reality (Garden City, N.Y., 1966) and Erving Goffman, *Interaction Ritual* (New York, 1967) for discussions of madness as phenomenologically threatening. Goffman calls psychosis an example of situational impropriety, "a failure to abide by the rules established for the conduct of face to face interaction" (p. 141).

15. Ernest Becker argued that human beings need to create elaborate structures of meaning that they see as existing independently of human origin, because investment in such social constructions distracts them from contemplation of their own end and the existential terror accompanying this realization. See Becker, *The Birth and Death of Meaning* (New York, 1962). Berger and Luckman offer a similar argument in *The Social Construction of Reality.*

16. One anthropologist reported that the threat of madness, even the apprehension of madness, is culturally variable. Robert Edgerton noted: "In folk societies as well as in the West, the consequences of mental illness, and the deviant label itself, are often negotiable. I have reported cases from East Africa where psychotic behavior was used to personal advantage, and other instances when apparently flagrant psychotic behavior was not labelled as such because there were compelling reasons not to do so." He cited instances in New Guinea where men have "gone wild" but have not been permitted to escape their social or economic obligations. See Edgerton, *Deviance: A Cross-Cultural Perspective* (Menlo Park, Calif., 1976), pp. 64–66. This evidence, as well as my own research, suggests that the notion of stigma or spoiled identity following an ascription of deviance, which was developed by Erving Goffman and Howard S. Becker to explain the constricted life opportunities of those labeled deviant, is not a historical or cultural constant but may refer only to some cultures at some times. See Goffman, *Stigma* (Englewood Cliffs, N.J., 1963); H. Becker, *The Outsiders: Studies in the Sociology of Deviance* (New York, 1963).

17. One way of explaining madness that has come to dominate our thinking is psychiatric nosology. The diagnostic category of *schizophrenia*, formulated by the medical profession at the beginning of the twentieth century, illustrates the way in which insanity challenges the most basic meanings of the social group. Psychiatric descriptions of schizophrenia emphasize the world of private meaning in which the victim lives. According to English and French, schizophrenics exhibit a "strong tendency to withdraw from reality." They "retreat into a world of their own making. To the normal person they seem odd and bizarre." (See Spurgeon O. English and Stuart M. French, *Introduction to Psychiatry* [New York, 1964], p. 11.) Standards for diagnosing schizophrenia repeatedly emphasize the oddness, bizarreness, and strangeness that mystify the observer and make him feel uncomfortable in the patient's company. The schizophrenic retreats from others, dresses in bizarre or ludicrous ways, refuses to bathe or shave—in other words to engage in

the social rituals that others depend on to maintain common meanings and order. Behaviors such as inappropriate affect and disassociation of thought processes, which separate the victim's emotional and intellectual responses from the outside world, tend to isolate the schizophrenic from the rest of society. Schizophrenics seems to be operating on the basis of their own reality, impelled by meanings and motivations not comprehensible to the observer. They "interpret external events in their own unique way." For similar descriptions see Jack R. Ewalt, *Textbook of Psychiatry* (New York, 1963), p. 216; Alfred Freedman *et al.*, *Modern Synopsis of Psychiatry* (Baltimore, 1972).

18. See especially Thomas Szasz, *The Myth of Mental Illness: Foundations of a Theory of Personal Conduct* (New York, 1961), *Law, Liberty and Psychiatry: An Inquiry into the Social Uses of Mental Health Practice* (New York, 1963), and *The Manufacture of Madness: A Comparative History of the Inquisition and the Mental Health Movement* (New York, 1970); Ronald Leifer, *In the Name of Mental Health* (New York, 1969); Thomas Scheff, ed., *Labeling Madness* (Englewood Cliffs, N.J., 1975); R. D. Laing, *The Politics of Experience* (New York, 1968); E. Fuller Torrey, *The Mind Game: Witchdoctors and Psychiatrists* (New York, 1973).

19. See, for example, Walter Reich, "Psychiatry's Second Coming," *Psychiatry* 45 (August 1982): 189–96.

20. Grob has provided a very full history of the steps in the asylum-building process in the state in *The State and the Mentally Ill*, but he did not systematically address the question of why the asylums were built, since he was more interested in their history once they were established. Rothman has addressed this question directly in *The Discovery of the Asylum*, but his argument has been subject to several rounds of critiques. See the following reviews: Gerald Grob, *Reviews in American History* 1 (March 1973): 43–52; James Banner, *Journal of Interdisciplinary History* 5 (Summer 1974): 167–74; and Jacques M. Quen, *Journal of Psychiatry and Law* 2 (Spring 1974): 105–22.

Chapter 1: The Supernatural Face of Madness
(pages 12–30)

1. In *Mystical Bedlam*, MacDonald demonstrated how a mixture of natural and supernatural causes also had served as a viable model to explain madness in seventeenth-century England. Evidence about conceptions of insanity in seventeenth-century New England is extremely limited but suggests a strong continuity with the ideas elaborated in the early eighteenth century.

2. "Warnings From the Dead: A Blessed Medicine for Sinful Madness," in Clifford K. Shipton, ed., *Early American Imprints, 1639–1800* (New York, 1963–), p. 12.

3. *Magnalia Christi Americana; Or the Ecclesiastical History of New England,* 1702 (Hartford, 1853), 1:438.

4. Ibid., p. 439.

5. Ibid., pp. 440–41.

6. These accounts are found in a collection of early eighteenth-century poems written by Thompson's family and friends. See Kenneth Murdock, ed., *Handkerchiefs from Paul* (Cambridge, Mass., 1927). The exact date when the poems were written is unknown. Murdock dates those of Benjamin Thompson (son of William) to sometime between 1700 and 1715. The others were presumably written in the same period, and all were recorded in the journal of Joseph Thompson (another son of William) in 1722.

7. Ibid., p. 12–18.

8. John Demos showed how withchcraft was used to define the "boundaries between good and evil" and "bolster traditional religious values." See Demos, *Entertaining Satan: Witchcraft and the Culture of Early New England,* (New York. 1982), p. 307.

9. *Diary of Cotton Mather, 1719,* ed. Worthington Ford (Boston, 1912), p. 583. The belief that men could be possessed by the devil survived in some places through the eighteenth century. In 1792 a monograph was written about the case of George Zukens, who had been "possessed by evil spirits for 18 years." Zukens had fits, declared he was the devil, could not stand to hear anything about God or religion, all behaviors reminiscent of many bewitched persons. He was cured not by doctors, who could no nothing for him, but by prayer. See "A Narrative of the Extraordinary Case of George Zukens" (Philadelphia, 1792), in Clifford K. Shipton, ed., *Early American Imprints 1639–1800* (New York, 1963–).

10. Cotton Mather, "A Brand Pluck'd Out of the Burning" (1693), in George Lincoln Burr, ed., *Narratives of the Witchcraft Cases, 1648–1706* (New York, 1914), p. 260

11. Frenzied movements, convulsions, and fits were commonly thought to suggest witchcraft. One observer, Samuel Willard, was not convinced that Elizabeth Knapp was a "demonic" until the "devil" drew out her tongue to an extraordinary length. She was "subject to violent body motions, leaping, straining and strange agitations." See Willard, "A Brief Account of a Strange and Unusual Providence of God Befallen to Elizabeth Knapp of Groton" (1672), in John Demos, ed., *Remarkable Providences* (New York, 1972), p. 367; C. Mather, "A Brand," pp. 261, 264.

12. Robert Calef, "More Wonders of the Invisible World," in George Lincoln Burr, ed., *Narratives of the Witchcraft Cases, 1648–1706* (New York, 1941), p. 298. Calef's remarks corroborate that possession and bewitchment were not viewed as the same phenomenon, although Mather sometimes referred to the bewitched girls as "posses'd." The be-

havior of the victims of witchcraft at the end of the seventeenth century was more bizarre and more formalized than that of people thought to be merely possessed by the devil in the early eighteenth century. The distinction between distraction and bewitchment was clear; the relationship of possession by the devil to both was muddier.

13. For a fuller discussion of colonial ideas about witchcraft, see the introduction to Thomas J. Holmes, ed., *Increase Mather: A Bibliography of His Works*, (Cambridge, 1943), 1:117; and Demos, *Entertaining Satan*. Demos discussed the difference between insanity and witchcraft in New England on pp. 90–92. Psychiatrists and social scientists writing about the witchcraft era have attempted to diagnose the behavior of the girls in psychiatric terms; the most common assumption is that they were suffering from hysteria and conversion reactions. See Richard Shyrock, "The Beginnings," in J. K. Hall and Gregory Zilboorg, eds., *One Hundred Years of American Psychiatry* (New York, 1944), p. 6; Ernest Caulfield, "Pediatric Aspects of the Salem Witchcraft Tragedy: A Lesson in Mental Health," *American Journal of Diseased Children* 65 (December 1943): 788–802. Suspected witches were also examined to determine their sanity. In the Goodwin case, the court appointed five physicians to examine Goodwife Glover, the persecutor of the Goodwin children and determine whether or not the accused witch were "crazed in her Intellectuals, and had not procured to herself by Folly and Madness the Reputation of a witch." They reported that, "diverse hours did they spend with her; and in all that while no Discourse came from her, but what was pertinent and agreeable." Doctors declared her to be compos mentis, and she was executed in 1688. See Cotton Mather, "Memorable Providences, Relating to Witchcraft and Possessions" (Boston, 1689), in Clifford K. Shipton, ed., *Early American Imprints, 1639–1800* (New York, 1963–), p. 107.

14. See *Magnalia*, p. 441 for Mather's comments on Warham; p. 438 for his more general remarks about pious New Englanders.

15. For Mather's sympathetic account of this problem, see "The Case of a Troubled Mind" (Boston, 1717), in Clifford K. Shipton, ed., *Early American Imprints, 1639–1800*, (New York, 1963–).

16. *Magnalia*, p. 392.

17. "Insaniabilia, An Essay upon Incurables" (Boston, 1714) in Clifford K. Shipton, ed., *Early American Imprints, 1639–1800* (New York, 1963–), p. 2. For serious warning of the consequences of sin, see John Rogers, "Death the Certain Wages of Sin to the Impenitent" (Boston, 1701), and "Warning to the Unclean" (Boston, 1700), in ibid.

18. Demos noted that the seventeenth-century Bay colonists "regarded themselves as participants in a cosmic struggle between the forces of God and of Satan for the control of their universe" (*Entertaining Satan*, p. 310). Christopher M. Jedrey found a perdurance of belief in witchcraft and other supernatural phenomena in one parish in Ips-

wich in the eighteenth century. See Jedrey, *The World of John Cleaveland: Family and Community in Eighteenth-century New England* (New York, 1979), pp. 95–97. Gary Nash described the power of this supernatural belief system in the early eighteenth century in *Urban Crucible: Social Change, Political Consciousness, and the Origins of the American Revolution* (Cambridge, 1979). "As late as 1727 an earthquake that shook most of New England was interpreted by lettered and unlettered alike as evidence of God's displeasure with his people in this corner of the earth" (p. 6). Demos described the various signs and portents taken as direct messages from the supernatural in seventeenth-century New England. The early New Englander believed that events were interconnected, that "every particular happening was inwardly linked to many others" (*Entertaining Satan*, pp. 373–79, 399). Patricia Tracy found that many residents of Northampton saw both the great earthquake of 1727 and the diphtheria epidemic of the mid 1730s as "signs that God was displeased with his covenanted people." See Tracy, *Jonathan Edwards, Pastor: Religion and Society in Eighteenth-century Northampton* (New York, 1979), p. 87.

19. For example, Max Weber has shown how work was given religious significance in Calvinist theology with the idea of the calling. See Weber, *The Protestant Ethic and the Spirit of Capitalism*, trans. Talcott Parsons (New York, 1958).

20. See Perry Miller, *The New England Mind: The Seventeenth Century* (Boston, 1961), especially pp. 16, 33–34, 39, for a discussion of this point.

21. *The Angel of Bethesda* (1724), ed. Gordon Jones (Barre, Mass., 1972), p. 130. Only in suicide did Satan continue to play a major role. In 1682 Mather's father, Increase Mather, who represented an earlier generation, explained how the devil could drive a man to self-murder: "Sometimes, the ill Humours of Vapours in the bodies of such Good Men, do so harbour the Devil that they have this woeful notion every day thence made to them: You must kill yourself—you must! You must!" See I. Mather, "A Call to the Tempted" (Boston, 1682) in Clifford K. Shipton, ed., *Early American Imprints, 1639–1800* (New York, 1963–). This sermon was reprinted in Massachusetts in 1723, after Increase Mather's death, a fact that suggests that its message was still important. MacDonald found that self-destructive thoughts were frequently linked to the devil by Napier and his clients (*Mystical Bedlam*, p. 136).

22. Demos in *Entertaining Satan* described the early New England religious experience as "distinctive in its intensity and in some qualitative aspects as well" (p. 310). Charles E. Hambrick-Stowe studied the daily devotional practices of seventeenth-century Puritans and revealed how important religion was to the colonists' daily life. See Hambrick-Stowe,

The Practice of Piety: Puritan Devotional Discipline in Seventeenth Century New England (Chapel Hill, N.C., 1982). Clearly this religiousness continued to be important during much of the eighteenth century. According to Richard D. Brown, "by 1700 it was public policy that everyone in Massachusetts was gathered in congregations." Even by the middle of the eighteenth century, although enforcement of mandatory church attendance had fallen off, "membership was not entirely voluntary since the weight of habit, tradition and the declared values of society continued to support participation in congregational life." The majority of colonists in eighteenth-century Massachusetts were likely to be regularly exposed to the outlines of the Calvinist symbolic order. See Brown, "The Emergence of Urban Society in Rural Massachusetts, 1760–1820," *Journal of American History* 61 (June 1974): 34. The Great Awakening in 1740 served to revivify that original Calvinist enthusiasm. See Sidney Ahlstrom, *A Religious History of the American People* (New Haven, Conn., 1972), p. 288.

23. George Selement found a strong correspondence in the theology of one minister and his congregation in mid seventeenth-century Massachusetts, which led him to argue that "ministers and their flocks held a theology in common." See Selement, "The Meeting of Elite and Popular Minds at Cambridge, New England, 1638–1645," *William and Mary Quarterly* 41 (January 1984): 32–48. Demos found a "wide influence" in clerical opinion about witchcraft in seventeenth-century New England (*Entertaining Satan*, pp. 310–11). Donald M. Scott argued that the New England minister in the eighteenth century had a wide public role in the community; his influence was felt not solely in religious matters but also in his comments about public issues. This influence diminished in the nineteenth century, when he became less embedded in the social structure of the community and more dependent on his congregation's judgment of his performance and on their goodwill. Scott emphasized the "localism" of the minister's role in the eighteenth century in *From Office to Profession: The New England Ministry, 1750–1850* (Philadelphia, 1978).

24. *The Diary of Michael Wigglesworth, 1653–1657*, ed. Edmund S. Morgan (Boston, 1951), p. 400.

25. "On the Nature of the Spleen," *American Chronicle and Historical Magazine*, July 1745, p. 17.

26. See Richard Shryock, *Eighteenth-century Medicine in America* (Worcester, Mass., 1950), p. 10.

27. Quoted in Hunter and Macalpine, eds., *Three Hundred Years*, p. 109. In this collection of writing on madness, the authors traced the strong influence of humoral doctrine on English ideas about insanity from the sixteenth century on.

28. (London 1669).

29. *A New System of the Spleen, Vapours and Hypochondriak Melancholy; wherein all the decays of the nerves and lownesses of the spirits, are mechanically accounted for* (London, 1729), p. 310.

30. Richard Shryock discussed the appearance of this speculative pathology in *Medicine in America: Historical Essays* (Baltimore, 1966). For a discussion of medical views of melancholy in England and on the continent in this period, see Stanley W. Jackson, "Melancholia and Mechanical Explanation in Eighteenth Century Medicine," *Journal of the History of Medicine and Allied Sciences* 38 (July 1983): 298–319. Jackson noted that humoral theory was losing its potency in explanations of melancholy, to be replaced by mechanical explanations by the end of the seventeenth century. Hypochondriasis was gradually separated from madness during the eighteenth century, until it was seen as a syndrome of physical complaints. See also Stanley Jackson, "Force and Kindred Notions in Eighteenth Century Neurophysiology and Medical Psychology," *Bulletin of the History of Medicine* 44 (September-October 1970): 397–410. For a discussion of the importance of irregularities of motion in eighteenth-century theories of nervous disorders, see Eric T. Carlson and Meribeth Simpson, "Models of the Nervous System in Eighteenth Century Psychiatry," *Bulletin of the History of Medicine* 43 (April 1969): 101–15. For a general history of medical thought in the early eighteenth century, see Lester S. King, *The Philosophy of Medicine* (Cambridge, Mass., 1978).

31. According to Shryock, while English medical writings circulated among the elites of the colonies, they made little impact on the practice of medicine there. He characterized the period from 1620 to 1720 as marked by "quasi-medieval thoughts and crude empiricism." See Shryock, *Medicine and Society in America: 1660–1860* (New York, 1960). Paul Starr described colonial medical practices as domestic in nature, and guided by oral tradition for much of the colonial period. See Starr, *The Social Transformation of American Medicine* (New York, 1982), p. 32.

32. See Ibid., pp. 39–40, for a discussion of the mixing of medical and ministerial roles. The medical authority of ministers was to be undermined as the eighteenth century progressed.

33. *The Angel of Bethesda* was not published until 1962, and therefore the text itself cannot be said to have influenced contemporary thinking about insanity; rather, it was a reflection of where that thinking was moving. For a discussion of the wider significance of the *The Angel*, see Margaret-Humphreys Warner, "Vindicating the Minister's Medical Role: Cotton Mather's Concept of the *Nishmath-Chajim* and the Spiritualization of Medicine," *Journal of the History of Medicine and Allied Sciences* 36 (January 1981): 278–95. Warner argued that *Angel* was Mather's attempt to forge a link between science and religion and, in particular, to justify ministerial involvement in medical matters by elevating

the spiritual aspects of disease. The concept of *nishmath-chajim* (taken from Genesis) was used by Mather to signify the force ("breath of life") that united the physical and spiritual aspects of human nature. As Warner pointed out, early in his life Mather had studied medicine with the idea of becoming a doctor. Yet he was also convinced that the devil was a very real force in the natural world and sought to unite these two perspectives in *The Angel* by giving the devil and spiritual forces in general a role in disease. His familiarity with medical views of disease is evident throughout the book. Carlson and Simpson discuss the connection between Mather's ideas in *The Angel* and earlier European thought about disease (especially Galen's ideas) in "Models of the Nervous System," pp. 103–4.

34. *Angel*, pp. 135, 130. The linking of sin and madness was also common among preachers in seventeenth-century England (MacDonald, *Mystical Bedlam*, p. 168).

35. *Angel*, p. 132.

36. Ibid., pp. 129–34.

37. See Hunter and Macalpine, *Three Hundred Years*, pp. 14, 17, 24–27. Richard Baxter, in *The Signs and Causes of Melancholy* (London, 1716), described "Melancholy persons" as "exceeding fearful. . . . Their fantasie most erreth in aggravating their Sin, or Dangers or Unhappiness" (p. 241).

38. The use of *distracted* as a referrent for *mad* is confirmed by the *Oxford English Dictionary*. It was sometimes used as a synonym for *non compos mentis* even in Massachusetts legal records. *Distracted* appears far more frequently in records of overseers of the poor than does *non compos mentis*.

39. "The Case of a Troubled Mind."

40. *The Diary of Ebenezer Parkman, 1703–1782*, ed. Francis G. Walett (Worcester, Mass., 1974), pp. 38, 49, 193.

41. Samuel Chandler, Diary, 1740–94, 1741, no. 215, New England Historic Genealogical Society, Boston. In the mid seventeenth century, John Winthrop had described a youth suffering "an affliction of mind," because he could "not be brought to apprehend any comfort in God" but was "humbled and broken up for sins" and went about mourning and languishing." Winthrop also recounted several other cases of the same nature, including one of a woman who died after a long bout with madness, which was due, Winthrop believed, to her despair after her first child died. He too used this incident for instructive purposes, for he viewed her distraction as "God's punishment for her unruliness." See Winthrop, *History of New England, 1630–1649* (Boston, 1853), 1:149, 2:93.

42. *The Castel of Helth* (London, 1539), quoted in Hunter and Macalpine, *Three Hundred Years*, p. 7.

43. *A Treatise on the Passions and Faculties of the Soule of Man* (London, 1640), quoted in Hunter and Macalpine, *Three Hundred Years*, p. 119.

44. Ibid., p. 130.

45. For a discussion of the importance of the role of ministers in eighteenth-century New England, see Scott, *From Office to Profession*. Patricia U. Bonomi and Peter R. Eisenstadt found that participation in church life was high in eighteenth-century New England and cited "respectable figures" of attendance in the 1760s. They argued that the Great Awakening increased loyalty to churches as competition among sects became newly important. "Sabbath worship remained a highly significant activity." See Bonomi and Eisenstadt, "Church Adherence in the Eighteenth-century British-American Colonies," *William and Mary Quarterly* 39 (April 1982): 245–87. Kenneth Lockridge argued that the religious impulse was very strong in Dedham in the first half of the eighteenth century at least. See Lockridge, *A New England Town: The First One Hundred Years* (New York, 1970). See also Ahlstrom, *A Religious History* for a discussion of religion in eighteenth-century New England, especially the intensifying impact of the Great Awakening. All this suggests that ministerial opinion about the nature and causes of insanity was likely to have been very influential.

46. "The Frailty and Misery of Man's Life" (Boston), Clifford K. Shipton, ed., in *Early American Imprints, 1639–1800* (New York, 1963–), pp. 2–3.

47. Ibid., p. 4.

48. Ibid., p. 5.

49. See Miller, *The New England Mind: The Seventeenth Century* for a discussion of this. Miller noted that Puritans believed that "Adam no doubt was created as upright in his reason as in his will, but what now remains as the light of reason is almost certain to prove a will-o'-the-wisp" (p. 31).

50. "Idle Poor Secluded from the Bread of Charity by the Christian Law" (Boston) in Clifford K. Shipton, ed., *Early American Imprints, 1639–1800* (New York, 1963–), pp. 6, 7.

51. Quoted in Williams, "The Fraility," p. 4. In England also there was concern about the dangers of too much mental exertion. MacDonald found that Napier treated twenty-seven clients who had experienced some symptoms of mental disorder because of "too much study" (*Mystical Bedlam*, p. 186).

52. *Sibley's Harvard Graduates*, vols. 1–3 by John Langdon Sibley (Cambridge, Mass., 1873); Vol. 4 by Clifford K. Shipton (Cambridge, Mass., 1933); vols. 5–17 by Clifford K. Shipton (Boston, 1941–76). Hereafter referred to as *Sibley's*. Coolidge reference is from 7:330.

53. *Sibley's*, 8:97.

54. "The Sin of Suicide Contrary to Nature" (Boston), Clifford K. Shipton, ed., in *Early American Imprints* (New York, 1963–).

55. Ibid., p. 6.

56. A Massachusetts law of 1771, for example, referred to one who had "been deprived of his reason by the Providence of God" ("Resolve Empowering Abijah Burrage, I.N. Burrage Guardian to Execute a Deed," *Acts and Resolves, Public and Private, of the Province of Massachusetts Bay* (Boston, 1869–1922), 1771, vol. 18, chap. 30, p. 546).

57. Richard Bushman discussed the heightened emphasis given to individualism in New England after the Second Great Awakening in *From Puritan to Yankee: Character and Social Order in Connecticut, 1690–1765,* (New York, 1967); Nash described the rise of self-interest in economic transactions among Bostonians and the rise of competition in the 1790s in *Urban Crucible;* Gordon S. Wood argued that new assumptions about causality appeared in the colonies just before the Revolution that "supplanted divine providence and omnipotence of God" and were instead based on the assumption of "a world of freely acting individuals who are capable of directly and deliberately bringing about events through their decisions and actions, and who therefore can be morally responsible for what happens." This would ultimately lead to an abandoning of God's Providence and a search for moral laws that corresponded to physical laws in the effort to explain reality. See Wood, "Conspiracy and the Paranoid Style: Causality and Deceit in the Eighteenth Century," *William and Mary Quarterly* 39 (July 1982): 412.

Chapter 2: A Familiar and Pitiful Sight *(pages 31–48)*

1. *Sibley's,* 7:326. A thorny problem confronts a historian looking at the reaction to insanity in earlier periods. How can the scholar be sure that behavior that suggests madness to the contemporary sensibility, finely honed to appreciate the difficulties inherent in achieving mental health, would have been evidence of insanity in an earlier generation? The best assurance I have found for avoiding an undue presentism is to include only those persons who were thought to be mad by others or who described themselves as distracted.

2. Quoted in *Sibley's,* 7:326–27.

3. Ibid., p. 328.

4. Ibid., pp. 328–30.

5. Ibid., p. 330.

6. Ibid., 6:273.

7. Ibid., 7:528.

8. See Ibid., 6:261 for Moody's story.

9. *Diary,* 1746.

10. Ibid., 1750.

11. See Charles E. P. Moody, *Biographical Sketches of the Moody Family* (Boston, 1847), pp. 95–106, and *Sibley's,* 6:260–61.

12. Ibid., 12:54.

13. Ibid., 6:77. Richard Napier, MacDonald's English astrologist and healer, would have called Checkley a "melancholick."

14. George Francis Dow, *Everyday Life in the Massachusetts Bay Colony* (Boston, 1735), p. 209.

15. *Sibley's*, 7:145–46.

16. See William Tudor, *The Life of James Otis* (Boston, 1823), 1:475.

17. John Rowe Diary, 16 March 1770, Massachusetts Historical Society, Boston.

18. *Sibley's*, 11:281.

19. Quoted in Ibid., pp. 282–85.

20. *Genealogy of the Otis Family*, New England Historic Genealogical Society, Boston, p. 102.

21. Franklin Bowditch Dexter, *Biographical Sketches of the Graduates of Yale College*, 1701–1815 (New York: 1885–98), 1:227.

22. *Sibley's*, 14:450.

23. Ibid., 9:35.

24. Joseph B. Felt, *History of Ipswich, Essex and Hamilton* (Cambridge, Mass.: 1834), p. 204.

25. "Persons Warned Out of Boston, 1745–1792," in Records of the Overseers of the Poor for the Town of Boston, 1733–1890, Massachusetts Historical Society, Boston; Middlesex County Quarterly Courts Records, 1708–55, Middlesex County Court House, East Cambridge, Mass.

26. *Diary*, p. 586.

27. Ibid., p. 587.

28. "Letter from Robert Treat Paine to Jopseph Palmer about Mr. Leonard's Mental Illness," September 1762, Massachusetts Historical Society, Boston.

29. Fewer than a dozen cases have been cited by Deutsch in *The Mentally Ill in America* to support this argument.

30. *Records of the Town of Braintree, Mass., 1640–1793*, ed. Samuel A. Bates (Randolph, Mass., 1886), p. 26.

31. *Records of the Town of Watertown, 1649–1829*, ed. Fred G. Barker (Watertown, Mass., 1894–1906), 2:143.

32. Ibid., p. 150.

33. *Sibley's*, 4:388.

34. Middlesex County Quarterly Courts Records, 1708–55, Middlesex County Court House, East Cambridge, Mass.

35. *Sibley's*, 7:325.

36. *Boston News Letter*, 9 December 1736.

37. *Sibley's*, 7:330.

38. Ibid., 11:282.

39. Quoted in Dexter, *Biographical Sketches*, 2:278.

40. In seventeenth-century England, too, violent lunatics were pre-

vented from roaming around freely, wreaking destruction. MacDonald found that it was violent lunatics who were chained and confined. English folk in the rural counties from which Napier's patients were drawn were frightened of the madman who had run amok: "a violent lunatic was a terrifying threat to everyone's safety." As in New England, "chains and fetters were reserved for the most violent and menacing mad men, people who terrrified their families and neighbors." MacDonald adds that a chained lunatic was not a sign of cruelty or barbarism, but rather a sign of fear. Napier's clients seem to have been wilder, noisier, and more out of control than were the insane of eighteenth-century Massachusetts. See MacDonald, *Mystical Bedlam,* especially chapter 4 and pp. 141–142.

41. "Confession of a Counterfeiter" (Boston 1769), in Clifford K. Shipton, ed., *Early American Imprints, 1639–1800* (New York, 1963–).

42. Mary B. Claflin (New York, 1890).

43. Ibid., p. 113–20.

44. Ibid., p. 120. There is, of course, some problem with taking these accounts at face value. Town histories written a century later cannot be considered first-hand information and are not as reliable as contemporary sources. Yet these accounts reflect a similar pattern found in first-hand evidence and so can be given credence.

45. Charles Atwood, *Reminiscences of Taunton* (Taunton, Mass., 1880).

46. Henry Smith Chapman (Winchester, Mass., 1936), p. 87.

47. See Demos, *Entertaining Satan,* especially p. 304, for discussion of the harm thought to be done by witches and the way they were blamed for misfortune. Witchcraft did not die out in New England at the end of the seventeenth century; on the contrary, as Demos pointed out, it was an important, if informal, part of New England life throughout the eighteenth century (p. 387).

48. I am indebted to John Demos for suggesting that madness and witchcraft set off different stress points in colonial New England. See *Entertaining Satan,* chapter 9 for a discussion of the "stress . . . points" set off by witchcraft in early New England.

49. Robinson, *A New System or The Spleen, Vapours and Hypochrondiak Melancholy; wherein all the decays of the nerves, and lownesses of the spirits, are mechanically accounted for,* 2d ed., (London, 1729); Battie, *A Treatise on Madness* (London, 1758); Nicholas Culpeper, *The Practice of Physick* (London, 1665).

50. One wealthy "mad woman" was offered the following treatment by her physician. "I bled her plentifully in the Cephalick Vein, on both arms, at the Saphena in both feet, . . . under the Tongue, and by leeches to the Hemorrhoids Vein. . . . I either bled her or vomited her strongly, or purged her . . . she would vomit twelve times, and purge two or three times downward" (Daniel Oxbridge, *General Observations and Prescrip-*

tions in the Practice of Physick [London, 1715], quoted in Hunter and Macalpine, *Three Hundred Years*, p. 122).

51. Tomes, *A Generous Confidence*, pp. 22–27.

52. MacDonald, *Mystical Bedlam*. John Demos, who has done extensive research on colonial Massachusetts, found no evidence that quasi-magical practices were used to treat the distracted (personal communication).

53. John Blake, *Public Health in the Town of Boston, 1680–1822* (Cambridge, Mass. 1959), pp. 3–10.

54. Sewall, *The Diary of Samuel Sewall, 1674–1729*, ed. M. Halsey Thomas (New York, 1973), 1:19, 147.

55. Parkman, *Diary*, p. 90.

56. Ibid., pp. 49, 69, 86, 193; C. Mather, *Diary*, p. 589.

57. C. Mather, *Magnalia*, 1:441, 447.

58. See, for example, entries for 1741, 1743, 1744, 1746, Chandler Diary.

59. "Letter from Robert Treat Paine to Joseph Palmer."

60. Parkman, *Diary*, p. 193.

61. "Letter from David Kingman to Cotton Tufts," 23 January 1768, Massachusetts Historical Society, Boston.

62. For a discussion of the rationale behind heroic remedies, see Charles E. Rosenberg, "The Therapeutic Revolution: Medicine, Meaning and Social Change in Nineteenth Century America," in Morris J. Vogel and Charles E. Rosenberg, eds., *The Therapeutic Revolution* (Philadelphia, 1979), pp. 3–25.

63. *A Treatise on Madness*, p. 74–76.

64. *A New System*, pp. 328–29.

65. *Angel*, pp. 130–34.

66. *A Generous Confidence*, p. 26. Blake discusses the smallpox hospitals in Boston in *Public Health in the Town of Boston*, p. 38.

67. For example, see *Records of the Suffolk County Court*, 2 vols, Publications of the Colonial Society of Massachusetts, vols. 29, 30 (Boston, 1933), 1:304, 90, 95; 2:784, 850; 851.

68. For example, see ibid., 1:436.

Chapter 3: Non Compos Mentis in Colonial Massachusetts
(pages 49–64)

1. *Probate Records of Essex County, Massachusetts* (Salem, Mass., 1916–20), 3:237.

2. Frederick Lewis Weiss, *Genealogy of the Atherton Family* (Boston, 1911), New England Historic Genealogical Society, Boston.

3. *Sibley's*, 10:371.

4. Dexter, *Biographical Sketches*, vol. 4.

5. *Sibley's*, 6:434.

6. See Hunter and Macalpine, *Three Hundred Years*, p. 293 for a discussion of private madhouses in England.

7. *Sibley's*, 11:283.

8. *Genealogy of the Otis Family* (1833), p. 103, New England Historical Genealogical Society, Boston.

9. *The Colonial Laws of Massachusetts, Reprinted from the Edition of 1672 with Supplements through 1686* (Boston, 1887), p. 248.

10. *The Charters and General Laws of the Colony and Province of Massachusetts Bay, 1634–1779* (Boston, 1814), p. 276.

11. The only evidence I found of town action of this kind was Watertown's efforts to control Samuel Coolidge. *Damnifie* meant "to cause injury," "to damage," or "to hurt" (*Oxford English Dictionary*).

12. Salem, Danvers, and Concord all boarded out some insane residents before 1770. Watertown, it will be recalled, boarded out Samuel Coolidge with local families. See Miscellaneous Papers, 1746–1832, in Records of the Overseers of the Poor for the Town of Salem, Essex Institute, Salem, Mass.; Records of the Overseers of the Poor for the Town of Danvers, vol. 1, 1767–74 and Notices of Boarders, 1766–73," in Records of the Overseers, Danvers Historical Society, Danvers, Mass.; Records of the Overseers of the Poor for the Town of Concord, Concord Public Library, Concord, Mass.

13. *Probate Records of Essex County*, 1:435.

14. *Records of the Town of Braintree*, pp. 41, 63, 65.

15. Records of the Overseers of the Poor for the Town of Haverhill, Haverhill Public Library, Haverhill, Mass. See also William Barry, *A History of Framingham, Massachusetts from 1640 to 1847* (Boston, 1847), p. 71; *Early Records of Dedham, Massachusetts*, ed. Benjamin Fisher (Dedham, 1968), p. 279, for examples of towns boarding out their insane.

16. "Petition of Groton Selectmen to Superior Court of Massachusetts on Behalf of Barrow," Massachusetts Historical Society, Boston, Mass.

17. Records of the Overseers, Concord, Mass.

18. Samuel Abbot Green, *History of Groton, Massachusetts*, (Cambridge, Mass., 1914–15), 1:114.

19. "The Confession of Samuel Frost" (Boston, 1783), in Clifford K. Shipton, ed., *Early American Imprints, 1639–1880* (New York, 1963–).

20. Josiah H. Benton, *Warning Out in New England 1656–1817* (Boston, 1911), pp. 1–52. The designation *stranger* was a negative one in both legal and social terms during the eighteenth century. It was usually used to imply a person not only without residential status but also bereft of family or property and hence without visible means of support.

21. Such was Samuel Coolidge, in 1742, "being in town and likely to

be a charge" (*Reports of the Record Commissioners of the City of Boston: Selectmen's Minutes, 1716–1810* [Boston, 1885–97], 17:366. [Hereafter cited as *Selectmen's Minutes*]).

22. Quoted in *Sibley's*, 9:35–37.

23. Middlesex County Quarterly Courts Records, 1708–55. Middlesex County Court House. Thirteen such cases were found.

24. Original Papers Relating to the Acts of the Massachusetts General Court, 1769, Massachusetts State Archives, State House, Boston.

25. The first mention of distracted paupers being kept in the Boston almshouse occurs in 1729 (*Selectmen's Minutes*, 13:194). Almshouse Records, in Records of the Overseers of the Poor, Massachusetts Historical Society, Boston, indicate that insane residents were kept there in the period 1750–71. The bulk of the Boston overseers of the poor records for the colonial period, which contained the almshouse records, were probably destroyed in fires, according to the director of archives of the Boston Public Library, repository of the city of Boston records. Those that have survived and are publicly held are at the Massachusetts Historical Society and Boston Public Library, Archives. The Massachusetts Historical Society (MHS) collection (1735–1911) includes incomplete almshouse records for the period 1750–71; correspondence for 1738–1911; some account books for the period 1750–70; and "Records of Persons Warned out of Boston," 1745–92. (BPL) Boston Public Library holdings include vote books of the overseers of the poor, 1788–1838 and other documents, 1793–1832.

26. See, for example *Selectmen's Minutes*, 19:166.

27. Ibid., 20:246.

28. See ibid., 15:98, 351.

29. Ibid., 19:177.

30. Ibid., 20:236.

31. Ibid., p. 190.

32. Ibid., 17:237.

33. Ibid., 23:120.

34. Almshouse Records, 1750–71, and Correspondence 1735–1911, in Records of the Overseers, Boston, MHS, Boston.

35. Josiah Quincy, *A Municipal History of the Town and City of Boston* (Boston, 1852), p. 9.

36. *Selectmen's Minutes*, 17:239.

37. Ibid., 13:194.

38. Ibid., 14:101.

39. Ibid., p. 77.

40. Ibid., p. 89.

41. Ibid., 20:98.

42. Ibid., p. 179.

43. I have identified a total of twenty-seven insane almshouse residents from 1757 to 1779, thirty-five male and twelve females according

to various sources. Four insane were sent to the workhouse in 1771, two males and two females. I identified almshouse insane from Almshouse Records, 1750–1911, in Records of the Overseers, MHS, Boston; and *Selectmen's Minutes*, 1716–1810.

44. See Nash, *Urban Crucible*, pp. 251–53.

45. Nash discusses the rising stratification in Boston and the growing number of poor in this period in ibid., pp. 117–18.

46. Ibid., pp. 182–86. The growing economic stratification was evident as early as the 1740s, when revivalist preachers began complaining about the fortunes made out of the growing entrepreneurial spirit and the rising numbers of poor (p. 217). Political and social factionalism grew in the town in this period. Nash noted that in the early 1760s "the town was no longer one community, a corporate entity with several pyramidically arranged but interdependent parts. Only in the geographical sense did it remain a community at all; in social terms Boston had become fragmented, unsure of itself, ridden with internecine animosities." Yet even in 1737 Nash found Bostonians to be traditional, conservative, and "strenuously egalitarian in their values" (pp. 137, 281).

47. See *Probate Records of Essex County*, 2:33; *Selectmen's Minutes*, 12:246; "Order Appointing John How Guardian of his Brother Elijah," *Acts and Resolves*, 1708–19, vol. 9, chap. 132, p. 505.

48. See "An Act in Further Addition to an Act Intitled an Act for the Relief of Idiots and Distracted Persons," in *The Charters and General Laws*, pp. 515–16.

49. Records of Probate Appeals Courts, 1775–87 (uncatalogued), Massachusetts State Archives, State House, Boston.

50. It is interesting that the criteria for determining sanity apparently bore little relation to contemporary measures, such as hallucinations, loss of contact with reality, disturbed thought patterns, and so forth.

51. Records of Probate Appeals Courts, 1775–87. Fourteen appeals were found for this period; all were granted.

52. Suffolk County Quarterly Courts Records, 1760, Suffolk County Court House, Boston.

53. *Sibley's*, 9:3.

54. Suffolk County Probate Court Records, 1771, no. 315, Suffolk County Court House, Boston.

55. *Selectmen's Minutes*, 12:246, 275, 313; 15:127; 17:57, 263; 19:169, 291; 20:117, 203, 235, 136, 99, 270; 23:132, 172, 198, 14, 23; 25:82, 271, 210, 113; 27:110, 333, 205.

56. See *Charters and General Laws*, p. 516.

57. Suffolk County Probate Court Records, 1746, #6878. Suffolk County Court House, Boston.

58. The colonial New England town, especially the Massachusetts town, has been subjected to intense scrutiny by historians over the last fifteen years. Most accounts have portrayed these towns as tight-knit

communities, characterized by a great deal of face-to-face interaction, social and psychic density, and commitment to communitarian values and consensus. See John Demos, *A Little Commonwealth: Family Life in Plymouth Colony* (New York, 1970); Kenneth Lockridge, *A New England Town: The First Hundred Years* (New York, 1970); Sumner Chilton Powell, *Puritan Village: The Formation of a New England Town* (Middletown, Conn., 1963); Philip J. Greven, Jr., *Four Generations: Population, Land and Family in Colonial Andover, Massachusetts* (Ithaca, N.Y., 1970); Michael Zuckerman, *Peaceable Kingdoms* (New York, 1970); Robert Gross, *The Minutemen and Their World* (New York, 1976); Tracy, *Jonathan Edwards, Pastor;* Jedrey, *The World of John Cleaveland.* All these studies have argued that, to a greater or lesser degree, communitarian and religious values were the most fundamental ones shaping the life experience of the residents of these towns for much of the colonial period.

Some scholars have painted a somewhat more complex picture of New England towns caught up in severe factional and religious battles or existing in an uneasy state of tension between values of community and individualism. Demos argued that the early New England towns demonstrated the tension between these competing values (*Entertaining Satan,* chapter 9). Paul Boyer and Stephen Nissenbaum described the social and religious divisions in Salem on the eve of the witchcraft trials in *Salem Possessed: The Social Origins of Witchcraft* (Cambridge, Mass., 1974). Stephen Innes found that Springfield, Massachusetts was a hotbed of acquisitiveness, competitive spirit, and individualism in the seventeenth century, largely because of its strong commercial cast and the preponderance of skilled workers seeking employment and opportunity. It was not until the eighteenth century that communal values, harmony, and equality began to characterize the town. See Innes, *Labor in a New Land: Economy and Society in Seventeenth-Century Springfield* (Princeton, N.J., 1983). Nash found that the rise of commercialism led to an emphasis on individual self-interest in eighteenth-century Boston. (*Urban Crucible*). These corrective views are important to a real understanding of the diversity of the colonial New England experience; nevertheless, the dominant experience for most members of Massachusetts Bay Colony was far different from what was to follow in the late eighteenth and early nineteenth centuries, when acquisitiveness and individualism would become values as well as reality.

Clearly, there was a great emphasis on communitarianism in most Massachusetts towns, at least in value and preference, throughout much of the colonial period. Jedrey found this to be true of the small parish in Ipswich he studied until the Revolution (*The World of John Cleaveland*). Tracy found that there was a surprising degree of individualism, ambition, and materialism in eighteenth-century Northampton; however, she also found that the community remained strictly committed ideologically to "the communitarian model of social life" until the Revolutionary era. She argued that community and consensus were still very important in the eighteenth century, and the changes that did occur then were small compared to those that occurred from 1650 to the nineteenth century. See Tracy, *Jonathan Edwards, Pastor* p. 92–93. Demos found that even in seventeenth-century New England towns, while individualism struggled against the deeply held values of community, the former could not be acknowledged, while the latter were the measure by which Puritans judged themselves (*Entertaining Satan*, chapter 9). David Thomas Konig in *Law and Society in Puritan Massachusetts: Essex County, 1629–1692* (Chapel Hill, N.C., 1979) argued that the high degree of litigation in Essex County in the seventeenth century did not suggest a deterioration of communities but rather was a way of promoting community stability by an orderly resolution of social problems. Kerry Arnold Trask studied the writings of New England ministers in the eighteenth century and found that for them individual rights were not as important as the welfare of the community. See Trask, "In the Pursuit of Shadows: A Study of Collective Hope and Despair in Provincial Massachusetts in the Era of the Seven Years War, 1748–1769," Ph.D. diss., University of Minnesota, Minneapolis, 1971.

The vast majority of towns in Massachusetts were quite small; in 1710 there were fewer than one hundred adult males in the average town. Even by 1765 a majority of towns in the Province had fewer than one thousand inhabitants. See Zuckerman, *Peaceable Kingdoms*, p. 19; and Evarts B. Greene and Virginia D. Harrington, *American Population Before the Federal Census of 1790* (New York, 1932), pp. 21–30. These towns were ethnically homogeneous; most residents of Massachusetts in the eighteenth century were English. Thomas Parvis estimated that the population of Massachusetts was 84.4 percent English as late as 1790 ("The European Ancestry of the U.S. Population, 1790," *William and Mary Quarterly* 41 [January 1984]: 85–101). There was comparatively less migration in and out of these towns, especially in the first half of the eighteenth century, than was to characterize Massachusetts in the second half of the eighteenth and certainly the nineteenth centuries. Most people lived and died in the same towns as their fathers and mothers had. While the subject of persistence and migration in the colonial period has become controversial, evidence suggests that migration was not an important factor in New England until the second half of the eighteenth century. Lockridge estimated that in the early eighteenth century, nine out of ten men born in Dedham would remain there for the rest of their lives (*A New England Town*, p. 40). Greven found a high level of persistence in Andover in the early eighteenth century (*Four Generations*, p. 175); Tracy found low levels of migration in Northampton until the 1760s (*Jonathan Edwards*, p. 94); Douglass Jones found higher rates of persistence in Beverly and Wenham in the first part of the eighteenth century than he did in the latter decades (*Village and*

Seaport: Migration and Society in Eighteenth Century Massachusetts [Hanover, N.H., 1981]). For a countervailing view that posits a high level of mobility throughout eighteenth-century New England based on a study of American militiamen, see George Villaflor and Kenneth Sokoloff, "Migration in Colonial America: Evidence from the Militia Muster Rolls," *Social Science History* 6 (Fall 1982): 539–70.

Massachusetts towns constructed elaborate systems of surveillance in the eighteenth century. Strangers were noticed; selectmen searched out possible lawbreakers and deviants; neighbors concerned themselves with each other's activities to an often extraordinary extent. Boston's selectmen's records make it clear how important was the role of town selectmen in checking on possible infractions of community mores. See *Selectmen's Minutes, 1700–1773*, passim. See also Nancy Cott, "Eighteenth Century Family and Social Life Revealed in Massachusetts Divorce Records," *Journal of Social History* 9 (Fall 1976): 20–42. Kinship ties within local communities probably contributed to this concentration on local affairs, which in turn increased commitment and communitarian values. Greven showed how strong kinship ties, based partly on inheritance patterns, led family members to live close to one another in seventeenth- and eighteenth-century Andover. (*Four Generations*). Jedrey found similar patterns in Ipswich (*The World of John Cleaveland*, pp. 73–74), as did Tracy in Northampton in the eighteenth century (*Jonathan Edwards, Pastor*, pp. 101–2).

While it is a truism that the New England way was transformed into the Yankee way sometime during the eighteenth century, historians disagree on when this happened. Gross in *The Minutemen and Their World* did not see it taking hold until after the Revolution in Concord. In *Urban Crucible*, Nash argued that Boston's character began changing toward a much more individualistic and unequal society after the 1740s. While James Henretta saw similar changes in Boston, he argued that "these changes did not constitute a basic economic and social transformation; rather this did not occur until the rise of manufacture in the 1790's." See Henretta, "Wealth and Social Structure," in Jack P. Greene and J. R. Pole, eds., *Colonial British America: Essays in the New History of the Modern Era* (Baltimore, 1984), pp. 278–84.

59. John Demos suggested this in "Shame and Guilt in Puritan Society," *Journal of Social History*, forthcoming. Townsfolk in Massachusetts were extremely concerned with their reputations. I found many (approximately eighty-five) suits for slander and libel in the Middlesex County Quarterly Court Records for the period 1708–55.

60. The most prominent and wealthy members of these towns tended to be returned to office regularly. Jedrey found this to be true in Ipswich, which he described as suggesting "the stable, conservative character of rural New England before the Revolution" (*The World of John Cleaveland*, p. xii). See Robert Joseph Dinkin, "Provincial Massachu-

setts—A Deferential or a Democratic Society?" (Ph.D. diss., Columbia University, 1960) for a fuller treatment of this subject.

61. The vast majority of towns were agricultural in nature, with relatively low levels of intensive economic growth. For a discussion of the extensive rather than intensive growth of the colonial economy, see James Henretta, "The Morphology of New England Society in the Colonial Period," *Journal of Interdisciplinary History* 11 (Winter 1971): 379–98, and "Wealth and Social Structure," pp. 262–89, 271; Stuart Bruchey, *The Roots of American Economic Growth, 1607–1860* (New York, 1965), p. 22; Alice Hanson Jones, *Wealth of a Nation To Be: The American Colonies on the Eve of the Revolution* (New York, 1980), pp. 72–85. Bruchey characterized the colonial economy as "overwhelmingly agricultural in character" and noted the preponderance of subsistence farming in the North (*The Roots of American Economic Growth*, pp. 23, 30–31). See also Henretta, "Wealth and Social Structure," p. 284. Henretta argued that the price system was subordinate to barter transactions and direct exchanges in the Northern colonies ("Families and Farms: Mentalities in Pre-Industrial America," *William and Mary Quarterly* 35 (January 1978): 3–33. He also noted an "elaborate system of local exchange among farmers, artisans and storekeepers" in colonial New England, sometimes based on family ties ("Wealth and Social Structure," pp. 283–84). Jedrey found that a credit and barter system was important in eighteenth-century Ipswich (*The World of John Cleaveland*, p. 92). Tracy found that in eighteenth-century Northampton, economic transactions were characterized by reciprocity rather than the cash nexus (*Jonathan Edwards, Pastor*, p. 104). W. T. Baxter found that merchants in eighteenth-century Boston had an informal economic relationship, in which an elaborate system of credits and debits he called "bookkeeping barter" replaced cash payments (*The House of Hancock: Business in Boston, 1724–1725* [Cambridge, Mass. 1945]). Lockridge argued that the Dedham farmer was not connected to the market economy in the eighteenth century, although Dedham was only ten miles from Boston (*A New England Town*, p. 141).

Stephen Innes showed the importance of paternalism in the economic life of Springfield under the patriarchal control of the Pynchon family (*Labor in a New Land: Economy and Society in Seventeenth Century Springfield* [Princeton, N.J., 1983]). Peter Dobkin Hall found that "by the middle of the eighteenth century, the merchants of eastern Massachusetts seem to have developed a remarkably stable system of activity in which family and business concerns were highly integrated." He argued that the family was the "major social and economic organization in Massachusetts," until the "late eighteenth century." See P. D. Hall, "Family Structure and Economic Organizations: Massachusetts Merchants, 1700–1850," in Tamara Haraven, ed., *Family and Kin in Urban Communities, 1700–1930* (New York, 1977), pp. 39, 43.

David Hackett Fischer argued that, insofar as wealth was measured by land, colonial New England was more equal than any society that existed at the time or was to follow it ("America: A Social History, 1650–1975," [manuscript, 1974], chapter 5, p. 16). Gloria Main discussed the relative equality of wealth distribution in the smaller towns of colonial Massachusetts ("Inequality in Early America. The Evidence from Probate Records of Massachusetts and Maryland," *Journal of Interdisciplinary History* 7 [Spring, 1977]: 558–81). Whether there existed what we consider equality or not, it is clear that, up to the time of the Revolution, the wealth distribution remained relatively stable, and that increasing inequality was to follow in the nineteenth century. See Henretta, "Wealth and Social Structure," pp. 276–78, for a review of recent studies of colonial wealth distribution. See also Jedrey, *The World of John Cleaveland*, pp. ix–x.

62. Communities were central to life in colonial New England. Jedrey found a great deal of parochialism and a strong sense of community in Ipswich (ibid., p. 95). David Grayson Allen argued that in the seventeenth century New England towns were characterized by a strong degree of localism, which derived from the fact that towns were modeled after the different regions in England from which their founders came. In the eighteenth century, he argued, the towns became more alike because of the homogenizing effect of a process of centralization in the Province, though they were not necessarily less parochial. See Allen, *In English Ways: The Movement of Societies and the Transferral of English Local Law and Custom to the Massachusetts Bay in the Seventeenth Century* (Chapel Hill, N.C., 1981). William E. Nelson argued that community standards of justice were enforced far more consistently than legal standards and that the judgment of local communities was far more important than the courts in enforcing sanctions. See Nelson, "The Legal Restraint of Power in Pre-Revolutionary America: Massachusetts as a Case Study, 1760–1775," *American Journal of Legal History* 18 (January 1974): 1–32. Elsewhere, Nelson argued that the primary purpose of law in pre-Revolutionary Massachusetts was to give "legal effect to the community's sense of sin and to punish those who breached the community's taboos" ("The Americanization of Common Law During the Revolutionary Period: A Study of Legal Change in Massachusetts, 1760–1830" [Ph.D. diss., Harvard University, 1971], p. 120). Zuckerman maintained that well into the eighteenth century the local community was largely autonomous from the authority of the Massachusetts Provincial government (*Peaceable Kingdoms*, p.18).

63. See Innes, *Labor in a New Land,* and P. D. Hall, "Family Structure and Economic Organizations" for discussions of the personal context of economic relationship in Springfield and Boston.

64. See *Selectmen's Minutes,* passim for examples.

65. MacDonald noted that the "governing elite" was responsible for

the fact that asylums "proliferated all over the country in the century after the English Revolution" (*Mystical Bedlam,* p. 230). I am indebted to Robert Gross for suggesting the comparison of colonial New England with early modern Europe.

Chapter 4: The Medical Face of Madness *(pages 65–89)*

1. Richard D. Brown, "The Healing Arts in Colonial and Revolutionary Massachusetts: The Context for Scientific Medicine," in *Medicine in Colonial Massachusetts, 1620–1820,* (Boston, 1980), pp. 35–49. Brown discussed the growth of the medical profession in post-Revolutionary Massachusetts and placed special emphasis on the Revolutionary War as a catalyst in this development (p. 45).

2. Ibid., p. 46.

3. Whitfield J. Bell, Jr., "Medicine in Boston and Philadelphia: Comparisons and Contrasts, 1750–1820," in *Medicine in Colonial Massachusetts, 1620–1820* (Boston, 1980), p. 65.

4. Barnes Riznik, "The Professional Lives of Early Nineteenth Century New England Doctors," *Journal of the History of Medicine and Allied Sciences* 19 (January 1964): 1–17.

5. W. Bell, "Medicine in Boston and Philadelphia," p. 164. Massachusetts General Hospital was the first hospital in the state.

6. Philip Cash makes this point in "The Professionalization of Boston Medicine, 1760–1803," in *Medicine in Colonial Massachusetts, 1620–1820* (Boston, 1980), pp. 69–101.

7. See Joseph F. Kett, *The Formation of the American Medical Profession* (New Haven, Conn., 1968), p. 10.

8. W. Bell, "Medicine in Boston and Philadelphia," p. 164.

9. Ibid., pp. 165–66.

10. See Carlson and Simpson, "Models of the Nervous System," pp. 101–15. "The dissertations of M.D. candidates are of particular value as barometers. . . . These writers were informed, had to please others besides themselves, and, despite youth's impetuousity, were extremely careful creatures at that point of their careers" (p. 114).

11. See W. Bell, "Medicine in Boston and Philadelphia," pp. 176–82.

12. The medical school in New York was located at King's College, Columbia University. See Kett, *The Formation of the American Medical Profession,* p. 35.

13. For a discussion of the important role passions played in speculations about madness in eighteenth-century European psychiatry, especially in the thinking of Pinel, see Kathleen M. Grange, "Pinel and Eighteenth-Century Psychiatry," *Bulletin of the History of Medicine* 35 (September-October 1961): 442–53.

14. See Vieda Skultans, ed., *Madness and Morals: Ideas on Insanity in*

the Nineteenth Century (London, 1975) for a discussion of English writing on madness in the early nineteenth century by John Haslam and Alexander Morison, among others. In a very thorough introduction Skultans discussed the importance of "moral force" and "will" in earlier nineteenth-century discussions of madness, concepts to be succeeded later in the century by notions of "hereditary endowment" and "character" (pp. 1–31). Grange also discussed the role of passions in English writing on madness in "Pinel and Eighteenth-Century Psychiatry."

15. Henry May argued that there were four phases to the Enlightenment in America; the first phase he named the moderate Enlightenment. For a discussion of its impact, see May, *The Enlightenment in America* (New York, 1978).

16. Cutbush, *An Inaugural Dissertation on Insanity* (Philadelphia, 1794); Rose, *An Inaugural Dissertation on the Effects of Passion upon the Body* (Philadelphia, 1794); Anderson, *An Inaugural Dissertation on Chronic Mania* (New York, 1796). Dain noted that these early medical dissertations represented the most "important medical writings on the chosen topic" (*Concepts of Insanity*, p. 23).

17. Cutbush, *Inaugural Dissertation on Insanity*, p. 40. This explanation sounds somewhat similar to the one offered by Robinson sixty years earlier in emphasizing vibration and motions in parts of the body. Cutbush differs from Robinson in locating the seat of madness in the brain (Robinson had written more vaguely of "nervous fibers"); and, more importantly, in reversing the order of causation. While Robinson had argued that irregular motion in the nerves caused "wrong turns of thoughts and judgements" (*A New System*, p. 3), Cutbush thought that madness began with passions, which affected the brain and eventually reason. Passions and psychological factors in general thus have a more important role in Cutbush's explanation.

18. All three dissertations imply that mania is connected to negative emotions.

19. *An Inaugural Dissertation on the Influence of the Passions upon the Body in the Production and Cure of Diseases* (Philadelphia, 1805), p. 14.

20. *An Inaugural Dissertation on Hypochondriasis* (Philadelphia, 1805), p. 8.

21. Edward Augustus Holyoke, Daybook, vol. 120, box 16, Holyoke Collection, Essex Institute, Salem, Mass. Holyoke never went mad. William Bentley from Gloucester noted in his diary in 1791 that a young man of his acquaintance who had "become crazy" was reaping the fruits of an idle, intemperate, and dissolute life. Later, in 1808, Bentley discussed the case of a "crazy man" in Gloucester who refused to eat. He remarked, "It may be depression, but then nothing but vice could have occasioned it as he could have had full employment and he might have left the house when he pleased" (*Diary of William Bentley, 1784–1819* [Gloucester, 1962], 1:214, 374).

22. "Pardons Issued by the General Court of Massachusetts" (uncatalogued), Massachusetts State Archives, State House, Boston.

23. "Remarkable Cases of Madness," *Medical Repository* 5 (April 1802): 408–12.

24. *A Discourse on the Disease of Mrs. Martha Russell* (Bennington, Vt., 1805), p. 3.

25. *Medical Inquiries and Observations upon the Diseases of the Mind* (Philadelphia, 1812), pp. 17, 50, 66. Carlson and Simpson discussed William Cullen's influence on medical writings on madness (which included those of Rush) in the latter half of the eighteenth century. Cullen, who was associated with the medical college at Edinburgh, emphasized the importance of nervous excess and deficiency in causing disease, including madness. Cullen's work was published in this country in the early nineteenth century. While Rush moved the seat of excitement from the nervous system to the vascular system, the ideas of excess and deficiency were nevertheless important to him. See Carlson and Simpson, "Models of the Nervous System."

26. *An Inquiry into the Influence of Physical Causes on the Moral Faculty* (Philadelphia, 1786).

27. For an extensive discussion of Rush's theories and his significant contribution to American psychiatry, see Dain, *Concepts of Insanity,* pp. 14–23. He noted that Rush in his day "probably had more effect on medical thought and practice concerning the insane than any other American" (p. 15). According to Richard H. Shryock, when Rush died he was considered to be the greatest figure in American medicine, but by 1843 he was thought to have been talking nonsense (*The Development of Modern Medicine* [New York, 1969], p. 4).

28. For a discussion of the evolution of the concept of moral insanity, see Eric T. Carlson and Norman Dain, "The Meaning of Moral Insanity," *Bulletin of the History of Medicine* 36 (January-February 1962): 130–39. Rush discussed moral insanity in *An Inquiry into the Influences of Physical Causes.*

29. Grange discussed Pinel's interest in the moral faculties (by which the French physician meant emotions and passions) as the cause of insanity and demonstrated how this conviction led him to the attempt to manipulate the passions by "opposing and balancing" them in what he called moral treatment ("Pinel and Eighteenth Century Psychiatry").

30. *Treatise on Insanity,* trans. D. D. Davis (Sheffield, England, 1806), p. 113.

31. In spite of his belief in the largely functional nature of insanity, Pinel sometimes used the language of somaticism in what seems to contemporary ears a fanciful way, suggesting that insanity might involve a "lesion" of the nervous system or even "lesion of the will and understanding" (*Treatise,* p. 84).

32. For a discussion of Pinel's scientific contribution to psychiatry, see

Evelyn A. Woods and Eric T. Carlson, "The Psychiatry of Philippe Pinel," *Bulletin of the History of Medicine* 35 (January-February 1961): 14–21. Grange discussed the careful records kept by Pinel ("Pinel and Eighteenth-Century Psychiatry.")

33. Jean E. D. Esquirol, *Des Passions*, Paris, 1805.

34. For a discussion of the transformation from custody to treatment wrought by Pinel, see Woods and Carlson, "The Psychiatry of Philippe Pinel"; Dora B. Weiner, "Health, and Mental Health in the Thought of Philippe Pinel: The Emergence of Psychiatry During the French Revolution," in Charles E. Rosenberg, ed., *Healing and History* (New York, 1979), pp. 59–86. Weiner pointed out that although Pinel did not free the patients at Bicêtre from chains, he did free 80 women at La Salpêtrière from similar confinement in 1796. According to Weiner, one of Pinel's contributions to humane psychiatry was the substitution of straitjackets for chains.

35. Carlson and Simpson described Rush as an anachronism because of his commitment to a monistic pathology at a time when Pinel and others had forsaken the attempt to offer unitary theories and were concentrating on "circumscribed and specific investigations" (Carlson and Simpson, "Models of the Nervous System," p. 114).

36. William F. Bynum has shown how physicians in early nineteenth-century England struggled to bring the treatment of the insane under their professional aegis, in the face of the implication that moral treatment did not demand the services of physicians. Nancy Tomes has described a similar, more philosophical effort by American superintendents of lunatic asylums in the same period. See Bynum, "Rationales for Therapy in British Psychiatry, 1780–1835," *Medical History* 18 (September 1964): 315–25; Tomes, *A Generous Confidence*, pp. 75–89.

37. Dain called Rush a "transitional figure in the history of psychiatry" (*Concepts of Insanity*, p. 15). Tomes argued that Rush's humanitarian contributions were not based on Pinel but derived largely from his own thinking, though by 1812 it is clear that he had read Pinel (*A Generous Confidence*, p. 336). Rush and other physicians writing about madness in this period were also influenced by the Scottish school of common-sense philosophy. Proponents of this school believed that the mind was composed of fixed moral qualities and was not merely the receptacle of sense impressions, as John Locke taught. Their ideas helped to contribute the strong moral flavor to the discussions of madness in this country. Locke's empiricism was also influential in broadening the range of causes of madness, since he argued that the mind was formed by an accumulation of all external stimuli. See May, *The Enlightenment in America* and Walter Jackson Bate, *From Classic to Romantic* (New York, 1946), for discussions of these influences.

38. W. Bell, "Medicine in Boston and Philadelphia," pp. 165–66. Massachusetts physicians also wrote to Rush seeking medical advice. See

also J. Worth Estes, "Therapeutic Practice in Colonial New England," in *Medicine in Colonial Massachusetts, 1620–1820* (Boston, 1980), p. 363. Dain discussed Rush's wide influence in this country and in Europe (*Medical Inquiries* went through five editions between 1812 and 1835) in *Concepts of Insanity,* pp. 21–23.

39. See Tomes, *A Generous Confidence,* p. 63 for a discussion of the Quaker connection.

40. Grob discussed this influence of the Retreat at York on the asylum movement in this country in *Mental Institutions in America,* pp. 43–44.

41. (Philadelphia), p. 40. See Anne Digby, *Madness, Morality and Medicine: A Study of the York Retreat* (Cambridge, 1985) for an in-depth study of the York Retreat.

42. Quoted in L. Vernon Briggs, et al., *History of the Psychopathic Hospital in Boston, Massachusetts* (Boston, 1922), p. 8.

43. *An Inaugural Dissertation on Insanity* (New York, 1811).

44. Anonymous, *American Medical and Philosophical Register* 2 (January 1812): 350.

45. *Management of Lunatics with Illustrations of Insanity* (Boston, 1817), pp. 10, 12.

46. *Massachusetts Reports: Report of Cases Argued and Determined in the Supreme Judicial Court of the Commonwealth of Massachusetts* (Boston, 1812), 9:225.

47. Ibid. (Boston 1831), 28:304.

48. Records of the Overseers, Haverhill.

49. See *Massachusetts Reports* (Boston 1805), 1:543. In this case the physician's testimony was also discounted.

50. Ibid. (Boston 1817), 14:223.

51. Ibid. (Boston 1810), 8:168; ibid. (Boston, 1815), 12:439.

52. See *Massachusetts House Documents* no. 2, 1835, p. 44.

53. The question of marriage was finally decided in favor of the insane person provided he seemed to be in possession of "some of his senses" (Correspondence, in Records of the Overseers of the Poor for the Town of Deerfield, 1802, Pocumtuck Valley Memorial Association, Deerfield, Mass.) An insane person was determined not to be able to inherit an estate, however (Deerfield Town Records, 1795–1828, p. 649, Henry N. Flint Library, Deerfield, Mass.).

54. See *Massachusetts Reports* (Boston, 1805), 1:543; ibid. (Boston, 1825), 22:174.

55. See Records of the Overseers, Salem; Records of the Overseers, Concord; and Records of the Overseers, Boston, MHS and BPL passim.

56. In one source *lunatic* was defined as a "dangerous insane person" (Correspondence, in Records of the Overseers, Deerfield, 1824).

57. Miscellaneous Papers, 1748–1832, no. 19, in Records of the Overseers, Salem.

58. Records of the Overseers, vol. 2, 1774–1818, Danvers.

59. February 1817.

60. Brigham made these remarks as a result of his experience at the Hartford Retreat, the first asylum in Connecticut, which opened in 1824. In 1844 Brigham established the *American Journal of Insanity;* at that time he was superintendent of Utica State Lunatic Asylum. Brigham and other superintendents (including Samuel Woodward) were influenced by phrenology, an important cultural influence in America in the period. Phrenologists believed that the mind was not unitary but composed of independent faculties that influenced the size and contour of the cranium. They thought that it was possible for people to cultivate virtues and limit vices and other undesirable tendencies through an exercise of these faculties. Phrenology was therefore both an optimistic system of beliefs that posited a way of overcoming disordered mental states and a way of explaining why some people were affected negatively by stresses that left others untouched. See John D. Davies, *Phrenology: Fad and Science: A Nineteenth-century American Crusade* (New Haven, Conn., 1955). For Brigham's remarks, see "Insanity and Insane Hospitals," *North American Review* 44 (January 1837): 101.

61. *Remarks on the Influence of Mental Cultivation Upon Health,* (Hartford, 1832), pp. 7, 76.

62. *The Discovery of the Asylum.* Rothman elaborated this search fully in pp. 109–30.

63. In 1835 Brigham made this relation clearer in discussing the effects of the Second Great Awakening. "If a number of people be kept for a long time in a state of great terror and mental activity, no matter whether from vivid descriptions of hell . . . or from any other cause, the brain and nervous system of such a people is as liable to be injured as the stomach and digestive organs are from the frequent use, during the same length of time, of very stimulating food and drink" (*Observations on the Influence of Religion upon the Health and Physical Welfare of Mankind* [Boston, 1835], p. 269).

64. "Insanity Produced by Masturbation," *Boston Medical and Surgical Journal* 12 (25 March 1835): 110. See Gerald Grob, "Samuel Woodward and the Practice of Psychiatry in Early Nineteenth Century America," *Bulletin of the History of Medicine* 36 (September-October 1962): 420–43 for an analysis of the intellectual foundations of Woodward's conceptions of insanity, which he identified as coming from a combination of Enlightenment ideas, Christian principles, and phrenology. Elsewhere Grob argued that Woodward's New England Protestant upbringing led him to indict alcohol, masturbation, and other breaches of this sensibility as causes of madness (*The State and the Mentally Ill,* pp. 56–57). Of course, his thinking is also linked to earlier theories of insanity found in the medical dissertations of Cutbush and others.

65. Superintendent's Report, in Fifth Annual Report of the Trustees of the State Lunatic Hospital at Worcester for the Year 1837, Massa-

chusetts Senate Document no. 5, 1838, p. 49. Hereafter the annual reports of the trustees of Worcester are referred to as Trustees' Reports. Trustees' Reports from 1833 to 1842 appear here as Senate documents; Trustees' Reports from 1843 to 1854 are from *Report of the Trustees of the State Lunatic Hospital*, vol. 2 (1843–54) (Boston, 1844–55). Trustees' Reports from 1855 on appear here as Senate documents. Intemperance was the most frequently listed cause in the admissions records in the early years of Worcester's existence. The causes listed in these records were based on reports of family, friends, and sometimes patients themselves.

66. Superintendent's Report, in Trustees' Report for 1836, Massachusetts Senate Document no. 13, 1837, p. 35.

67. Ibid., p. 50.

68. See especially Superintendent's Report, in Trustees' Report for 1834, Massachusetts Senate Document no. 16, 1835, p. 22; Superintendent's Report, in Trustees' Report for 1835, Massachusetts Senate Document no. 7,1836, p. 34. Grob discussed Woodward's belief in the necessity of early treatment in "Samuel Woodward," p. 429.

69. Superintendent's Report, in Trustees' Report for 1837, Massachusetts Senate Document no. 5, 1838, p. 46.

70. For Brigham's views on insanity and women, see *Remarks on the Influence*, p. 74; for Woodward's views, see Superintendent's Report, in Trustees' Report for 1836, Massachusetts Senate Document no. 13, 1837, p. 46.

71. Superintendent's Report, in Trustees' Report for 1837, Massachusetts Senate Document no. 5, 1838, p. 48.

72. Ibid., p. 51.

73. See "Moral Insanity," *Boston Medical and Surgical Journal* 18 (28 March 1838): 124–26. Woodward commented on the fact that some of his patients seemed no more deranged than he did.

74. See Dain, *Concepts of Insanity*, pp. 84–113 for a discussion of medical perceptions of the causes of insanity in the antebellium period.

75. *Annual Report to the Board of Trustees of the Massachusetts General Hospital* and *Report of the Superintendent of McLean Asylum for the Insane*, 1837 (Boston, 1837), p. 7.

76. Trustees' Reports for 1838, Massachusetts Senate Document no. 8, 1839, pp. 13–14.

77. Ibid., pp. 5–6.

78. Alcohol became a problem in the period independently of madness, as the realization that drink was a threat to the social order led to the formation of temperance societies and eventually, in the antebellum period, to a movement to prohibit alcohol by law. See Joseph Gusfield, *Symbolic Crusade* (Urbana, Ill., 1972) and W. J. Rorabaugh *The Alcoholic Republic* (New York, 1979). For discussion of some of the problems posed by sexuality in the early nineteenth century see Nancy Cott, "Pas-

sionlessness: An Interpretation of Victorian Sexual Ideology, 1790–1850," in Nancy Cott and Elizabeth Pleck, eds., *A Heritage of Her Own* (New York, 1979), pp. 162–82.

79. See Peter Gay, *The Enlightenment: An Interpretation,* (New York, 1967), especially vol. 1, for a discussion of the way the Enlightenment transformed the thinking about individual responsibility. Of course, as far as New England was concerned, the Enlightenment was a tide, not a tidal wave. It did not sweep away the old Protestant establishment, yet it did extend the influence of rationalism. Sidney Ahlstrom noted that in Boston "the waves of enlightenment were sipped with cautious moderation" (*A Religious History*, p. 358).

80. Trustees' Report for 1838, Massachusetts Senate Document no. 8, 1839, p. 6.

81. Gordon S. Wood argued that the search for moral laws characteristic of the Enlightenment meant that moral deeds were presumed to have moral doers, which resulted in a "moral identity between cause and effect." "Evil motives caused evil actions," whereas good intentions would lead to good actions. It is clear how this perspective could lead to a conviction that the condition of madness was caused by immoral acts. See Wood, "Conspiracy and the Paranoid Style: Causality and Deceit in the Eighteenth Century," *William and Mary Quarterly* 39 (July 1982): 418.

Chapter 5: Dangerous to Go at Large *(pages 90–105)*

1. Tomes found a similar pattern in early nineteenth-century Pennsylvania (*A Generous Confidence*, especially chapter 3).

2. *Selectmen's Minutes*, 29:6, 106.

3. According to the minutes of the overseers of the poor, "lunatics" in the almshouse became a problem in 1805, when the overseers called a town meeting to discuss "further provisions for lunatics in the almshouse." The word *maniak* (the first use of this term in Boston town records) was substituted for *lunatic* in 1807. Use of this term suggests that the medical category and the person had been joined together in the town officials' minds. The insane person had become the disease (Vote Book of the Overseers of the Poor for the Town of Boston, 1788–1809, Boston City Archives, BPL, Boston).

4. Vote Book, 1810–27. In 1810, 403 paupers lived in the Boston almshouse.

5. Quoted in Jacques Quen, "Early Nineteenth-century Observations of the Insane in the Boston Almshouse," *Journal of the History of Medicine* 23 (January 1968): 82. See also Vote Book of the Overseers of the Poor, 1810–27 for discussion of the confinement of all insane in cells in the "small wooden house" next to the almshouse.

6. See *Selectmen's Minutes*, 35:353 for mention of insane in the bridewell.

7. "An Act in Addition to Act Entitled an Act for Suppressing Rogues, Vagabonds, Common Beggars and Other Idle, Disorderly and Lewd Persons," *Acts and Resolves*, 1796–97, chap. 62, p. 451; *Records of the State of Connecticut*, (Hartford, 1881), 8:87.

8. "Original Papers Relating to Pardons Issued by the Governor of Massachusetts," 1776–1800, Massachusetts State Archives, State House, Boston.

9. Bentley, *Diary*, 1808, 1:3, 88.

10. Any increase in insanity in the period after the Revolution seems to have been proportional to population growth. Between 1799 and 1819, 48 Boston residents were placed in guardianship because of their non compos mentis status. Although this is almost twice the number of residents given guardians between 1720 and 1780, Boston's population increased by 250 percent from 1790 to 1820, and this factor accounts for the increase. See guardianship petitions, *Selectmen's Minutes*, vols. 35, 38. Robert McCaughey discussed Boston's population increase in this period in "From Town to City: Boston in the 1820s," *Political Science Quarterly* 88 (June 1973): 194.

11. John P. Marquand, *Timothy Dexter Revisited* (Boston, 1925), especially, p. 243.

12. Details of Payson and Porter are found in *Sibley's*, 16:86–87, 147. For other examples of family care of the insane in post-Revolutionary New England, see "Ebenezer Bradish" (class of 1769) ibid., 17:128; "Aaron Kellogg" (class of 1778), "Josiah Spaulding" (class of 1778), and "Charles Goodrich" (class of 1786), *Dexter's*, 4:41, 56, 475; "David Haskell" (class of 1802), ibid., p. 500.

13. I found seventeen insane residents of Cambridge listed as incarcerated in the Cambridge jail between 1799 and 1820. In addition I found four from Salem who were incarcerated there between 1802 and 1816 and three from Danvers between 1802 and 1812. See Middlesex County Court Records, Middlesex County Court House, Cambridge, Mass.; Poor Ledger, 1815–27, no. 29, in Records of the Overseers, Salem; Correspondence, 1760–1845, in Records of the Overseers, Danvers.

14. In 1800 the populations of these towns were as follows: Salem 9,457; Danvers 2,643; and Concord 1,679 (U.S. Department of Commerce, Bureau of the Census, *Second Census of the United States: 1800*).

15. Louis Piccarello, "Social Structure and Public Welfare Policy in Danvers, Massachusetts, 1750–1850," *Essex Institute Historical Collections* 118 (October 1982): 248–64.

16. Two insane paupers were put in one room in 1803 and were confined there; other paupers were not confined in the almshouse (Cor-

respondence, 1760–1845, Notices of Boarders, 1760–73, and Poor Records, vol. 1, 1767–74, and vol. 2, 1774–1818, in Records of the Overseers, Danvers).

17. Correspondence 1760–1845 in ibid.

18. Another private home for the mad was run by Abraham Goodele of Chatham, who operated a board and care facility that seems to have specialized in would-be suicides. Two Danvers residents who had attempted suicide were sent there in 1809 (Correspondence, 1760–1845, in Records of the Overseers, Danvers).

19. Another insane pauper was put in the room with Parsons and one other insane pauper in 1805 (ibid.).

20. Archelaus Putnam, Diary, 1805–17, Danvers Historical Society, Danvers, Mass.

21. See Robert Doherty, *Society and Power in Five New England Towns 1800–1860* (Amherst, Mass., 1977), pp. 13–14 for a discussion of Salem in this period.

22. Information about the treatment of the insane in Salem comes from Miscellaneous Papers, 1746–1832, Poor Ledgers, 1719–1840, and Lists of Inmates of the Salem Almshouse, 1815–41, in Records of the Overseers, Salem. There were eleven insane paupers in the Salem almshouse from 1769 to 1815.

23. The plans for the almshouse called for a separate section for the insane and specified that cells be provided. When the new almshouse opened, a total of 150 paupers were admitted, 8 of whom were insane paupers locked in the cells. Information from Miscellaneous Papers, 1746–1832, and List of Inmates, 1815–41, in ibid.

24. Miscellaneous Papers, 1746–1832, and List of Inmates, 1815–1841, in ibid. Towns could confine the insane in whatever facilities were available.

25. Miscellaneous Papers, 1746–1832.

26. Between 1816 and 1823, six letters were written by the overseers to other towns demanding the removal of insane paupers. Payment to town residents was made nine times between 1820 and 1827 for the purpose of apprehending insane townsfolk in order that they could be confined in the almshouse (Journal of Proceedings, Overseers of the Poor, and Miscellaneous Papers, 1746–1832, in Records of the Overseers, Salem).

27. See Gross, *The Minutemen and Their World,* pp. 171–92 for a discussion of the economic boom Concord experienced after the Revolution.

28. Evidence about the treatment of the insane in Concord was found in Records of the Overseers, Concord.

29. In some years (1801–1804 and 1812–1813) no insane surface in the records. After 1816 an average of two insane paupers were boarded with private families each year (ibid.).

30. Twelve residents were retrieved from neighboring towns from 1800 to 1838.

31. *Records of the Visiting Committee of the Board of Trustees of Massachusetts General Hospital, Asylum for the Insane at Charlestown, 1818* (Boston, 1818) and Records of the Overseers, Concord.

32. Ibid.

33. Records of the Overseers, Haverhill.

34. Letters from these towns to Danvers overseers mention that insane residents from these towns were confined in this manner. Seven such persons were confined; it is impossible to tell whether or not they were paupers. These letters were written to Danvers overseers in order to ask their advice about putting these people in the Ipswich jail. See Records of the Overseers, Correspondence, 1760–1845, in Danvers.

35. Records of the Overseers of the Poor for the Town of East Sudbury (now known as Wayland), Wayland Archives, Wayland Public Library, Wayland, Mass.

36. Four insane residents were kept in irons at this time, according to a bill submitted to the overseers of Deerfield for the purchase of their irons. Three "lunatics" were sent to the house of corrections in Greenfield between 1824 and 1829. See Records of the Overseers, Correspondence, in Deerfield.

37. Records of the Overseers of the Poor for the Town of Greenfield," Greenfield Town Hall, Greenfield, Mass.

38. Records of the Overseers, Concord. The records do not indicate whether any of the insane confined there were paupers.

39. Correspondence, 1760–1845, in Records of the Overseers, Danvers.

40. Actual almshouse records for 1832 have been lost. *Documents on the Subject of the Salem almshouse, Reported by a Committee of the Town and Ordered to be Printed, March, 1832,* Records of the Overseers, Salem. Some insane, like other paupers, were auctioned off to the lowest bidder and cared for in a group. A state legislative committee reported in 1832 that some towns had made private contracts with keepers of jails or houses of correction to "keep the insane poor at a low price and imprison them in some of their unoccupied cells, where no person has been held responsible for their treatment, nor has the law delegated authority to any one to examine into their condition. Other towns have annually offered the keeping of their insane poor at auction, and struck them off to the lowest bidder, by whom they have been taken and treated with various degrees of attention or of cruelty, according to the character of the individual, who, in this competition for the profits of keeping them, would be likely to prevail" ("Report of Commissioners Appointed under a Resolve of the Legislature of Massachusetts to Superintend the Erection of a Lunatic Hospital at Worcester," Massachusetts Senate Document no. 2, 1832).

41. Report of a Committee on the Subject of Lunatics and Persons Furiously Mad in 112 Towns of Massachusetts, 1829," Massachusetts State Archives, State House, Boston. Since not all the towns in the state responded to the survey, the report probably does not give a completely accurate picture. On the other hand, those towns that did not respond may have had no insane to report.

42. Vote Book, 1820–27, in Records of the Overseers, Boston, BPL. The number of insane at the House of Industry was thirty-nine in 1829, according to the "Report of a Committee on the Subject of Lunatics."

43. *Massachusetts House Document* no. 12, 1835.

44. For an especially eloquent plea, see Annual Report of Director of the House of Industry for 1835, Boston City Document no. 7, 1835.

45. *Second Annual Report of the Boston Prison Discipline Society,* 1827 (Boston, 1827), pp. 19, 57. It is impossible to tell whether more men or women were confined as insane persons in the state. While discrete evidence from the smaller towns suggests that there were more men, the 1829 census reports only slightly more men (155 men, 134 women).

46. *Massachusetts House Document* no. 50, 1827, p. 9.

47. See Grob, *The State and The Mentally Ill,* pp. 22–25 for a discussion of the circulation and significance of these reports.

Chapter 6: The Place for Lunatics *(pages 106–30)*

1. Holyoke Family Papers, Box 5f5, Holyoke Collection.

2. George Wallis, *The Art of Preventing Diseases and Restoring Health Founded on Rational Principles and Adapted to Persons of Every Capacity* (New York, 1794), pp. 119, 438.

3. Cutbush, *An Inaugural Dissertation on Insanity,* p. 40.

4. Anderson, *An Inaugural Dissertation on Chronic Mania,* p. 3.

5. Vaughan, "Remarkable Cases of Madness," p. 412.

6. G. G. Brown, "The Efficacy of Cold in Madness," *Medical Repository* 4 (1801): 210. The water treatment enjoyed brief but wide popularity during the antebellum period. See Dain, *Concepts of Insanity,* pp. 160–61. Brown was probably from England, but his ideas were published and influential here. See ibid., p. 218, n. 71.

7. *An Inaugural Dissertation on Hypochondriasis,* p. 17.

8. See William L. Russell, *The New York Hospital: A History of the Psychiatric Service* (New York, 1945) for a discussion of early nineteenth-century somatic treatment of insanity.

9. *Medical Inquiries,* pp. 104–5. His restraining chair he described in the following way: "I have contrived a chair and introduced it to our Pennsylvania Hospital to assist in curing madness. It binds and confines every part of the body. By keeping the trunk erect, it lessens the impetus of the blood toward the brain. By preventing the muscles from acting,

it reduces the force and frequency of the pulse, and by the position of the head and feet favors the easy application of cold water or ice to the former, and warm water to the latter. Its effects have been truly delightful to me. It acts as a sedative to the tongue and temper as well as to the blood vessels. In 24, 12, 6 and in some cases in 4 hours, the most refractory patients have been composed. I have called it Tranquillizer" (quoted in Andrew Scull, ed., *Madhouses, Mad-Doctors, and Madmen: The Social History of Psychiatry in the Victorian Era* [Philadelphia, 1981], p. 34). William F. Bynum discussed similar rigorous treatment of the insane by physicians in the eighteenth century. King George III was chained to a stake, beaten, and starved by his doctors. See Bynum, "Rationales for Therapy in British Psychiatry, 1780–1835," *Medical History* 18 (September 1964): 15–332. Pinel, it will be recalled, suggested the use of the straitjacket as a temporary measure of discipline (Weiner, "Health and Mental Health in the Thought of Philippe Pinel," pp. 59–86).

10. *Medical Inquiries*, pp. 108.

11. Quen, "Early Nineteenth-century Observations, pp. 82–85.

12. Quoted in Henry M. Hurd, *Institutional Care of the Insane in the United States and Canada*, rev. ed. (New York: 1973), p. 585.

13. Kittredge's establishment is described in *Sibley's*, 17:351.

14. Hurd. *Institutional Care*, p. 586.

15. See Tuke, *Description of the Retreat*, pp. 11, 29.

16. *Proposals for Establishing a Retreat for the Insane* (Boston, 1814). According to Dain, Parkman was trained by Pinel in Paris and owned a small private asylum in Massachusetts, which was probably an establishment like Kittredge's (*Concepts of Insanity*, p. 216, n. 63).

17. *Management of Lunatics*. The idea of the rotary swing was not new, but the simulation of seasickness seems to have been unique to Parkman.

18. See Tuke, *Description of the Retreat*, pp. 110–12.

19. The asylum movement in this country was also part of a larger reform movement in the early nineteenth century. A religious sensibility directly connected to the evangelical Protestant temperament, combined with the sense of efficacy inspired by the Revolution and the impact of the Enlightenment, led to a new conviction that human beings had far more power over their social world than earlier generations had realized. A great deal of this reform effort in New England was directed toward the insane. Horace Mann, Louis Dwight, and Dorothea Dix, all important to the asylum-building movement in Massachusetts, were members of the Protestant elite, and as such were strongly influenced by religious motives. For a somewhat cynical view of this early reform effort, see Clifford S. Griffin, *Their Brothers' Keepers: Moral Stewardship in the United States, 1800–1865* (New Brunswick, N.J., 1960). For a discussion of the evangelical roots of reform in this period, see Lois Banner, "The Protestant Crusade: Religious Missions, Benevolence and Re-

form in the United States, 1790–1840" (Ph.D. diss., Columbia University, 1973). For a description of New England Protestant elite, see Paul Goodman, "Ethics and Enterprise: The Values of the Boston Elite, 1800–1860," *American Quarterly* 18 (Winter 1966): 437–52.

20. This asylum was originally known as the Asylum for the Insane at Charlestown and was established as a section of Massachusetts General Hospital. It was renamed McLean Asylum for the Insane in 1826 in honor of a donor. Other early asylums based on Tuke's model were the Hartford Retreat, which opened in Connecticut in 1824, and Bloomingdale Asylum, which opened in New York in 1821. See Thomas Eddy, "Hints for Introducing an Improved Mode of Treating the Insane in the Asylum" (New York, 1815) for a description of Bloomingdale Asylum. See Grob, *Mental Institutions in America*, pp. 58–59 for a discussion of the Hartford Retreat; and pp. 51–55 for a full treatment of the early efforts by reformers to establish a hospital for the insane in Massachusetts in the early nineteenth century.

21. One of its first patients had been confined at home since 1815 and had been attended by a physician who "sweated him profusedly and whipped him" (Luther Bell, Journal, 1838, McLean Hospital Archives, McLean Hospital, Belmont, Mass.).

22. See *Rules of Admission, Massachusetts General Hospital, Asylum for the Insane,* 1818 (Boston 1818), for a statement about a sliding scale to allow the "richer patients to pay for the poor." Norman Dain and Eric T. Carlson estimate that 15 to 20 percent of McLean's inmates were from the lower classes ("Social Class and Psychological Medicine in the United States, 1789–1824," *Bulletin of the History of Medicine* 33 (September-October 1959): 461. Later the number of poorer inmates declined drastically. See *Rules and Regulations for the Government of the Asylum for the Insane Adopted December, 1822. Additional to those adopted by July 5, 1821 (Boston 1822);* and *Rules and Regulations of the McLean Asylum for the Insane,* 1828 (Boston, 1828).

23. Ibid. See Dain, *Concepts of Insanity,* p. 22 for a discussion of Pinel and Tuke's influence on Wyman.

24. See ibid., p. 22 for a discussion of the significance of these early asylums; see also Grob, *Mental Institutions in America,* p. 65.

25. Superintendent's Report to the Trustees, 1825, quoted in Morrill Wyman, "The Early History of the McLean Asylum for the Insane," *Boston Medical and Surgical Journal* 97 (December 1877): 671.

26. Ibid.

27. See Superintendent's Report to the Trustees in *Annual Report to the Board of Trustees of Massachusetts General Hospital, 1825;* "Diary of an Attendant," quoted in Nina Fletcher Little, *Early Years of the McLean Hospital* (Boston, 1972), p. 49.

28. See "Diary of the Upper Story," 1827, McLean Hospital Archives, McLean Hospital, Belmont, Mass. for examples.

29. Little, *Early Years*, p. 54.

30. Mann's committee extrapolated from a census of 112 towns in Massachusetts (Report of a Committee on the Subject of Lunatics) to come up with a figure of 500. There were 310 towns in the state, and many did not report. Mann's 1830 report can be found in *Reports and Other Documents Relating to the State Lunatic Hospital at Worcester, Massachusetts* (Boston, 1837), pp. 4–6, and "Resolve to Erect a Lunatic Hospital," *Acts and Resolves*, 10 March 1830, vol. 18, chap. 83, p. 19. The legislation creating Worcester mandated that the hospital accept all persons who had been committed by the courts to jails or houses of correction on the basis of the law of 1796 and an 1816 statute. See Grob, *The State and the Mentally Ill*, especially chapters 1 and 2, for a comprehensive discussion of the origins of this first public mental hospital in Massachusetts.

31. *Reports and Other Documents*, p. 20–21.

32. See Grob, *The State and the Mentally Ill*, pp. 26–30 for an elaboration of Mann's arguments for the opening of Worcester State Lunatic Hospital. Mann's belief that one-half of the insane were curable was offered in a speech he gave in 1830, which was quoted in the *Independent Chronicle and Boston Patriot*, 17 February 1830.

33. Trustees' Report for 1833 Massachusetts Senate Document no. 10,1834, p. 25. The state legislature appropriated $30,000 for the erection of the asylum; towns and relatives of the insane were to pay for the care of those admitted there (Grob, *The State and the Mentally Ill*, p. 84).

34. Trustees' Report for 1834, Massachusetts Senate Document no. 16, 1835, p. 26.

35. Artemus Simmons to Horace Mann, 17 August 1832, Horace Mann Papers, Massachusetts Historical Society, Boston.

36. "An Act Concerning Commitments to the State Lunatic Hospital," *Acts and Resolves*, 13 March 1833, vol. 12, B, chap. 95, p. 629. The first group to be sent to Worcester consisted of those designated as furiously mad, whether already or about to be confined; the second consisted of pauper insane cared for in towns (but not considered dangerous) who could be cared for at the hospital at town option and expense; the third consisted of nonviolent insane cared for by their families. See Grob, *The State and the Mentally Ill*, pp. 35–38.

37. Trustees' Report for 1833, Massachusetts Senate Document no. 10, p. 11.

38. Case Records, 1833–40, passim, Worcester State Lunatic Hospital, Francis A. Countway Library, Boston. Grob discussed Woodward's heavy reliance on drugs in *The State and the Mentally Ill*, p. 64.

39. Superintendent's Report, in Trustees' Report for 1836, Massachusetts Senate Document no. 13, 1837, p. 50.

40. In the early years the voluminous case records were written by Woodward himself, who was clearly involved with every patient. See

Grob, *The State and the Mentally Ill,* pp. 69–74 for a discussion of Woodward's treatment of the patients at Worcester.

41. The Worcester case records demonstrate this, though Woodward chided his fellow physicians in Massachusetts for continuing to bleed their insane patients excessively ("Insanity," *Boston Medical and Surgical Journal* 12 (3 June 1835): 264–66.

42. For examples, see Case Records, Worcester State Lunatic Hospital, passim, especially Casebook no. 3, 1834; no. 4, 1835; no. 5, 1835.

43. Ibid., no. 9, 1836.

44. Ibid., no. 11, 1837.

45. Ibid., no. 9, 1836; no. 10, 1836; no. 11, 1837; no. 13, 1837, passim.

46. Case records demonstrate this. By 1837 there were twenty-three strong rooms at Worcester (Trustees' Report for 1837, Massachusetts Senate Document no. 5, 1838, p. 10).

47. Trustees' Report for 1835, Massachusetts Senate Document no. 7, 1836, p. 4. See Grob, *The State and the Mentally Ill,* pp. 74–77 for a discussion of the percentage of patients cured in the early years of Worcester. Although Woodward inflated his figures (claiming a cure rate of between 82 and 91 percent), a later study showed that "51 per cent of those discharged before 1840 had never again become insane" (p. 77).

48. See Caseboook nos. 1–3, 1833.

49. Trustees' Report for 1834, Massachusetts Senate Document no. 16, 1835, p. 5.

50. That is, if the towns of residence or families would pay for their keep at the hospital.

51. *Annual Report to the Board of Trustees of Massachusetts General Hospital, and Report of the Superintendent of McLean Asylum for the Insane,* 1837, p. 19.

52. See L. Bell, Journal, 1838, for a discussion.

53. Lee to Boston Prison Discipline Society, 1836, quoted in *Eleventh Annual Report of the Boston Prison Discipline Society* (Boston, 1836), p. 9.

54. L. Bell, Journal, 1838.

55. *An Account of the Imprisonment and Sufferings of Robert Fuller of Cambridge* (Boston, 1833).

56. See Dain, *Concepts of Insanity,* pp. 195–97. Dain discussed several reports by former inmates that attempted to impugn the reputation of mental hospitals.

57. See "Diary of the Upper Story," 1827, for examples.

58. See *Rules of Admission,* 1818.

59. *An Account of the Imprisonment,* pp. 27–28.

60. Luther Bell, Superintendent's Report, in *Annual Report to the Board of Trustees of Massachusetts General Hospital 1839,* p. 11.

61. Over 350 were confined in local jails and almshouses. Towns

themselves often preferred to keep pauper lunatics rather than send them to Worcester, which they viewed as more expensive. See "Report on Gaols and Houses of Correction," *Massachusetts House Document* no. 36, 1834; *Massachusetts Documents, 1834–37*; *Annual Report of the House of Industry for 1835* (Boston, 1835), p. 3; *Annual Report of the House of Corrections, 1837* (Boston, 1837); Trustees' Report for 1837, Massachusetts Senate Document no. 5, 1838, p. 6.

62. "An Act to Provide for the Confinement of Idiots and Insane Persons," *Acts and Resolves*, 13 April 1836, vol. 13, chap. 223, p. 917.

63. These were Suffolk County, which established Boston Lunatic Hospital in 1839; Middlesex County, which established a receptacle for the insane at the East Cambridge jail; and Essex County, which reopened a receptacle for the mad in the Ipswich jail that had been used earlier in the century. See *Annual Report of the State Board of Charities* (Boston, 1865), 1:155. As early as 1835 the legislature passed a law that mandated the release from Worcester of those insane "least susceptible to improvement in the hospital" and their return to jails and houses of correction. The furiously mad, however, had to be kept at the hospital ("An Act in Addition to an Act Concerning the State Lunatic Hospital," *Acts and Resolves*, 7 April 1835, vol. 13, chap. 129, p. 481).

64. P. 13.

65. See *Report of the Board of Visitors of the Boston Lunatic Hospital and the Annual Report of the Superintendent,* 1844 and 1846 (Boston, 1844, 1846). See also Grob, *Mental Institutions in America*, pp. 125–26.

66. After a visit to the hospital in 1840, the inspector of prisons reported that although "the lunatics know quite well that *they are prisoners, subject to greater or lesser degrees of confinement,* they also know that they are 'diseased of mind' and that this house is for their cure" (*Report of the Inspector of Prisons, 1840: Boston City Document no. 21, 1840* [Boston, 1840], p. 13. Emphasis added).

67. *Not fit to go at large* was a common phrase used by overseers and other town officials when discussing the need to confine an insane resident.

68. David Rothman argued that moral treatment was also designed to be illustrative of an ordered, disciplined world that could replace the chaos and flux of Jacksonian society, so alarming to the superintendents and asylums in this period. The proscriptive nature of moral treatment, according to Rothman's analysis, faced both ways: inside and outside the asylum walls. See *Discovery of the Asylum*, chapters 4 and 5, especially p. 133.

69. In *The State and the Mentally Ill*, pp. 80–102 Grob discussed the overcrowding at Worcester, which was the main reason why the legislature ordered the release of incurables and other patients.

70. *Annual Report to the Board of Trustees of Massachusetts General Hospital*, 1828, p. 11.

71. Ideas of what constitutes madness are culturally as well as temporally relative. Herbert Goldhammer and Andrew W. Marshall found the same rate of mental hospital admissions in Massachusetts in 1840 and in 1940, and on this basis they argue that "social changes of the last century . . . have not been sufficient to alter the incidence of psychoses," but they admitted they might have come to different conclusions if they had compared 1740 with 1840. A significant increase in the incidence of psychosis may have taken place before 1840. See Goldhammer and Marshall, *Psychosis and Civilization* (Glencoe, Ill., 1949), p. 3. In rural Laos, investigators recently found that folk criteria for madness centered primarily on socially dysfunctional behavior rather than on disturbances in thought and affect. Villagers were reluctant to label as mad even those with longstanding patterns of violent or other socially disruptive behavior. In rural Africa and Puerto Rico, hallucinations were virtually never reported as criteria for madness. By contrast, in the modern postindustrial state, we have extended the idea of madness to encompass many kinds of nonconforming behaviors, and we are almost as concerned with thought as we are with actions. This extension of the meaning of insanity begins to be evident in Massachusetts in the Jacksonian period in asylums, jails, and almshouses. See Joseph Westermeyer and Ronald Wintrob, "Folk Criteria for the Diagnosis of Mental Illness in Rural Laos: On Being Insane in Sane Places," *American Journal of Psychiatry* 136 (June 1979): 775–61.

72. I am indebted to Gerald Grob for the idea that the existence of an asylum encourages its use (personal communication). See also *The State and the Mentally Ill*, p.82.

73. James Henretta, *The Evolution of American Society, 1700–1815*, tables 1, 3, p. 27; Douglass Jones, "Geographic Mobility and Society in Eighteenth-century Essex County" (Ph.D. diss., Brandeis University, 1975), pp. 201–3.

74. Maris Vinovskis, "Demographic Changes in America to the Civil War. An Analysis of the Socio-economic Determinants of Fertility Differentials and Trends in Massachusetts from 1765 to 1860" (Ph.D. diss., Harvard University, 1975), p. 310. Only 4 percent of the state's population lived in towns of 8,000 or more in 1790 as compared to 8.1 percent in 1800. In 1790, 27.6 percent lived in towns of over 2,500; ten years later this percentage increased to 37.2 (pp. 308, 324).

75. See Jones, *Village and Seaport* for a discussion of decline in persistence rates in the state. Doherty found "surprisingly high levels of out-migration from 1800—1810" in his study of five New England towns (*Society and Power*, p. 34).

76. See Douglass Jones, "The Strolling Poor," *Journal of Social History* 8 (1975): 29–54. Jones noted that in 1794 the Commonwealth of Massachusetts passed a law that standardized the process of removing transients from the towns and eliminated the older warning out system.

77. Brown discussed the rise of supralocal attachments in "The Emergence of Urban Society."

78. See ibid., p. 37 for a discussion of the distribution of political office holding in the state. Gordon S. Wood noted that the Revolution meant that the citizens of the Republic viewed the political order not as one "tied together by . . . unity of interest but rather [as] an agglomeration of hostile individuals coming together for their mutual benefit to construct a society" (*The Creation of the American Republic, 1776–1787,* [New York, 1969], p. 607). Stephen Lukes characterized this new order as one in which citizens must necessarily be viewed as "independent and rational beings, who are the sole generation of their own wants and preferences, and the best judges of their interests" (*Individualism* [New York, 1973], p. 79). David Hackett Fischer found a significant expansion of voter participation in the period 1796–1816. He argued that the election of 1800 marked the decline of deference in the state and the rise of the party system, which accompanied the intense competition for office. See Fischer, *The Revolution of American Conservatism* (Chicago, 1975), p. 187. Ronald Formisano argued that deferential politics and elite influence persisted until the 1830s in Massachusetts; he viewed the period from 1790 to 1840 as a transitional one as the state was moving from deferential to mass politics. Yet he agreed that the change in the 1790s was greater than the one that was to occur in the 1840s, and he found high voter turnouts early in the century. See Formisano, *The Transformation of Political Culture: Massachusetts Parties, 1790–1840* (New York, 1982).

79. Brown discussed this in "The Emergence of Urban Society." He found that over 1,900 voluntary associations were created in Massachusetts between 1760 and 1820. These societies included literary and debating clubs, musical and library societies, religious societies, and societies created to perform social welfare functions such as fire prevention, education, and aid to the poor (pp. 38–39). Of course, political parties were another form of voluntary association that sprang up in this period. Gross also found a growth of these voluntary associations in Concord after the Revolution (*The Minutemen and Their World,* pp. 173–75). I am indebted to David Hackett Fischer for the idea that multiple association patterns increasingly characterized Massachusetts in the early nineteenth century.

80. Nelson found much more litigation, most of it of a commercial nature, in the towns of Plymouth County after than before the Revolution. Tracy has argued that the Revolution legitimized competition and individualism in Northampton. Melchior found much more divisiveness and competition in Massachusetts towns after the Revolution, as town officials increasingly had to mediate between opposing interests within the towns. Howe argued that after the Revolution local communities were characterized not by harmony but by "contention and

disagreement." See William Nelson, "The Larger Context of Litigation in Plymouth Colony, 1725–1825," in David Thomas Konig, ed., *Plymouth Court Records, 1686–1859* (Wilmington, Del., 1978); Tracy, *Jonathan Edwards, Pastor,* p. 92; Alan Melchior, "Town and Community in Massachusetts, 1760–1860," Brandeis University, mimeo 1978; John R. Howe, *From the Revolution to the Age of Jackson* (Englewood Cliffs, N.J., 1973), p. 15.

81. This increase in the number of persons without regular means of subsistence resulted in visible numbers of able-bodied men who were without work and rootless. Much of the information on wealth stratification and the growing number of propertyless men is from Boston, but it is probable that these trends were also evident to some degree in other parts of the state. See Gary B. Nash, "Urban Wealth and Poverty in Pre-Revolutionary America," *Journal of Interdisciplinary History* 6 (Spring 1976): 545–84. By 1771 the top 25 percent of the taxable population controlled 78 percent of the assessed wealth in the city. An elite controlled much of the capital invested in the town's major enterprises by 1790. See James Henretta, "Economic Development and Social Structure in Colonial Boston," in Stanley Katz, ed., *Colonial America* (Boston, 1971), pp. 450–66. By the Revolution, Boston was characterized by an increased concentration of capital available for commercial investment and a growing number of capitalless workers (Marc Egnal "The Economic Development of the Thirteen Colonies, 1720 to 1775," *William and Mary Quarterly* 32 [October 1975]: 220). Alan Kulikoff found a growing number of poor and propertyless people in Revolutionary Boston. By 1790 the top 1 percent of the population owned 27 percent of the wealth. He also found "an excess population in the working ages . . . who were outside the occupational structure" after the Revolution. By 1790 the poor accounted for 34–47 percent of the population of the town. Kulikoff described the poor class as "composed of widows, blacks, seamen, laborers and poorer artisans who might dip below the minimum level of subsistence when unemployment increased." He found occupational mobility declining, especially among the transient. See Kulikoff, "The Progress of Inequality in Revolutionary Boston," *William and Mary Quarterly* 28 (July 1971): 375–412. This trend in Boston was the beginning of a larger Northern trend accompanying urbanization and the rise of manufacturing in the early decades of the nineteenth century, according to Peter H. Lindert and Jeffrey C. Williamson, who called it "a marked rise" in inequality ("Three Centuries of American Inequality," in Paul Usselding, ed., *Research in Economic History: An Annual Compilation of Research* [Greenwich, Conn., 1976], 1: 101–3). A. H. Jones argued that while the Northern colonies were characterized by wealth concentration during the eighteenth century, the situation got substantially worse in the beginning of the nineteenth century (*Wealth of A Nation To Be,* pp. 317–18). Nash found a

decline in bound labor in Massachusetts in the 1760s (*Urban Crucible,* p. 320). Jones found that indentured servants were rarely used in Massachusetts after the early 19th century ("The Strolling Poor," p. 33). The appearance of a class of unattached workers was related to this decline of bound labor.

82. Kulikoff found that Boston produced mostly for her own consumers for most of the eighteenth century. He also found that by 1820 the city had become a center of market activity. See Kulikoff, "The Progress of Inequality," p. 376. Winifred Rothenberg found an increase in market-oriented agricultural production in the state in the second half of the eighteenth century; this resulted in a trend toward price uniformity and suggested a "very wide market indeed" ("The Market and Massachusetts Farmers, 1750–1855," *Journal of Economic History,* 41 [Winter, 1981], 283–314.) Christopher Clark found an extension of market relations in the Connecticut Valley after 1780, a trend accompanied by increasing inequality. ("The Household Economy, Market Exchange and the Rise of Capitalism in the Connecticut Valley, 1800–1860," *Journal of Social History* 13 [Winter 1979], pp. 169–91). See Caroline D. Ware for a discussion of the proliferation of textile manufacturing in New England. Twenty textile mills were founded in southern New England before 1807. See Ware, *The Early New England Cotton Manufacture* (Boston, 1931), pp. 36–38 and Appendix A, p. 301. Manufacturing output increased substantially from 1820 to 1830 in Massachusetts, the growth centered mainly in textiles and the boot and shoe industry (Douglass North, *The Economic Growth of the United States, 1790–1860* [New York, 1966], p. 165). For an exploration of the impact of early industrialization (especially in the form of textile mills) in early nineteenth-century Massachusetts and the concomitant tensions and dislocations experienced by workers and New England farmers, see Jonathan Prude, *The Coming of the Industrial Order: Town and Factory Life in Rural Massachusetts, 1810–1860* (Cambridge, 1983).

83. According to C. C. Goen, the Great Awakening set in motion a disintegrating process that resulted in the "permanent shattering of the Congregational establishment in New England" by the time of the Revolution. One hundred separatist churches were created in New England. See Goen, *Revivalism and Separatism in New England, 1740–1800; Congregationalists and Separate Baptists in the Great Awakening* (New Haven, Conn., 1962), pp. vi–x. The disestablishment of Congregationalism primarily benefited the Baptists, who were the largest dissenting group at the time. One historian of the New England Baptists, William A. McLoughlin, sees their rise as the story of the "transformation of New England from a conformist, elitist, corporate Christian commonwealth to an atomistic, individualistic, laissez-faire, quasi-secular democracy." After religious pluralism was legalized in Massachusetts, a "new rash of dissenting movements" began to appear, including the Universalists, the

Methodists, and the Shakers. See McLoughlin, *New England Dissent, 1630–1833* (Cambridge, Mass., 1971), 1:21. Perry Miller discussed a growing secularism before the Revolution in New England, which represented another alternative to the Puritan symbolic world ("From Covenant to Revival," in James Smith and A. Leland Jamieson, eds., *Religion in American Life* [Princeton, N.J., 1961], 2:321–43). Sidney Ahlstrom noted a "rise of rationalism" in New England at the end of the eighteenth century, which contributed its own momentum (however small) to the shift away from the Congregational establishment (*A Religous History*, p. 351). Carl F. Kaestle and Maris Vinovskis found an increased secularism in Massachusetts society in the early nineteenth century (*Education and Social Change in Nineteenth Century Massachusetts* [Cambridge, 1980]).

84. Gross argued that the Revolution had a profound impact in Concord, Massachusetts in ways both concrete and intangible, as the town's citizens transformed their political system, grew more cosmopolitan in their outlook, and generally unleashed a wave of energy and optimism that would have significant economic and social consequences (*The Minutemen and Their World*, especially pp. 171–91). Peter Russell argued that a "far-reaching transformation of its social, economic and political life" took place in Massachusetts at the end of the eighteenth century ("The Development of Judicial Expertise in Eighteenth Century Massachusetts and a Hypothesis Concerning Social Change," *Journal of Social History* 16 [Spring 1983]: 143–55).

85. Participation in a market economy increases the responsibility of the individual to make independent economic transactions. The move to wage labor was accompanied by a dissolution of the bonds of paternalism, which limited the individual mobility and freedom in all aspects of work life. The search for work and the necessity of bargaining for one's economic survival call for an internal commitment to the proposition on which wage labor is founded—that of isolated, competitive units of labor. Those who participate must shoulder sole responsibility for their own survival. Rationality and a strong system of internal controls are demanded of them. The need for both would be most crucial and most problematic in the period of transition from paternalism to wage labor. Weber realized that some internalized drive was necessary to motivate people to participate in a labor market. For him, this motivation was provided by the secularization of the Puritan concept of *calling*. "One's duty in a calling is what is most characteristic of the social ethic of capitalistic culture, and is in a sense the fundamental basis of it. It is an obligation which the individual is supposed to feel and does feel towards the content of his professional activity, no matter in what it consists" (*The Protestant Ethic*, p. 54).

86. Here is where my evidence intersects most significantly with Rothman's argument in *The Discovery of the Asylum*. Rothman focused on the

confinement of the insane in the Jacksonian asylum; my evidence suggests that confinement in Massachusetts began almost a generation earlier and was *not* linked to medical treatment. The Jacksonian reformers were rescuing the insane from a great deal of attention, not from a lack of it.

Epilogue *(pages 131–39)*

1. They were McLean Asylum for the Insane (1818); Worcester State Lunatic Hospital (1833); Boston Lunatic Hospital (1839); Taunton State Lunatic Hospital (1854); Northampton State Lunatic Hospital (1858); and Massachusetts State Almshouse at Tewksbury, Insane Department (1866) (Grob, *Mental Institutions in America*, pp. 379–80).

2. The trustees there remarked that Worcester State Lunatic Hospital was "one of the poorest, if not the poorest in the country." (quoted in ibid., p. 369).

3. Northampton State Lunatic Hospital was opened in 1858 as the result of concern over deteriorating conditions at Worcester (ibid., p. 369–70).

4. Woodward began mentioning physical causes in his reports more frequently after 1840. See Superintendent's Report, in Trustees' Report for 1840, in *Report of the Trustees of the State Lunatic Hospital*, 1:16; Superintendent's Report, in Trustees' Report for 1844, in ibid., 2:44; Superintendent's Report, in Trustees' Report for 1846, in ibid., p. 76.

5. Superintendent's Report, in Trustees' Report for 1850, in ibid., p. 53. In 1851 Chandler counted "physical causes and heredity" as the most important causes of madness (Superintendent's Report, in Trustees' Report for 1851, in ibid., p. 46).

6. Dain, *Concepts of Insanity*, pp. 84–113.

7. See Woodward's Superintendent's Report, in Trustees' Report for 1846, in *Report of the Trustees of the State Lunatic Hospital*, 2:76. Woodward was convinced by 1846 that insanity could be cured only if it was treated before organic brain lesions appeared. In the same report he gave heredity a primary role in causing madness (p. 77). George Chandler found in 1855 that "heredity" and "physical causes" accounted for over 70 percent of admissions to Worcester (Superintendent's Report, in Trustees' Report for 1855, Massachusetts Senate Document no. 16, 1856, p. 11). Charles Stedman, appointed superintendent of Boston Lunatic Hospital in 1844, cited heredity as the major cause of the madness of most of his pauper patients (*Report of the Board of Visitors of the Boston Lunatic Hospital and the Annual Report of the Superintendent* for 1850, p. 5–6).

8. The idea that insanity was inherited was in itself not necessarily pessimistic; early in the nineteenth century some physicians felt that

those with a hereditary predisposition could avoid the disease through proper living. As Charles E. Rosenberg has argued, the idea of heredity was a protean concept for much of the nineteenth century, embodying an optimism about the possibility both of passing on positive acquired traits and of avoiding the most serious consequences of negative tendencies. Environmental manipulation was believed to be crucial not only to producing positive acquired traits, but also to preventing the realization of the potentialities of hereditary predisposition. In the case of insanity, the idea of heredity began to have a pejorative thrust in the middle of the century. Certain conditions, if not prevented through sound personal habits, diet, and other aspects of wholesome living, were thought to be much less susceptible to change than conditions without hereditary predispositions. This gloomier conception of hereditarian theory convinced many that hereditary insanity was unlikely to be cured. See Charles E. Rosenberg, "The Bitter Fruit: Heredity, Disease and Social Thought," in Charles E. Rosenberg, ed., *No Other Gods: Science and American Social Thought* (Baltimore, 1976), pp. 25–54.

9. See Grob, *The State and the Mentally Ill* for a full account of Worcester's decline. This began with Chandler's appointment as superintendent in 1846; he was beset with rising admissions and other administrative problems that made the practice of moral treatment very difficult (pp. 121–43).

10. Dain noted the increasing tendency after 1850 of physicians in the older asylums in the Northeast to cite hereditary factors as the sole cause of insanity among those under their care. Other precipitating causes began to be ignored as "the predisposition was thought to be so strong that insanity could occur without precipitating causes or as a result of minor ones, so that frequent relapses were common." This emphasis on the role of heredity "indicated a growing pessimism about cure," until "heredity and incurability became linked together." Dain noted that the assumption of heredity was more likely to be made for the poor, who seemed to "recover less frequently than the middle and upper-class patients receiving better care in select corporate and private institutions" (*Concepts of Insanity*, pp. 112–13).

11. *Report of the Board of Visitors of the Boston Lunatic Hospital* for 1845, p. 17.

12. Trustees' Report for 1851, in *Report of the Trustees of the State Lunatic Hospital*, 2:1. Woodward's successor, Chandler, was horrified at the number of Irish immigrants coming to the hospital in the late 1840s. In 1847 he warned the legislature that "if this bad class continues to press in upon us, I shall be obliged to ask you to send a portion to the jails of the counties from which they come." See Superintendent's Report, in Trustees' Report for 1847, in ibid., p. 22.

13. Trustees' Report for 1848, in ibid., p. 4. There were 242 Irish at Worcester in 1852 out of a total population of 515. Throughout the

1850s the trustees continued to deplore the number of Irish patients, calling them on several occasions "vicious and depraved." For expressions of despair over the increasing numbers of Irish patients, see Trustees' Report for 1855, Massachusetts Senate Document no. 16, 1856, p. 8; and especially Trustees' Report for 1858, Massachusetts Senate Document no. 5, 1859, p. 7. In 1848 Chandler noted regretfully, "As a class, we are not so successful in our treatment of them as with the native population in New England" (Superintendent's Report, in Trustees' Report for 1848, in *Report of the Trustees of the State Lunatic Hospital*, 2:4. At Boston Lunatic Hospital, Stedman noted that the Irish were "unused to the manners and customs of our countrymen" and were "very suspicious" of the staff, "making it quite difficult to win their confidence and, of course to treat them satisfactorily" (*Report of the Board of Visitors of the Boston Lunatic Hospital and the Annual Report of the Superintendent* for 1850, p. 5).

14. See Grob, *Mental Institutions in America*, p. 159 for a discussion of the cultural homogeneity of the asylum superintendents. The superintendents were in the process of establishing themselves as a distinct specialty within the medical profession in the 1840s and 1850s (ibid., pp. 172–73).

15. *Insanity and Idiocy in Massachusetts: Report of the Commission on Lunacy, 1855*, rev. ed. (Cambridge, Mass., 1971), p. 52, 63.

16. *Causes of Insanity, An Address Delivered Before the Norfolk, Massachusetts, District Medical Society* (Norfolk, 1851), p. 17.

17. Jarvis also discussed Irish insanity in a similarly pessimistic tone in *Insanity and Idiocy*, p. 63. His ideas about social causes of madness did not change, for he repeated them in 1856. He clearly had different explanations for different groups. See *Address Delivered at the Laying of the Cornerstone of the Insane Hospital, at Northampton, Massachusetts* (Northampton, 1856).

18. This decline of treatment occurred in the state mental hospitals all over the country. See Rothman, *The Discovery of the Asylum*, chapter 11. See also Dain, *Concepts of Insanity*, pp. 204–10 for a discussion of the decline of the curative aspects of the state mental hospitals. Grob discussed the "therapeutic nihilism" that followed the "emphasis on somatic ideology" in public mental hospitals in the 1870s. (*The State and the Mentally Ill*, p. 231).

In the late nineteenth century some articles appeared in popular journals warning readers against excesses of emotion, intellection, ambition, and sexuality as causes of madness. The authors did not deny the organic nature of insanity, but they used the subject as an opportunity for a moral lesson, just as had their predecessors in the early nineteenth century. The authors of these articles had little contact with the insane in the asylum. The superintendents themselves were overwhelmingly convinced that biological causes were the most important factors. For discussion of these warnings, see Barbara Sicherman, "The Paradox of Prudence: Mental Health in the Gilded Age," *Journal of American History* 62 (March 1976), 890–912.

19. Trustees' Report for 1855, Massachusetts Senate Document no. 16, 1856, p. 26–27.

20. "Memorial from the Trustees of the State Lunatic Hospital at Worcester," Massachusetts Senate Document no. 60, 1854. Woodward had noticed the increased passivity and withdrawal of many patients and announced in 1843 that he had discovered a new kind of insanity he called "dementia." In this condition "the whole brain is torpid and the mind is dull. The physical energies are as much blunted as the mental powers and the mind seems to be obliterated." He was no doubt noticing what Gorham had noticed earlier in the century; the effects of long-term custodial confinement and administration of drugs. See Superintendent's Report, in Trustees' Report for 1843, in *Report of the Trustees of the State Lunatic Hospital,* 2:21.

21. *Report of the Board of Visitors of Boston Lunatic Hospital* for 1848, pp. 16, 10–12.

22. Ibid., 1850, p. 14; ibid., 1851, p. 20. The vast majority of inmates were Irish. In 1848, 124 out of 188 patients were Irish, according to the annual report of 1848. The hospital was continually overcrowded, with little or no room for exercise.

23. Bell discussed McLean's treatment in the *Annual Report to the Board of Trustees* for 1844 (Boston, 1844), p. 3, 14, 26. Fletcher described the living situation there in *Early Years at McLean Hospital,* p. 120.

24. See *Annual Report to the Board of Trustees* for 1843 (Boston, 1843), p. 34; ibid., 1844, p. 17; ibid., 1855, pp. 25–27. See also Grob, *Mental Institutions in America,* chapter 2 for discussion of the homogeneous, affluent population of this and other private asylums in the period.

25. Bell thought the precipitating causes of insanity were improper early education and "long continued pressure of unusual business anxieties." He admitted that he had failed to find physical causes in the patients he had treated and confessed he had no idea how to find them. See L. Bell, *Annual Report to the Board of Trustees* for 1843, pp. 20, 36. Ibid., 1849, p.15. Bell believed that the insanity of his patients was curable through moral rather than medical treatment. He reiterated this conviction in all his reports that have survived (1843, 1844, 1849, and 1853).

26. The number of elderly insane admitted to asylums did not grow proportionately with their numbers in the population. In a study of these patients in Massachusetts in 1854, Maris Vinovskis and Barbara G. Rosenkrantz found that although the elderly insane comprised 16.8 percent of the insane among the general population, they made up only 9.8 percent of the inmates in Massachusetts asylums. They concluded that "the extent of insanity among the elderly was two to three times as

great as that among individuals in their twenties and thirties" and suggested that age discrimination was the key factor in limiting the number of elderly admitted in the 1830s, 1840s, and 1850s. The authors based their argument on the assertions that the asylums in this period were curative places and that the public image of them, at least, was one of optimism and efficacy. Limiting access of the aged was therefore denying them "equal access" to the possibility of cure. Superintendents of Massachusetts asylums became "hostile" to the admission of elderly patients in the 1840s and 1850s and began to neglect their treatment. The authors hypothesized that these attitudes were part of a larger pattern of negative attitudes toward the elderly in antebellum America. See Vinovskis and Rosenkrantz, "The Invisible Lunatic: Old Age and Insanity in Mid-Nineteenth Century Massachusetts," in Stuart Spicker et al., eds., *Aging and the Elderly* (New York, 1978), pp. 100–103.

27. Trustees' Report for 1843 in *Report of the Trustees of the State Lunatic Hospital,* 2:8.

28. Sixty-two lunatics were reported confined in jails and houses of correction in the state. One jail keeper complained that "the House of Correction in Dedham was built since the state lunatic hospital at Worcester and as it was then the duty of all keepers of jails, houses of correction and almshouses to send all lunatics to Worcester, no provision was made for them in this building. Considerable expense has since been incurred to provide for their confinement since the change of the laws authorizing the return of lunatics back upon the counties, but the accommodations are wholly inadequate for the proper care and treatment of furious lunatics and not well adapted to the confinement and treatment of such as are moderately so." "Returns Concerning the Condition of Pauper Lunatics and Idiots," 1843, Massachusetts State Archives, State House, Boston. Descriptions of the deranged were handwritten by local officials.

29. Ibid. One woman in Westford had been confined in chains for ten years to prevent her from "running away and tearing her clothes." Thirty-two persons were described as furiously mad, and 224 as occasionally furiously mad. Of those in almshouses, 134 had already been in a hospital, 113 of them at Worcester. Women were apparently more aggressively mad than men: the number of "furiously mad women greatly exceeds the males and this proportion is found to exist in each and all of the counties." However, there was no significant difference in the numbers of male and female mad confined in almshouses.

30. Ibid.

31. Ibid.

32. *Annual Report of the State Board of Charities* 1865, 1:326.

33. Dorothea Dix (perhaps the most famous of the advocates of hospitalization of the insane), Horace Mann, and Samuel Gridley Howe, other important reformers, all believed that insanity was a disease that

could be cured with early medical intervention (Dain, *Concepts of Insanity*, pp. 168–75). Dix and Howe launched a massive campaign to improve conditions for the insane in the state, after Dix had been appalled at the sight of insane women at the Cambridge jail. Her speech to the Massachusetts legislature in 1843 was heart wrenching. "I come to place before the Legislature of Massachusetts the condition of the miserable, the desolate, the outcast. I come as the advocate of helpless, forgotten, insane, idiotic men and women; of beings sunk to a condition from which the most unconcerned would start with real horror; of beings wretched in our prisons, and more wretched in our almshouses" (Memorial to the Legislature of Massachusetts, 1843, Old South Leaflets 6, no. 148, p. 2). Dix moved on to other states, but not until she succeeded in having another wing added onto Worcester in 1844.

34. The Massachusetts reformers thought that the public asylums could and would provide moral treatment. They certainly were not interested in creating custodial institutions or a situation of repressive confinement. See Dain, *Concepts of Insanity*, p. 171; Grob, *The State and the Mentally Ill*, pp. 112–14.

Reformers probably knew more about the condition of the mad in jails and almshouses than they did about their condition at Worcester; this would explain some of their eagerness to put more insane in asylums. One reformer, Robert Waterson, believed that insanity became "fixed" in almshouses and jails, whereas it was cured in lunatic hospitals ("The Insane in Massachusetts," *Christian Examiner* 32 [January 1843]: 338–52).

35. Many of the patients at Worcester in the 1840s and 1850s were described as harmless in the case records. At Boston Lunatic Hospital "noisy and filthy" patients were kept in the strong rooms, while the majority stood silently in the halls (*Report of the Board of Visitors of Boston Lunatic Hospital* for 1846, p. 6; ibid., 1844, pp. 14–16). The 1843 census reported only 32 persons as furiously mad, yet many more were confined.

36. *Insanity and Idiocy*, pp. 168–74. Jarvis polled all practicing physicians as well as the keepers of all almshouses, jails, and houses of correction and the superintendents of all public and private hospitals, in order to determine the number of insane in the state. He concluded that there were 2,632 insane persons in the state, an increase of 1,100 since the report of the Committee on Charitable Institutions in 1848. The majority (2,007) were natives. There were 1,284 in homes or in almshouses, 1,141 in hospitals, and 207 in receptacles for the insane, jails, and houses of correction. Those submitting figures determined whether the insane were curable or incurable. One important result of Jarvis's report was the establishment of Northampton State Lunatic Hospital in 1858.

37. In 1852 the Superior Court of the state committed a pauper to

Worcester State Lunatic Hospital, saying "This dangerous class of persons belongs in the hospital" (*Massachusetts Reports* [Boston, 1852], 63:582).

38. U.S. Department of Health, Education, and Welfare, National Institute of Mental Health, Mental Health Statistical Note no. 153, Washington, D.C., August 1979.

39. A description of life inside Pennsylvania Hospital in the eighteenth century is offered by Tomes, *A Generous Confidence,* pp. 3–5. The story of Virginia's first asylum was thoroughly told by Norman Dain in *Disordered Minds: The First Century of Eastern State Hospital in Williamsburg, Virginia, 1766–1866* (Williamsburg, Va., 1971). For the early years, see pp. 5–40.

40. All these histories dealt in one way or another with the removal of the insane from the larger society. So did Tomes in her lucid history of Pennsylvania Hospital (*A Generous Confidence*). MacDonald described but did not focus on the confinement of the insane in asylums in England in the eighteenth century (*Mystical Bedlam*). See also Andrew Scull, *Museums of Madness: The Social Organization of Insanity in Nineteenth Century England* (New York, 1982). Scull argued that the psychiatric profession in England achieved control over the market in lunacy in the nineteenth century with the opening of medical establishments for the mad (pp. 43–44). In this way his history is similar to mine, for physicians became the experts on madness and established lunatic hospitals around the same time in this country. However, at least as far as New England is concerned, the history of madness was telescoped compared to that of England's. Whereas insane had been controlled under nonmedical auspices in England for much of the eighteenth century, in New England this secular confinement did not take place until the beginning of the nineteenth century, for reasons related to the social and economic characteristics of each society.

Selected Bibliography

Primary Sources

Abstract of Returns from the Several Towns, Jails and Houses of Correction Concerning the Condition of Pauper Idiots and Lunatics in Almshouses and Jails, 1843. Prepared in Obedience to an Order of the House of Representatives on January 25, 1843. Boston: Dutton & Wentworth, 1843.

Abstract of Returns of Inspectors and Keepers of Jails and Houses of Correction. Massachusetts House Document No. *39* (7 February 1840). Boston: Dutton & Wentworth, 1840.

Acts and Laws of the Commonwealth of Massachusetts, 1796–97. Boston: Young & Minns, 1896.

Acts and Resolves, Public and Private, of the Province of Massachusetts Bay. 21 vols. Boston: Wright & Porter, 1869–1922.

American Journal of Insanity. Editorial. 16 (October 1859): 239–40.

Anderson, Alexander. *An Inaugural Dissertation on Chronic Mania.* New York: T. & J. Swords, 1796.

Annual Report of the House of Corrections, 1837. Boston City Document no. 11, 1837. Boston: J. H. Eastburn, 1837.

Annual Report of the State Board of Charities. 2 vols. Boston: John H. Eastburn, 1865.

Annual Reports of the Director of the House of Industry, 1832–1844. Boston: J. H. Eastburn, 1832–44.

Annual Reports of the State Lunatic Hospital at Worcester
   1833. Massachusetts Senate Document no. 10, 1834.
   1834. Massachusetts Senate Document no. 16, 1835.
   1835. Massachusetts Senate Document no. 7, 1836.
   1836. Massachusetts Senate Document no. 13, 1837.
   1837. Massachusetts Senate Document no. 5, 1838.
   1838. Massachusetts Senate Document no. 8, 1839.
   1839. Massachusetts Senate Document no. 9, 1840.
   1855. Massachusetts Senate Document no. 16, 1856.
   1858. Massachusetts Senate Document no. 5, 1859.

Annual Reports to the Board of Trustees of Massachusetts General Hospital, and Report of the Superintendent of McLean Asylum for the Insane, 1827–1855. Boston: Press of James Loring, 1827–55.

Barry, William. *A History of Framingham, Massachusetts from 1640 to 1847.* Boston: James Monroe & Co., 1847.

Battie, William *A Treatise on Madness.* London: J. Whitson & B. White, 1758.

Beck, Theodoric Romeyn. *An Inaugural Dissertation on Insanity.* New York: J. Seymour, 1811.

Bell, Luther. Journal, 1838. McLean Hospital Archives, McLean Hospital, Belmont, Mass.

Bentley, William. *The Diary of William Bentley, 1784–1819.* 2 vols. Gloucester, Mass: Peter Smith, 1962.

Brigham, Amariah. "Definition of Insanity—Nature of the Disease." *American Journal of Insanity* 2 (January 1844): 97–116.

———. "Insanity and Insane Hospitals." *North American Review* 44 (January 1837): 91–121.

———. "The Medical Treatment of Insanity." *American Journal of Insanity* 4 (April 1847): 353–58.

———. "The Moral Treatment of Insanity." *American Journal of Insanity* 4 (July 1847): 111–16.

———. *Observations on the Influence of Religions upon the Health and Physical Welfare of Mankind.* Boston: Marsh Capen & Lyon, 1835.

———. *Remarks on the Influence of Mental Cultivation upon Health.* Hartford, Conn.: F. J. Huntington, 1832.

Brown, G. G. "The Efficacy of Cold in Madness." *Medical Repository* 4 (1801): 209–10.

Calef, Robert. "More Wonders of the Invisible World." In George Burr, ed., *Narratives of the Witchcraft Cases, 1648–1706,* pp. 296–398. New York: Barnes & Noble, 1916.

Case Records, Worcester State Lunatic Hospital. Francis A. Countway Memorial Library, Boston.

Chandler, Samuel. Diary, 1740–94. New England Historic Genealogical Society, Boston.

The Charters and General Laws of the Colony and Province of Massachusetts Bay, 1634–1779. Boston: T. B. Wait & Co., 1814.

Chauncey, Charles. "Idle Poor Secluded from the Bread of Charity by the Christian Law" (Boston, 1752). In Clifford K. Shipton, ed., *Early American Imprints 1639–1800,* New York: Readex Microprint 1963–.

The Colonial Laws of Massachusetts. Reprinted from the Edition of 1672 with Supplements through 1686. Boston: Rockwell & Churchill, 1887.

Culpeper, Nicholas. *The English Physician.* London: John Streater, 1669.

———. *The Practice of Physick.* London: Peter Cole, 1655.

Currier, John J. *Ould Newbury: Historical and Biographical Sketches.* Boston: Damsell & Upham, 1896.

Cutbush Edward. *An Inaugural Dissertation on Insanity.* Philadelphia: Zachariah Poulson, 1794.

Dedham Town Records, 1706–1736. 8 vols. Dedham, Mass.: Transcript Press, 1930–36.

Dexter, Franklin Bowditch. *Biographical Sketches of the Graduates of Yale College, 1701–1815.* 6 vols. New York: Henry Holt & Co., 1885–98.

"Diary of the Upper Story," 1827. McLean Hospital Archives, McLean Hospital, Belmont, Mass.

Dickinson, Timothy. Diary, 1787–1808. New England Historic Genealogical Society, Boston.

Dix, Dorothea L. "Memorial to the Legislature of Massachusetts, 1843." Old South Leaflets 6, no. 148. Boston, 1843. n.p. n.d.

Fuller, Robert. *An Account of the Imprisonment and Sufferings of Robert Fuller of Cambridge, Who, While Peaceably and Quietly and Rationally in Possession of His Own House, Was Seized and Detained in the McLean Asylum For the Insane at Charlestown, Mass. 65 Days, From June 24th to August 28th, 1832. Together With Some Remarks on That Institution.* Boston: Printed for the author, 1833.

Gibbons, William. *An Inaugural Dissertation on Hypochondriasis.* Philadelphia: Joseph Rakestraw, 1805.

Holyoke Collection. Essex Institute, Salem, Mass.

Howe, Samuel Gridley. "Insanity in Massachusetts." *North American Review* 36 (January 1843): 171–91.

Hunter, Richard, and Ida Macalpine, eds. *Three Hundred Years of Psychiatry, 1535–1860.* London: Oxford University Press, 1963.

"The Insane in Massachusetts." *Christian Examiner* 32 (January 1843): 338–52.

Jarvis, Edward. *An Address Delivered at the Laying of the Cornerstone of the Insane Hospital at Northampton, Massachusetts.* Northampton: J. L. Metcalf, 1856.

———. *Causes of Insanity, An Address Delivered Before the Norfolk, Massachusetts District Medical Society.* Norfolk, 1851.

———. *Insanity and Idiocy in Massachusetts: Report of the Commission on Lunacy, 1855.* Rev. ed. Cambridge, Mass.: Harvard University Press, 1971.

Jubeart, John. "Confessions of a Countefeiter" (Boston, 1769). In Clifford K. Shipton, ed., *Early American Imprints, 1639–1800,* New York: Readex Microprint, 1963–.

"Lunatic Hospital at Worcester." *Christian Examiner* 26 (May 1839): 247–59.

Massachusetts House Documents

No. 50, 1827. Boston: Dutton & Wentworth, State Printers, 1827.
No. 28, 1828. Boston: Dutton & Wentworth, State Printers, 1828.
No. 1, 1831. Boston: Dutton & Wentworth, State Printers, 1831.
No. 12, 1835. Boston: Dutton & Wentworth, State Printers, 1835.
No. 36, 1834. Boston: Dutton & Wentworth, State Printers, 1834.

No. 12, 1842. Boston: Dutton & Wentworth, State Printers, 1842.

No. 47, 1842. Boston: Dutton & Wentworth, State Printers, 1842.

No. 38, 1843. Boston: Dutton & Wentworth, State Printers, 1843.

No. 110, 1850. Boston: Dutton & Wentworth, State Printers, 1850.

No. 48, 1852. Boston: Dutton & Wentworth, State Printers, 1852.

Massachusetts Reports: Reports of Cases Argued and Determined in the Supreme Judicial Court of the Commonwealth of Massachusetts. 109 vols. Boston: Little, Brown, 1809–89.

Mather, Cotton. *The Angel of Bethesda* (1724). Edited by Gordon Jones. Barre, Mass.: American Antiquarian Society, 1972.

————. "A Brand Plucked Out of the Burning" (1693). In George Lincoln Burr, ed., *Narrative of the Witchcraft Cases, 1648–1706,* pp. 259–87. New York: Barnes & Noble, 1914.

————. "The Case of a Troubled Mind" (Boston, 1717). In Clifford K. Shipton, ed., *Early American Imprints, 1639–1800.* New York: Readex Microprint, 1963–.

————. *Diary of Cotton Mather, 1719.* Edited by Worthington Ford. Boston: Massachusetts Historical Society, 1912.

————. "Insanabilia, An Essay upon Incurables" (Boston, 1714). In Clifford K. Shipton, ed., *Early American Imprints, 1639–1800,* New York: Readex Microprint, 1963–.

————. *Magnalia Christi Americana; or the Ecclesiastical History of New England* (1702). 2 vols. Hartford, Conn.: Silas Andrus & Son, 1853.

————. "Memorable Providences, Relating to Witchcraft and Possessions" (Boston, 1689). In Clifford K. Shipton, ed., *Early American Imprints, 1639–1800,* New York: Readex Microprint, 1963–.

————. "Speedy Repentance Urged" (Boston, 1690). In Clifford K. Shipton, ed., *Early American Imprints, 1639–1800,* New York: Readex Microprint, 1963–.

————. "Warnings from the Dead: A Blessed Medicine for Sinful Madness" (Boston, 1693). In Clifford K. Shipton, ed., *Early American Imprints, 1639–1800,* New York: Readex Microprint, 1963–.

————. *Wonders of the Invisible World* (1693). London: John Russell Smith, 1862.

Mather, Increase. "A Call to the Tempted" (Boston, 1682; reprinted 1723). In Clifford K. Shipton, ed., *Early American Imprints, 1639–1800,* New York: Readex Microprint, 1963–.

Middlesex County Quarterly Courts Records, 1708–55. Middlesex County Court House, East Cambridge, Mass.

Miscellaneous File. Massachusetts State Archives, State House, Boston.

Moody, Charles C. P. *Biographical Sketches of the Moody Family.* Boston: Samuel G. Drake, 1847.

Murdock, Kenneth, ed. *Handkerchiefs from Paul.* Cambridge, Mass.: Harvard University Press, 1927.

"A Narrative of the Extraordinary Case of George Zukens" (Philadelphia, 1792). In Clifford K. Shipton, ed., *Early American Imprints, 1639–1800,* New York: Readex Microprint, 1963–.

"On the Nature of the Spleen." *American Chronicle and Historical Magazine,* July 1745, pp. 17–23.

"Original Papers Relating to Acts of the Massachusetts General Court." Massachusetts State Archives, State House, Boston.

Parkman, Ebenezer. *The Diary of Ebenezer Parkman, 1703–1782.* 3 vols. in 1. Edited by Francis G. Walett. Worcester, Mass.: American Antiquarian Society, 1974.

Parkman, George. *Management of Lunatics with Illustrations of Insanity.* Boston: John Eliot, 1817.

———. *Proposals for Establishing a Retreat for the Insane.* Boston: John Eliot, 1814.

Parrish, Joseph. *An Inaugural Dissertation on the Influence of Passions upon the Body, in the Production and Cure of Diseases.* Philadelphia, 1805.

Phillips, Samuel. "The Sin of Suicide Contrary to Nature" (Boston, 1767). In Clifford K. Shipton, ed., *Early American Imprints, 1639–1800,* New York: Readex Microprint, 1963–.

Pinel, Philippe. *A Treatise on Insanity.* Translated by D. D. Davis. Sheffield, England: W. Todd, 1806.

Putnam, Archelaus. Diary, 1805–17. Danvers Historical Society, Danvers, Mass.

Records and Files of the Quarterly Courts of Essex County, Massachusetts. 8 vols. Salem, Mass.: Essex Institute, 1921.

Records of the Overseers of the Poor for the Town of Boston. Massachusetts Historical Society, Boston.

Persons Warned Out of Boston, 1745–92.

Almshouse Records, 1735–1911.

Correspondence, 1735–1911.

———. Boston City Archives at Boston Public Library, Boston.

Vote Books for the Overseers of the Poor of the Town of Boston, 1788–1838.

Other Documents, 1793–1832.

Records of the Overseers of the Poor for the Town of Concord. Concord Public Library, Concord, Mass.

Records of the Overseers of the Poor for the Town of Danvers. Danvers Historical Society, Danvers, Mass.

Poor Records. 7 vols. 1767–1887.

Notices of Boarders, 1760–73.

Correspondence, 1760–1845.

Records of the Overseers of the Poor for the Town of Deerfield. Pocumtuck Valley Memorial Association, Deerfield, Mass.

Records of the Overseers of the Poor for the Town of Greenfield.

Greenfield Town Hall, Greenfield, Mass.

Records of the Overseers of the Poor for the Town of Haverhill. Haverhill Public Library, Haverhill, Mass.

Records of the Overseers of the Poor for the Town of Salem. Essex Institute, Salem, Mass.

Poor Ledger, 1812–41, no. 39.

Poor Ledger, 1815–27, no. 29.

Poor Letters, 1815–37, no. 19.

List of Inmates of the Salem Almshouse, 1815–41.

Miscellaneous Papers, 1746–1832.

Documents on the Subject of the Salem Almshouse, Reported by a Committee of the Town and Ordered to be Printed, March 1832.

Records of Probate Appeals Courts, 1775–87. Massachusetts State Archives, State House, Boston.

Records of the Town of Braintree, Massachusetts, 1640–1793. Edited by Samuel A. Bates. Randolph, Mass.: Daniel H. Huxford, 1886.

Records of the Town of Watertown, 1649–1829. 7 vols. Edited by Fred G. Barker. Watertown, 1894–1939.

Records of the Visiting Committee of the Board of Trustees of Massachusetts General Hospital, Asylum for the Insane at Charlestown, 1818–1828. Boston: Russell & Gardner, 1818–28.

Report and Resolve Making Appropriations for State Lunatic Hospital. Senate Document No. 62 (March 1838). Boston: Dutton & Wentworth, 1838.

"Report of a Committee on the Subject of Lunatics and Persons Furiously Mad in 112 Towns of Massachusetts, 1829." Massachusetts State Archives, State House, Boston.

Report of Commissioners Appointed Under a Resolve of the Legislature of Massachusetts, to Superintend the Erection of a Lunatic Hospital at Worcester, and to Report a System of Discipline and Government for the Same, Made January 4, 1832. Senate Document no. 2, 1832. In *Massachusetts House and Senate Documents, 1832.* Boston: Dutton & Wentworth, 1832.

Report of the Committee on Public Charitable Institutions. Senate Document No. 43 (March 1840). Boston: Dutton & Wentworth, 1840.

Report of the Inspector of Prisons, 1840: Boston City Document no. 21, 1840. Boston: J. H. Eastburn, 1840.

Reports and Other Documents Relating to the State Lunatic Hospital at Worcester, Massachusetts. Boston: Dutton & Wentworth, 1837.

Reports of the Board of Visitors of Boston Lunatic Hospital, 1838–1855. Boston: J. H. Eastburn, 1838–55.

Reports of the Prison Discipline Society of Boston, 1826–1854. 6 vols. Montclair, N.J.: Patterson Smith, 1972.

Reports of the Record Commissioners of the City of Boston: Selectmen's Minutes, 1716–1810. 33 vols. Boston: Rockwell & Churchill, 1885–97.

Reports of the Trustees of the State Lunatic Hospital, 1833–1854. 2 vols. Boston: Dutton & Wentworth, 1833–54.

"Returns Concerning the Condition of Pauper Lunatics and Idiots, 1843." Massachusetts State Archives, State House, Boston.

Robinson, Nicholas. *A New System of the Spleen, Vapours and Hypochondriak Melancholy; wherein all the decays of the nerves, and lownesses of the spirits, are mechanically accounted for.* London: A. Bettesworth, W. Innys & C. Rivington, 1729. 2d ed., London: J. Whitson & B. White, 1758.

Rose, Henry. *An Inaugural Dissertation on the Effects of Passion upon the Body.* Philadelphia: William Woodward, 1794.

Rules and Regulations for the Government of the Asylum for the Insane. Adopted December 1, 1822, Additional to those Adopted July 5, 1821. Boston: Russell & Gardner, 1822.

Rules and Regulations of the McLean Asylum For the Insane, 1828. Boston: Russell & Gardner, 1828.

Rules of Admission, Massachusetts General Hospital, Asylum for the Insane, 1818. Boston: Russell & Gardner, 1818.

Rush, Benjamin. *An Inquiry into the Influences of Physical Causes on the Moral Faculty.* Philadelphia: Kimber & Richardson, 1786.

———. *Medical Inquiries and Observations upon the Diseases of the Mind.* Philadelphia: Kimber & Richardson, 1812.

Sanders, Daniel Clarke. *A Discourse on the Disease of Mrs. Martha Russell.* Bennington, Vt.: Haswell & Smead, 1805.

Sewell, Samuel, *The Diary of Samuel Sewell, 1674–1729.* 2 vols. Edited by M. Halsey Thomas. New York: Farrar, Strauss & Giroux, 1973.

Shew, Joel. *Hydropathy or the Water Cure: Its Principles, Modes of Treatment and Cure.* New York: Wiley & Putnam, 1845.

Sibley's Harvard Graduates. 17 vols. Vols. 1–3 by John Langdon Sibley. Cambridge, Mass.: Charles William Sever, 1873. Vol. 4 by Clifford K. Shipton. Cambridge, Mass.: Harvard University Press, 1933. Vols. 5–17 by Clifford K. Shipton. Boston: Massachusetts Historical Society, 1941–76.

Suffolk County Probate Court Records, 1636–1800. Suffolk County Court House, Boston.

Suffolk County Quarterly Courts Records, Suffolk County Court House, Boston.

Topsfield Town Records, 1659–1778. 2 vols. Topsfield, Mass.: Topsfield Historical Society, 1919–20.

Tuke, Samuel. *Description of the Retreat, An Institution Near York, for Insane Persons of the Society of Friends.* York, England: Dawson's of Pall Mall, 1813.

Vaughan, John. "Remarkable Cases of Madness." *Medical Repository* 5 (April 1802): 408–12.

Wallis, George. *The Art of Preventing Diseases and Restoring Health, Founded on Rational Principles and Adapted to Persons of Every Capacity.* New York: Samuel Campbell, 1794.

Wigglesworth, Michael. *The Diary of Michael Wigglesworth, 1653–1657.*

Edited by Edmund S. Morgan. Publications of the Colonial Society of Massachusetts, vol. 35. Boston: Colonial Society of Massachusetts, 1951.

Williams, Solomon. "The Frailty and Misery of Man's Life" (Boston, 1740). In Clifford K. Shipton, ed. *Early American Imprints, 1639–1800*, New York: Readex Microprint, 1963–.

Winthrop, John. *History of New England, 1630–1649*. 2 vols. Boston: Little, Brown & Co., 1853.

Woodward, Samuel. "Insanity." *Boston Medical and Surgical Journal* 12 (3 June 1835): 264–66.

———. "Insanity Produced by Masturbation." *Boston Medical and Surgical Journal* 12 (25 March 1835): 109–11.

———. "Moral Insanity." *Boston Medical and Surgical Journal* 18 (28 March 1838): 124–26.

———. "Observations on the Medical Treatment of Insanity." *American Journal of Insanity* 7 (July 1850): 1–34.

Wyman, Morrill. "The Early History of the McLean Asylum for the Insane." *Boston Medical and Surgical Journal* 97 (December 1877): 670–77.

Wyman, Rufus. "A Discourse on Mental Philosophy as Connected with Mental Disease." *Medical Communications of the Massachusetts Medical Society* 5 (Boston, 1836): 1–36.

Secondary Sources

Ahlstrom, Sidney. *A Religious History of the American People*. New Haven, Conn.: Yale University Press, 1972.

Alexander, Franz, and Sheldon Selznick. *The History of Psychiatry*. New York: Harper & Row, 1966.

Allen, David Grayson. *In English Ways: The Movement of Societies and the Transferral of English Local Law and Custom to Massachusetts Bay in the Seventeenth Century*. Chapel Hill: University of North Carolina Press, 1981.

Baxter, W. T. *The House of Hancock: Business in Boston, 1724–1725*. Cambridge, Mass.: Harvard University Press, 1945.

Becker, Ernest. *The Birth and Death of Meaning*. New York: Free Press, 1962.

Becker, Howard S. *The Outsiders: Studies in the Sociology of Deviance*. New York: Free Press, 1963.

Bell, Whitfield, Jr. "Medicine in Boston and Philadelphia: Comparisons and Contrasts, 1750–1820." In *Medicine in Colonial Massachusetts, 1620–1820*, pp. 159–87. Publications of the Colonial Society of Massachusetts, vol. 57. Boston: Colonial Society of Massachusetts, 1980.

Benton, Josiah H. *Warning Out in New England, 1656–1817*. Boston: W. B. Clarke Co., 1911.

Berger, Peter L., and Thomas Luckman. *The Social Construction of Reality*. Garden City, N.Y.: Doubleday, 1966.

Blake, John. *Public Health in the Town of Boston, 1680–1822*. Cambridge, Mass.: Harvard University Press, 1959.

Bockoven, J. Sanborn. "Moral Treatment in American Psychiatry." *Journal of Nervous and Mental Disorders* 124 (September 1956): 242–321.

Bonomi, Patricia U., and Peter R. Eisenstadt. "Church Adherence in the Eighteenth Century British-American Colonies." *William and Mary Quarterly* 39 (April 1982): 245–87.

Boyer, Paul, and Stephen Nissenbaum. *Salem Possessed: The Social Origins of Witchcraft*. Cambridge, Mass.: Harvard University Press, 1974.

Brown, Richard D. "The Emergence of Urban Society in Rural Massachusetts, 1760–1820." *Journal of American History* 61 (June 1974): 29–51.

———. "The Healing Arts in Colonial and Revolutionary Massachusetts: The Context for Scientific Medicine." In *Medicine and Society in Colonial Massachusetts, 1620–1820*, pp. 35–49. Publications of the Colonial Society of Massachusetts, vol. 57. Boston: Colonial Society of Massachusetts, 1980.

Bruchey, Stuart. *The Roots of American Economic Growth, 1607–1860*. New York: Harper Torchbooks, 1965.

Bushman, Richard. *From Puritan to Yankee: Character and Social Order in Connecticut, 1690–1765*. New York: W. W. Norton, 1967.

Bynum, William F. "Rationales for Therapy in British Psychiatry, 1780–1835." *Medical History* 18 (September 1964): 315–32.

Carlson, Eric T., and Norman Dain. "The Meaning of Moral Insanity." *Bulletin of the History of Medicine* 36 (January-February 1962): 130–39.

———. "The Psychotherapy That Was Moral Treatment." *American Journal of Psychiatry* 117 (December 1960): 519–24.

Carlson, Eric T., and Meribeth Simpson. "Models of the Nervous System in Eighteenth-century Psychiatry." *Bulletin of the History of Medicine* 43 (April 1969): 101–15.

Caulfield, Ernest. "Pediatric Aspects of the Salem Witchcraft Tragedy: A Lesson in Mental Health." *American Journal of Diseased Children* 65 (December 1943): 788–802.

Chapman, Henry Smith. *History of Winchester, Massachusetts*. Town of Winchester, 1936.

Clark, Christopher. "The Household Economy, Market Exchange and the Rise of Capitalism in the Connecticut Valley, 1800–1860." *Journal of Social History* 13 (Winter 1979): 169–91.

Cott, Nancy. "Eighteenth-century Family and Social Life Revealed in Massachusetts Divorce Records." *Journal of Social History* 9 (Fall 1976): 20–42.

————. "Passionlessness: An Interpretation of Victorian Sexual Ideology, 1790–1850." In Nancy Cott and Elizabeth Pleck, eds., *A Heritage of Her Own: Toward a New Social History of American Women*, pp. 162–82. New York: Simon & Schuster, 1979.

Dain, Norman. *Concepts of Insanity in the United States, 1789–1865*. New Brunswick, N.J.: Rutgers University Press, 1964.

————. *Disordered Minds: The First Century of Eastern State Hospital in Williamsburg, Virginia, 1766–1866*. Williamsburg, Va.: Colonial Williamsburg Foundation, 1971.

Dain, Norman, and Eric T. Carlson. "Social Class and Psychological Medicine in the United States, 1789–1824." *Bulletin of Historical Medicine* 33 (September-October 1959): 454–65.

Davies, John D. *Phrenology: Fad and Science: A 19th Century American Crusade*. New Haven, Conn.: Yale University Press, 1955.

Demos, John. *Entertaining Satan: Witchcraft and the Culture of Early New England*. New York: Oxford University Press, 1982.

————. "Shame and Guilt in Puritan Society." *Journal of Social History*. Forthcoming.

Deutsch, Albert. *The Mentally Ill in America*. New York: Columbia University Press, 1946.

Dinkin, Robert Joseph. "Provincial Massachusetts—A Deferential or a Democratic Society." Ph.D. diss., Columbia University, 1960.

Doherty, Robert. *Society and Power: Five New England Towns, 1800–1860*. Amherst: University of Massachusetts Press, 1977.

Egnal, Marc. "The Economic Development of the Thirteen Colonies, 1720 to 1775." *William and Mary Quarterly* 32 (October 1975): 191–221.

Estes, J. Worth. "Therapeutic Practice in Colonial New England." In *Medicine in Colonial Massachusetts, 1620–1820*, pp. 289–364. Publications of the Colonial Society of Massachusetts, vol. 57. Boston: Colonial Society of Massachusetts, 1980.

Felt, Joseph B. *History of Ipswich, Essex and Hamilton*. Cambridge, Mass.: Charles Folsom, 1834.

Fischer, David Hackett. "America: A Social History, 1650–1975." Manuscript. 1974.

————. *The Revolution of American Conservatism*. Chicago: University of Chicago Press, 1975.

Foucault, Michel. *Madness and Civilization: A History of Insanity in the Age of Reason*. Translated by Richard Howard. New York: Pantheon, 1965.

Gay, Peter. *The Enlightenment: An Interpretation*. 2 vols. New York: Alfred Knopf, 1967.

Goen, C. C. *Revivalism and Separatism in New England, 1740–1800: Congregationalists and Separate Baptists in the Great Awakening*. New Haven, Conn.: Yale University Press, 1962.

Goffman, Erving. *Interaction Ritual.* New York: Anchor Books, 1967.
———. *Stigma.* Englewood Cliffs, N.J.: Anchor Books, 1963.
Goldhammer, Herbert, and Andrew W. Marshall. *Psychosis and Civilization.* Glencoe, Ill.: Free Press, 1949.
Goodman, Paul. "Ethics and Enterprise: The Values of the Boston Elite, 1800–1860." *American Quarterly* 18 (Winter 1966): 437–52.
Grange, Kathleen M. "Pinel and Eighteenth-century Psychiatry." *Bulletin of the History of Medicine* 35 (September-October 1961): 442–53.
Green, Samuel Abott. *History of Groton, Massachusetts.* 2 vols. Cambridge, Mass.: Harvard University Press, 1914–15.
Greene, Evarts B., and Virginia D. Harrington. *American Population Before the Federal Census of 1790.* New York: Columbia University Press, 1932.
Greven, Phillip J., Jr. *Four Generations: Population, Land and Family in Colonial Andover, Massachusetts.* Ithaca, N.Y.: Cornell University Press, 1970.
Griffin, Clifford S. *Their Brothers' Keepers: Moral Stewardship in the United States, 1800–1865.* New Brunswick, N.J.: Rutgers University Press, 1960.
Grob, Gerald N. *Mental Institutions in America—Social Policy to 1875.* New York: Free Press,1973.
———. "Rediscovering Asylums: The Unhistorical History of the Mental Hospital." *Hastings Center Report* 7 (August 1977): 33–41.
———. "Samuel Woodward and the Practice of Psychiatry in Early Nineteenth-century America." *Bulletin of the History of Medicine* 36 (September-October 1962): 420–43.
———. *The State and the Mentally Ill: A History of Worcester State Hospital in Massachusetts, 1830–1920.* Chapel Hill: University of North Carolina Press, 1966.
Gross, Robert. *The Minutemen and Their World.* New York: Hill & Wang, 1976.
Hall, J. K., and Gregory Zilboorg, eds. *One Hundred Years of American Psychiatry.* New York: Columbia University Press, 1944.
Hambrick-Stowe, Charles E. *The Practice of Piety: Puritan Devotional Discipline in Seventeenth-century New England.* Chapel Hill: University of North Carolina Press, 1982.
Henretta, James. "Economic Development and Social Structure in Colonial Boston." In Stanley Katz, ed., *Colonial America,* pp. 450–66. Boston: Little, Brown, 1971.
———. *The Evolution of American Society, 1700–1815.* Lexington, Mass.: D. C. Heath,1973.
———. "Families and Farms: Mentalities in Pre-Industrial America." *William and Mary Quarterly* 35 (January 1978): 3–33.
———. "Wealth and Social Structure." In Jack P. Greene and J. R. Pole,

eds., *Colonial British America: Essays in the New History of the Modern Era*, pp. 278–84. Baltimore: Johns Hopkins University Press, 1984.

Howe, John R. *From the Revolution to the Age of Jackson.* Englewood Cliffs, N.J.: Prentice-Hall, 1973.

Innes, Stephen. *Labor in a New Land: Economy and Society in Seventeenth-century Springfield.* Princeton, N.J.: Princeton University Press, 1982.

Jackson, Stanley W. "Force and Kindred Notions in Eighteenth-century Neurophysiology and Medical Psychology." *Bulletin of the History of Medicine* 44 (September-October 1970): 397–410.

———. "Melancholia and Mechanical Explanations in Eighteenth-century Medicine." *Journal of the History of Medicine and Allied Sciences* 38 (July 1983): 298–319.

Jedrey, Christopher M. *The World of John Cleaveland: Family and Community in Eighteenth-century New England.* New York: W. W. Norton, 1979.

Johnson, Paul. *A Shopkeeper's Millennium.* New York: Hill & Wang, 1978.

Jones, Douglass. *Village and Seaport: Migration and Society in Eighteenth-century Massachusetts.* Hanover, N.H.: University Press of New England, 1981.

———. "Geographic Mobility and Society in Eighteenth-century Essex County." Ph.D. diss., Brandeis University, 1975.

———. "The Strolling Poor. " *Journal of Social History* 8 (Summer 1975): 29–54.

Kaestle, Carl F., and Maris Vinovskis. *Education and Social Change in Nineteenth-century Massachusetts.* Cambridge: Cambridge University Press, 1980.

Kett, Joseph. *The Formation of the American Medical Profession.* New Haven, Conn.: Yale University Press, 1968.

King, Lester S. *The Philosophy of Medicine.* Cambridge, Mass.: Harvard University Press, 1978.

Konig, David Thomas. *Law and Society in Puritan Massachusetts: Essex County, 1629–1692.* Chapel Hill: University of North Carolina Press, 1979.

Kulikoff, Alan. "The Progress of Inequality in Revolutionary Boston." *William and Mary Quarterly* 28 (July 1971): 375–412.

Leifer, Ronald. *In the Name of Mental Health.* New York: Aronson, 1969.

Lockridge, Kenneth. *A New England Town: The First Hundred Years.* New York: W. W. Norton, 1970.

McCaughey, Robert. "From Town to City: Boston in the 1820s." *Political Science Quarterly* 88 (June 1973): 191–99.

MacDonald, Michael. *Mystical Bedlam: Madness, Anxiety and Healing in Seventeenth-century England.* Cambridge: Cambridge University Press, 1981.

McLoughlin, William A. *New England Dissent 1630–1833.* 2 vols. Cambridge, Mass.: Harvard University Press, 1971.

Main, Gloria. "Inequality in Early America. The Evidence from Probate Records of Massachusetts and Maryland." *Journal of Interdisciplinary History* 7 (Spring 1977): 558–81.

May, Henry. *The Enlightenment in America.* New York: Oxford University Press, 1978.

Medicine in Colonial Massachusetts, 1620–1820. Publications of the Colonial Society of Massachusetts, vol. 57. Boston: Colonial Society of Massachusetts, 1980.

Melchior, Alan. "Town and Community in Massachusetts, 1760–1860." History Department, Brandeis University, 1978. Mimeo.

Miller, Perry. "From Covenant to Revival." In James Smith and A. Leland Jamieson, eds., *Religion in American Life*, 2:321–43. Princeton, N.J.: Princeton University Press, 1961.

———. *The New England Mind from Colony to Province.* Cambridge, Mass.: Harvard University Press,1953.

———. *The New England Mind: The Seventeenth Century.* Boston: Beacon Press, 1961.

Nash, Gary. *Urban Crucible: Social Change, Political Consciousness and the Origins of the American Revolution.* Cambridge, Mass.: Harvard University Press, 1979.

———. "Urban Wealth and Poverty in Pre-Revolutionary America." *Journal of Interdisciplinary History* 6 (Spring 1976): 545–84.

Nelson, William E. "The Americanization of Common Law During the Revolutionary Period: A Study of Legal Change in Massachusetts, 1760–1830." Ph.D. diss., Harvard University, 1971.

———. "The Legal Restraint of Power in Pre-Revolutionary America: Massachusetts as a Case Study, 1760–1775." *American Journal of Legal History* 18 (January 1974): 1–32.

Parvis, Thomas. "The European Ancestry of the U.S. Population, 1790." *William and Mary Quarterly* 41 (January 1984): 85–101.

Piccarello, Louis. "Social Structure and Public Welfare Policy in Danvers, Massachusetts, 1760–1850." *Essex Institute Historical Collections* 118 (October 1982): 248–64.

Prude, Jonathan. *The Coming of the Industrial Order: Town and Factory Life in Rural Massachusetts, 1810–1860.* Cambridge: Cambridge University Press, 1983.

Quen, Jacques. "Early Nineteenth-century Observations of the Insane in the Boston Almshouse." *Journal of the History of Medicine* 23 (January 1968): 82–85.

Quincy, Josiah. *A Municipal History of the Town and City of Boston.* Boston: Charles C. Little & James Brown, 1852.

Riese, Walther. "The Impact of Nineteenth-century Thought on Psychiatry." *International Record of Medicine* 173 (June 1960): 7–19.

———. "Psychiatry's Second Coming." *Psychiatry* 45 (August 1982): 189–96.

Riznik, Barnes. "The Professional Lives of Early Nineteenth-century New England Doctors." *Journal of the History of Medicine and Allied Sciences* 19 (January 1964): 1–17.

Rosen, George. *Madness in Society: Chapters in the Historical Sociology of Mental Illness*. New York: Harper & Row, 1967.

Rosenberg, Carroll Smith. *Religion and the Rise of the American City*. Ithaca, N.Y.: Cornell University Press, 1971.

Rosenberg, Charles E. "The Bitter Fruit: Heredity, Disease and Social Thought." In Charles E. Rosenberg, ed., *No Other Gods: Science and American Social Thought*, pp. 25–34. Baltimore: Johns Hopkins University Press, 1976.

Rosenberg, Charles E. "The Therapeutic Revolution: Medicine, Meaning and Social Change in Nineteenth-century America." In Morris J. Vogel and Charles E. Rosenberg, eds., *The Therapeutic Revolution*, pp. 3–25. Philadelphia: University of Pennsylvania Press, 1971.

Rothenberg, Winifred. "The Market and Massachusetts Farmers, 1750–1855." *Journal of Economic History* 41 (Winter 1981), 283–314.

Rothman, David. *The Discovery of the Asylum: Social Order and Disorder in the New Republic*. Boston: Little, Brown, 1979.

Russell, Peter. "The Development of Judicial Expertise in Eighteenth-century Massachusetts and a Hypothesis Concerning Social Change." *Journal of Social History* 16 (Spring 1983): 143–55.

Russell, William L. *The New York Hospital: A History of the Psychiatric Service*. New York: Columbia University Press, 1945.

Scheff, Thomas, ed. *Labeling Madness*. Englewood Cliffs, N.J.: Prentice-Hall, 1975.

Scott, Donald. *From Office to Profession: The New England Ministry, 1750–1850*. Philadelphia: University of Pennsylvania Press, 1978.

Scull, Andrew T. *Museums of Madness: The Social Organization of Insanity in Nineteenth-century England*. New York: Penguin Books, 1982.

———., ed. *Madhouses, Mad Doctors and Madmen: The Social History of Psychiatry in the Victorian Era*. Philadelphia: University of Pennsylvania Press, 1981.

Selement, George. "The Meeting of Elite and Popular Minds at Cambridge, New England, 1638–1645." *William and Mary Quarterly* 41 (January 1984): 32–48.

Shyrock, Richard H. *Eighteenth-century Medicine in America*. Worcester, Mass.: American Antiquarian Society, 1950.

———. *Medicine and Society in America: 1660–1860*. New York: New York University Press, 1960.

———. *Medicine in America: Historical Essays*. Baltimore: Johns Hopkins Press, 1966.

Sicherman, Barbara. "The Paradox of Prudence: Mental Health in the Gilded Age." *Journal of American History* 62 (March 1976): 890–912.

Smith, Daniel Scott, and Michael Hindus. "Prenuptial Pregnancy in America." *Journal of Interdisciplinary History* 4 (Spring 1975): 537–70.

Starr, Paul. *The Social Transformation of American Medicine.* New York: Basic Books, 1982.

Tarail, Mark. "Current and Future Issues in Community Mental Health." *Psychiatric Quarterly* 52 (Spring 1980): 47–59.

Tomes, Nancy. *A Generous Confidence: Thomas Story Kirkbride and the Art of Asylum-Building, 1840–1883.* Cambridge: Cambridge University Press, 1984.

Tracy, Patricia. *Jonathan Edwards, Pastor: Religion and Society in Eighteenth-century Northampton.* New York: Hill & Wang, 1979.

Trask, Kerry Arnold. *In the Pursuit of Shadows: A Study of Collective Hope and Despair in Provincial Massachusetts in the Era of the Seven Years War, 1748–1769.* Ph.D. diss., University of Minnesota, Minneapolis, 1971.

Tudor, William. *The Life of James Otis.* 8 vols. Boston: Wells & Tilly, 1823.

Viets, Henry R. *A Brief History of Medicine in Massachusetts.* Boston: Houghton Mifflin, 1930.

Vinovskis, Maris. "Demographic Changes in America to the Civil War. An Analysis of the Socio-economic Determinants of Fertility Differentials and Trends in Massachusetts from 1765 to 1860." Ph.D. diss., Harvard University, 1975.

Ware, Caroline. *The Early New England Cotton Manufacture.* Boston: Houghton Mifflin, 1931.

Warner, Margaret Humphreys. "Vindicating the Minister's Medical Role: Cotton Mather's Concept of the *Nishmath-Chajim* and the Spiritualization of Medicine." *Journal of the History of Medicine and Allied Sciences* 36 (January 1981): 278–95.

Waters, John J., Jr. *The Otis Family.* New York: W. W. Norton, 1968.

Weiner, Dora B. "Health and Mental Health in the Thought of Philippe Pinel: The Emergence of Psychiatry During the French Revolution." In Charles E. Rosenberg, ed., *Healing and History,* pp. 59–86. New York: Neale Watson Academic Publisher, 1979.

Westermeyer, Joseph, and Ronald Wintrob. "Folk Criteria for the Diagnosis of Mental Illness in Rural Laos: On Being Insane in Sane Places." *American Journal of Psychiatry* 136 (June 1979): 755–61.

Windsor, Justin. *The Memorial History of Boston.* 4 vols. Boston: Ticknor & Co., 1881.

Wood, Gordon S. "Conspiracy and the Paranoid Style: Causality and Deceit in the Eighteenth Century." *William and Mary Quarterly* 39 (July 1982): 401–42.

———. *The Creation of the American Republic, 1776–1787.* New York: W. W. Norton, 1969.

Woods, Evelyn A., and Eric T. Carlson. "The Psychiatry of Phillippe Pinel." *Bulletin of the History of Medicine* 35 (January-February 1961): 14–21.

Zuckerman, Michael. *Peaceable Kingdoms.* New York: Vintage Press, 1970.

Index

"Act for the Relief of Idiots and Distracted persons" (1694), 51
Africa, perceptions of insanity in, 180n.71
Ahlstrom, Sidney, 170n.79, 184n.83
Alcohol, 72, 168n.64, 169n.78. *See also* Intemperance
Allen, David Grayson, 162n.62
Almshouses, 60, 90, 91, 102, 104–5; 114, 115, 121, 123, 124, 130, 136, 190n.34; at Boston, 54, 55, 56, 91, 103, 115, 156–57nn.25, 43, 170n.3; at Danvers, 94; at Lynn, 99; at Newburyport, 99; at Salem, 96, 101, 173n.40
American Journal of Insanity, 168n.60
Amherst, Mass., Maria Bartlett case, 136
Anderson, Alexander, 68, 73
Andover, Mass.: demographic stability of, 159n.58; kinship ties at, 160n.58; private asylums at, 36, 95, 111
Angel of Bethesda, The (Mather), 20–22, 23, 25, 68, 148–49n.33
Appeals Court for the Province of Massachusetts, 57
Asylum for the Insane at Charlestown, 176n.20. *See also* McLean Asylum
Asylum movement, 5, 6, 76, 82–89, 104, 114, 137, 175n.19
Asylums, 8, 73, 75, 129, 131, 143n.20 (*see also individual asylums*); overcrowding of, 115, 121, 124, 132,

136, 179n.69; private, 36, 50, 94, 95, 110–11, 172n.18
Atherton, Stephen, 49
Atomistic conception of government, 126
Auction of pauper insane, 173n.40

Babcock, Henry, 40
Barnstable, Mass., *see* Otis, James, Jr.
Barron, Nancy, 98–99, 136
Barron, Rebecca, 98
Barrow, pauper at Groton, Mass., 52
Bartlett, Maria, 136
Battie, William, 43, 46
Baxter, W. T., 161n.61
Beck, Theodoric, 78
Becker, Ernest, 142n.15
Belcher, Joseph, 27, 35
Belknap, Thomas, mad spinster relative of, 42
Bell, Luther, 86, 118, 119, 135, 188n.25
Bentley, William, 164n.21
Bewitchment, vs. possession, 144–45n.12. *See also* Witchcraft
Bicêtre, asylum, 74, 166n.34
Biological models of insanity, 16, 18, 21, 24, 72–73, 79, 106, 185n.7, 186–87n.18. *See also* Humoral doctrine of insanity; Vascular theory of insanity
Bleeding (phlebotomy), 43, 46, 74, 76, 107, 108, 116, 117, 153n.50, 178n.41
Blistering, 46, 107, 108, 116, 117

Bloomingdale Asylum (N.Y.), 176n.20
Boarding out, *see* Home care of the
insane: nonfamily
Bonomi, Patricia U., 150n.45
"Bookkeeping barter," 161n.61
Boston, Mass., 62–63; almshouse, 54,
55, 56, 91, 103, 115, 156–57nn.25,
43, 170n.3; "bookkeeping barter"
at, 161n.61; confinement of the insane at, 90–93; Goodwife Glover
witchcraft episode, 145n.13; Henry
Dove case, 59; house of industry
(*see* Boston, almshouse); jail (bridewell), 54; sends insane paupers
back to Concord, 98; shift from
communitarianism to individualism
at, 160n.58; surveillance by select-
men, 160n.58; warns out Jonathan
How, 37; workhouse, 55. *See also*
Otis, James, Jr.
Boston Lunatic Hospital, 122, 125,
132, 134, 179n.63, 190n.35
Boston Prison Discipline Society re-
port (1827), 103
Boundaries of the self, 9
Bowen, Mr., of Woodstock, 55
Boyer, Paul, 158n.58
Braintree, Mass.: Abigail Neal case,
52; French doctor treats distracted
woman at (1768), 46; Goodwife
Witty case, 38–39
Brampton, Mass., *see* Hopkinton,
Mass.
Brampton Sketches, 41
Bridewell, 54, 56, 92
Bridges, Mrs., cares for Archelaus
Putnam, 95
Brigham, Amariah, 82, 168nn.60, 63
Brigham, Deborah, 22
Brintal, Ruth, 136
Brookline, Mass., Joseph Norcross
forcibly returned to, 54
Brown, Richard D., 181n.79
Buck, Billy, 41
Buckland, Mass., insane pauper
caged at, 136
Bureaucratic response to insanity,
141n.1
Bushman, Richard, 151n.57
Bynum, William F., 166n.36

Cages, 100, 135, 136
Calvinism, *see* Puritan symbolic world
Cambridge, Mass.: insane confined in
jail, 93, 171n.13, 179n.63; Samuel
Coolidge case, 32
Carney, Michael, 54
Causality, post-Revolutionary struc-
ture of, 29
Certificate of insanity, 119–20
Chains, 40, 100, 102, 166n.34. *See also*
Fettering; Manacles; Restraints
Chandler, George, 131, 185n.7,
186nn.9, 12
Chandler, Samuel, 23, 34, 45
Charlestown, Mass., "Tobe" case, 52
Chase, Benjamin, 80
Chatham, Mass., private asylum at,
172n.18
Chauncey, Charles, 26, 50
Chauncey, Israel, 39–40
Checkley, Samuel, 34–35
Chelsea, Mass.: insane man confined
at, 102; Ruth Brintal case, 136
Chemotherapy, *see* Digitalis; Drugs;
Laudanum; Opium
Clark, Atherton, 53, 58
Clark, Christopher, 183n.82
Coercion, as therapy, 107, 119
College of Philadelphia, 67. *See also*
University of Pennsylvania
Commercialism in New England
Towns, 158n.58
Communitarianism of town life, 61,
126, 158–59n.59
Community Mental Health Centers
Act, vii, 138
Community Mental Health move-
ment, 1960s, 5
*Concepts of Insanity in the United States,
1789–1865* (Dain), 6–7
Concord, Mass., 128; post-
Revolutionary social transformation
of, 184n.84; town response to its in-
sane, 52, 97–99, 136
Confinement of the insane, 4, 8, 38–
40, 63, 74, 118, 121, 123, 125, 135,
185n.86; Jacksonian society's need
for, 128, 130; non-paupers, 101–2;
and reversability of insanity, 115;
by town authorities, 90–105

Congregationalism, disestablishment of in Massachusetts state constitution, 127, 183n.83
Connecticut state law jailing the violent insane (1793), 92
Control: of insane by local authorities, 90–105, 128, 160n.58 (*see also* Almshouses; Home care of insane: nonfamily; Jails); of self (*see* Self-control); social, 122, 128
Coolidge, Samuel, 27, 31–33, 40, 52, 55, 155–56nn.11, 21
Courts, 53, 57–59, 79–81
"Crazy," 22, 37, 55, 81
Cullen, William, 165n.25
Culpeper, Nicholas, 19, 43
Custodial care, 118, 122, 138, 139, 188n.20; vs. moral treatment, 131
Cutbush, Edward, 68, 69, 73, 85, 107, 164n.17, 168n.64

Daily, James, 100–101
Dain, Norman, 6–7, 131–32, 166n.37, 191n.39
Danvers, Mass., 128; moral responsibility of insane charged by overseers, 81; suicide attempts at, 172n.18; town response to its insane, 93, 94–96, 100–101; witchcraft episode at, *see* Witchcraft, Salem Village episode
Decision making, individual, 61–62
Dedham, Mass.: demographic stability of, 159n.58; economy of, 161n.61
Deer Island (Boston), 91
Deerfield, Mass., sends insane paupers to Greenfield house of correction, 100
Deference, decline in, post-Revolutionary, 126, 160–61n.60, 181n.78
"Dementia," 188n.20
Democracy, political, 126
Demographics of New England Towns, 159–60n.58, 180n.74
Demonology, 16, 17
Demos, John, 144n.8, 145n.18, 146n.18, 147n.23, 153n.47, 154n.52, 158n.58, 160n.59

Depression, 164n.21. *See also* Melancholy/melancholia
"Deranged," 81
Description of the Retreat Near York . . . (Tuke), 77
Determination of sanity, 51, 57–58, 79–81, 157n.50, 180n.71
Deutsch, Albert, 5, 141n.1
Deviance, 8, 142n.16
Devil, the, *see* Satan
Dexter, Timothy, 93
Digestive theory of insanity (Parkman), 79
Digitalis, 109
Diphtheria epidemic of mid-1730s (Northampton), 146n.18
Discovery of the Asylum (Rothman), 6
Disease, insanity as, 77, 78, 81–88 passim, 113, 129, 131–32, 133
Dissertations, medical, 68–70, 163n.10, 168n.64
"Distracted," 149n.38
"Distraction," 22, 27, 28, 37, 38, 69, 81; vs. possession, 14
Dix, Dorothea, 10, 175n.19, 189–90n.33
Dove, Henry, 59
Downs, Jack, 41
Drugs, 113, 117, 188n.20. *See also* Digitalis; Laudanum; Opium
Dwight, Rev. Louis, 103–4, 114, 122, 175n.19

East Sudbury (Wayland), Mass., insane man sent to Ipswich jail, 100
Eastern State Lunatic Hospital, Williamsburg (Va.), 138, 191n.39
Easton, Mass., Rev. Belcher case, 35
Economic growth of towns, 161–62n.61
Economic stratification, 126–27, 157nn.45, 46
Economic transformation of Northeast, 127, 129
Edgerton, Robert, 142n.16
Edinburgh (Scotland): hospital, 67; medical school, 165n.25
Egnal, Marc, 182n.81
Eisenstadt, Peter R., 150n.45
Electric shock, 108

Elyot, Sir Thomas, 24
Emetics, 43, 46, 116, 153n.50
England: violent insane in, 152–
    53n.40; York Retreat, 76, 77, 111
English Physician, The (Culpeper), 19
Enlightenment, 164n.15, 170n.79;
    and moral responsibility for insan-
    ity, 28, 29
Epistemological dilemma posed by in-
    sanity, 8
Esquirol, Jean-Étienne-Dominique, 75
Eveleth, Edward, 54
Ewins's home-care facility, 94
Excesses, 70, 71, 73, 78, 165n.25,
    187n.18; of passions, 23–24, 75

Factionalism, 157n.46
Family care of the insane, 7, 38–40,
    49, 63, 93, 112
Fasting, as therapy, 109
Fear, as therapy, 69–70, 107, 108, 112
Fettering, 134. *See also* Chains; Mana-
    cles; Restraints
Financial dependence of the insane,
    51, 53, 59
Fischer, David Hackett, 162n.61,
    181nn.78, 79
Fitchburg, Mass., Rev. Payson case, 93
Folie à ménage: Smith Brothers' (Hop-
    kinton), 41–42; in a Vermont fam-
    ily, cited by Waughan, 71
Folly, 3
Foreigners, insane, 131, 132–33, 134
Formisano, Ronald, 181n.78
Foucault, Michel, 2, 63, 139, 141n.1
Friends' Asylum (Frankford, Pa.),
    76–77
Frost, Samuel, 52
Fuller, Robert, 119–20
Furiously mad, 92, 97, 103, 104, 115,
    121, 124, 179n.63, 189n.29,
    190n.35. *See also* Violent insane

General Court (Mass. legislature) laws
    governing the insane: of 1678, 50–
    51; of 1694, 51; of 1796, 92, 97; of
    1833, 115, 177n.36; of 1836, 121
Generous Confidence, A (Tomes), 7
George III (king), 175n.9
Gibbons, William, 70, 108

Gifford, Mary, 92
Gilver, Thomas, 35
Gloucester, Mass.: Bentley's account
    of two distracted persons at,
    164n.21; home confinement of
    nonviolent madman at, 92
Glover, Goodwife, 145n.13
God, 65; inscrutability of, 16–17;
    Providence of (*see* Providence,
    God's); tests righteous with mad-
    ness, 13, 38
Goffman, Erving, 142nn.14, 16
Goldhammer, Herbert, 180n.71
Goodele, Abraham, 172n.18
Goodrich, Charles, 50
Goose, Mary, 51–52
Gorham, John, 91, 109–10
Government, atomistic conception of,
    126
Great Awakening, 29, 127, 150n.45,
    183n.82; Second, 168n.63
Greenfield, Mass., Deerfield insane
    paupers confined at house of cor-
    rection at, 100
Greven, Phillip J., Jr., 159n.58,
    160n.58
Griswold, Solomon, 102
Grob, Gerald, 5–6, 8, 139, 141n.1,
    180n.72
Gross, Robert, 160n.58, 163n.65,
    184n.84
Groton, Mass.: Barrow case, 52; con-
    finement of the insane at, 102
Guardianship, 51, 57–59, 171n.10

Haislup, William, 59
Hale, Nathan (madman), 49
Hall, Benjamin, 57
Hall, Peter Dobkin, 161n.61
Hambrick-Stowe, Charles E., 146n.22
Hamilton, Alexander (madman), 98
Hancock, Thomas, 56
Hartford Retreat, 113, 168n.60,
    176n.20
Hartshorn, Sarah, 55
Harvard Medical School, 66, 67, 76
Harvey, William, 24
Haverhill, Mass.: jails insane man
    from neighboring town, 99; Lydia
    Smith case, 52

Hawkins, John, 19
Hawthorne, Nathaniel, 33
Healing arts, colonial, not limited to
 physicians, 19–20
Henretta, James, 160n.58, 161n.61,
 182n.81
Heredity, 86, 132, 164n.14, 185–
 86nn.7, 8, 10
Holyoke, Edward Augustus, 71, 106–
 7, 164n.21
Home care of the insane: nonfamily,
 91, 94, 97, 98, 102, 114, 130, 135,
 155n.12; by own family (*see* Family
 care of the insane)
Hometowns, insane sent back to, 53–
 54, 97, 98, 136
Hopkinton, Mass.: attempts to re-
 move Atherton Clark, 53; dis-
 tracted residents of, 41–42
Hosmer, Joel, 97
Hospitals (*see also individual hospitals*):
 smallpox (at Boston), 47
House of industry, Boston, *see* Bos-
 ton: almshouse
Houses of correction (county jails),
 100, 115, 121, 189n.28. *See also*
 Jails, town
How, Jonathan, 37
Howe, John R., 181–82n.80
Howe, Samuel Gridley, 10, 189–
 90n.33
Hull, Mass., Capt. Souther's home for
 distracted at, 50
Humiliation, as therapy, 109
Humoral doctrine of insanity, 3, 12,
 19, 46, 148n.30
Hunter, Richard, 3
Hypertension, 73
Hypochondriasis, 28, 70, 108,
 148n.30

Identity and insanity, 125, 142n.16
Idleness, repression of, 3
Immigrants, Irish, insane, *see* Irish
 immigrants, insane
Incapacity for work, 26
"Incurables," 115, 118, 123, 132, 135;
 and heredity, 186n.10
Independent Chronicle (Boston), 81
Individualism, 126, 128

Innes, Stephen, 158n.58, 161n.61
"Insanabilia" (Mather), 15
"Insane," as legal term, 81
Insane persons: civil rights of, 80–81,
 167n.53; and the Community Mental Health Centers Act, vii; confinement of (*see* Confinement of the insane); as "disabled" (Chauncey), 26;
 discharged as cured, 120; elderly,
 188–89n.26; financial dependence
 of, 51, 53, 59; immigrant, 131,
 132–33; nonviolent, confinement
 of, 91, 92, 103; paupers (*see* Paupers, insane; property of, 51; resocialization of, 120, 133; returned
 to hometowns, 53–54, 97, 98, 136;
 segregation of (*see* Segregation of
 the insane); and the towns (*see*
 Towns); violent (*see* Furiously mad;
 Violent insane)
Insanity: antebellum reformers' views
 on, 5 (*see also* Asylum movement);
 biological models for, 16, 18, 21,
 24, 72–73, 79, 106, 185n.7, 186–
 87n.18 (*see also* Humoral doctrine
 of insanity; Vascular theory of insanity); bureaucratic response to,
 141n. 1; certificate of, 119–20; and
 colonial law, 50–59; and cultural
 relativism, 142n.16, 180n.71; cure
 vs. confinement, 122; determination of (*see* Determination of sanity); as disease, 77, 78, 81–88 passim, 113, 129, 131–32, 133; and
 economics, 3, 4; episodic, 37, 84,
 124–25; epistemological dilemma
 posed by, 8–9; and heredity, 86,
 132, 164n.14, 185–86nn.7, 8, 10;
 historiography of, 1–8, 151n. 1;
 and identity, 125, 142n.16; induced
 by societal stress, 82–83, 117, 133–
 34; medical treatment of (*see* Medical treatment of insanity); medie-
 val-Renaissance views of, 2, 3–4;
 melancholy vs. raving, Puritan view
 of, 15; moral implications of, 13,
 70, 77, 83, 86, 88, 89, 121, 170n.81;
 as personal choice, 28, 29; reversability of, 25, 77–78, 88, 89, 114,
 123, 135, 178n.47; seventeenth-

and eighteenth-century English
views of, 18–19; supernatural models for, 12–30; terminology of, viii,
14, 22, 69, 81
Intemperance, 83, 88, 117, 169n.65.
See also Alcohol
Interaction, socially acceptable, 120.
See also Situational impropriety
Ipswich, Mass.: barter and credit at,
161n.61; communitarian character
of, 158n.58, 161n.61; Edward Eveleth forcibly returned to, 54; jail
used to house insane from other
towns, 99–100, 101, 173n.34,
179n.63; kinship ties at, 160n.58;
persistent belief in witchcraft at,
145–46n.18; receptacle for the insane at, 135
Irish immigrants, insane, 131, 132,
134, 186–87nn.12–13, 17, 188n.22
Irrationality, 124. *See also* Reason, loss
of; Unreason

Jackson, James, 77
Jackson, Stanley W., 148n.30
Jacksonian society: insanity-inducing
stresses of, 82–83, 117, 133–34;
need for social control in, 6, 8, 70,
128, 130; political structure of,
181n.78
Jails, town, 60, 90, 92, 97, 100, 102,
103–4, 114–35 passim, 171n.13,
179n.63, 189n.28, 190n.34. *See also*
Houses of correction
Jarvis, Edward, 133–34, 137–38,
190n.36
Jedrey, Christopher, 145n.18,
158n.58, 160n.58, 161n.61,
162n.62
Jewetts, Dummer, 37
Jones, A. H.. 182n.81
Jones, Douglass, 159n.58
Joseph, Captain, 106
Jubeart, John, 41
Justices of the peace, 51

King George's War, 56
Kingman, David, 46
Kinship ties, 160n.58; and economic
exchanges, 161n.61

Kirkbride, Thomas, 7
Kirtland, Daniel, 37
Kittredge, Joseph, 111
Kittredge, Thomas, 111
Knapp, Elizabeth, 144n.11
Konig, David Thomas, 159n.58
Kulikoff, Alan, 182n.81, 183n.82

Labor market, 127, 184n.85
Laos, perceptions of insanity in,
180n.71
Laudanum, 113, 116
Laws and the insane, 50–59. *See also*
General Court
Lee, Thomas, 119
Leominster, Mass., sends female van-
dal to Worcester county jail, 102
Leonard, Abiel, 37, 38, 45
Leonard, Charles, 42
Lindert, Peter H., 182n.81
Litigation, 159n.58, 181n.80
Lockridge, Kenneth, 150n.45,
159n.58, 161n.61
Lothrup, Samuel, 58
Lukes, Stephen, 181n.78
"Lunatic," 22, 81, 167n.56; vs. "ma-
niac," 170n.3
Lynn, Mass., confines insane in alms-
house, 99

Macalpine, Ida, 3
MacDonald, Michael, 3–4, 191n.40
McLean, Asylum, 86, 99, 100, 112–24
passim, 134–35, 138, 176n.20,
185n.1
McLoughlin, William A., 183n.83
"Mad," 22, 149n.38
Madness, vi. *See also* Insanity
Madness and Civilization (Foucault), 2
Madness in Society (Rosen), 2–3
Magnalia Christi Americana (Mather),
13, 15
Mahoney, insane pauper at Boston,
91
Main, Gloria, 162n.61
Malden, Mass., confinement of the in-
sane at, 103
Manacles, 113. *See also* Chains; Fetter-
ing; Restraints

Mania, 22, 69, 91, 164n.18
"Maniac house" at Boston, 91, 92
Manie sans délire, see Moral insanity
Mann, Horace, 10, 114, 122, 175n.19,
    177n.32, 189–90n.33
Mann Report to the Massachusetts
    Legislature (1830), 114, 177n.30
Manufacturing, 183n.82
Market economy, 127, 161n.61,
    183n.82, 184n.85
Marlborough, Mass., insane man con-
    fined at, 102
Marshall, Andrew W., 180n.71
Mascarene, John, 37
Massachusetts General Hospital, 112,
    176n.20
Massachusetts legislature: census of
    state's insane (1829), 102, 135,
    174n.41; report on insane state
    prisoners (1827), 104. See also Gen-
    eral Court
Massachusetts State Almshouse at
    Tewksbury, Insane Department,
    185n.1
Masturbation, 70, 83, 88, 117,
    168n.64
Mather, Cotton, 12–18, 20–22, 37–
    38, 44, 45, 46, 49, 148–49n.33
Mather, Increase, 146n.21
Mather, Lydia, 14, 37–38
May, Henry, 164n.15
Maynard, Jonathan, 39
Medfield, Mass., Benjamin Hall de-
    clared sane at, 57–58
Medical Papers, 66
Medical practice: colonial American,
    19–20, 43–48; folk, English, 20;
    professionalization of, 65–66
Medical publications, 66, 68, 71. See
    also Dissertations, medical; Medical
    writings, English
Medical schools, 65, 66, 67, 68, 71
Medical societies, 66
Medical treatment of insanity, 10, 28,
    65–89, 106–12, 136; merging of
    disease model and psychology, 114;
    reformers' faith in, 137; skepticism
    about, 136
Medical writings, English, 148n.31
Medicalization of insanity: in Amer-

ica, 121, 138–39; in England,
    166n.36. See also Medical treatment
    of insanity
Medicine: cultural influence of, 66–
    67
Melancholy/melancholia, 15, 20–21,
    69, 148n.30; religious, 22–23
Melchior, Alan, 181n.80
Mental illness, viii. See also Insanity
Mental Institutions in America (Grob), 6
"Mental therapy" (Rush), 109
Mentally Ill in America (Deutsch), 5
Middlesex General Sessions Court, 53
Migration, see Mobility
"Minister's Black Veil, The" (Haw-
    thorne), 33
Ministers: community influence of,
    147n.23, 148n.32, 150n.45; dis-
    tracted, 33–35, 38, 93; as mental
    health authorities, 16, 17, 26–28,
    43, 44–45, 65, 150n.45; subordina-
    tion of individual rights to commu-
    nity values by, 159n.58
Mobility, 126, 159–60n.58
Moderation, loss of, 69. See also Ex-
    cesses
Moody, Joseph, 33–34, 45
Moody, Samuel, 34
Moral insanity, 74, 85, 124, 165n.28
Moral irregularities, 23. See also Sin
Moral responsibility for insanity, 13,
    70, 77, 83, 86, 88, 89, 121, 170n.81
Moral treatment, 76, 82, 111–23 pas-
    sim, 133, 135, 138, 141n.13,
    165n.29, 179n.68; vs. custodial
    care, 118, 131. See also Traitement
    moral
Museums of Madness (Scull), 4
Mystical Bedlam (MacDonald), 3–4, 63

Napier, Richard, 3, 4, 44, 146n.21,
    152n.13, 153n.40
Nash, Gary B., 146n.18, 151n.57,
    157nn.45, 46, 158n.58, 160n.58,
    182–83n.81
Natural law, 23, 29, 77
Neal, Abigail, 52
Nelson, William E., 162n.62, 181n.80
New System of the Spleen, Vapors, and

Hypochondriak Melancholy . . . (Robinson),19
Newbury, Mass., Timothy Dexter case, 93
Newburyport, Mass.: confines insane in almshouse, 99; Elizabeth Petton case, 136
Newton, Mass., Atherton Clark case, 53
Nishmath-chajim, 148–49n.33
Nissenbaum, Stephen, 158n.58
Non compos mentis, 22, 52, 53, 149n.38. See also Determination of sanity
Nonproductivity, 2
Nonviolent insane, 121, 125
Norcross, Joseph, 54
Normative demands of post-Revolutionary social order, 70. See also Jacksonian society, need for social control
Northampton, Mass.: communitarian character of, 158–59n.58; demographic stability of, 159n.58; earthquake at (1727), 146n.18; economic exchange at, 161n.61; individualism and competition at, 181n.80; kinship ties at, 160n.58
Northampton State Lunatic Hospital, 185n. 1, 190n.36
Nosology, psychiatric, 142n.17. See also Insanity, terminology of
"Not fit to go at large," 179n.67

Opium, 46, 107, 110, 116, 119
Osgood's farm (Andover), private asylum at, 36
Otis, James, Jr., 35–36, 40, 50, 58, 63, 84, 92, 94
Overcrowding of asylums, 115, 121, 124, 132, 136, 179n.69

Pain, as therapy, 108
Paine, Robert Treat, 38, 45
Parkman, Ebenezer, 22, 44, 45–46, 49
Parkman, George, 78–79, 111, 175nn.16, 17
Parris, Noyes, 33
Parris, Samuel, 33
Parrish, Joseph, 69–70
Parsons, Ruth, 94–95

Parvis, Thomas, 159n.58
Passions, 68–70, 71, 75, 88; excess of, 23–24, 75
Paupers, 182–83n.81, 190–91n.37; insane, 52, 59–60, 121–22, 131–35 passim, 156n.25, 172nn. 19, 22, 23, 26, 29, 186–87nn.12, 13, 188n.22
Payson, Rev. John, 93
Pennsylvania Hospital, 7, 44, 47, 67, 76, 108, 141n.13, 191n.39; asylum at, 8, 133
Pepperell, Mass., home care of the insane at, 135
"Periodic insanity" (Woodward), 84, 125
Pexlen, Widow, 54–55
Philips, Samuel, 27–28
Phrenology, 168nn.60, 64
Physicians, 37, 136; as mental health experts, 28, 191n.40
Pinel, Philippe, 74–76, 79, 85, 111, 112, 123, 165–66nn.29–32, 34, 35
Pines, Mrs., boards Widow Pexlen at Boston, 54
Plymouth, Mass., John Porter case, 93
Portents, 16, 146n.18
Porter, John, 93
Possession, demonic, 144n.9; vs. bewitchment, 144–45n.12; vs. distraction, 14
Prayer and fasting, 44–45
Pride, insanity as punishment for, 15
Prince, Nathan, 33
Prisons, state, 135
Private asylums, 36, 50, 94, 95, 110–11, 172n.18
Probate Court, 58–59
Proliferation of religious sects, 127
Providence, God's, 17, 29, 56, 72, 81, 86, 151nn.56, 57
Provincial government's responsibility for the insane, 57
Psychiatric practice, private, 138
Puerto Rico, perceptions of insanity in, 180n.71
Purging, 43, 46, 74, 76, 107, 116, 153n.50
Puritan symbolic world, 16–17, 60, 129, 146–47n.22, 184n.83
Putnam, Archelaus, 95–96, 111

Quarterly Courts, Suffolk County, 58

Ray, Isaac, 110–11
Reality: of everyday life, 9; post-Revolutionary transformation of, 129
Reason, 25, 29, 88; loss of, 57, 89; Puritan view of, 150n.49. *See also* Irrationality; Unreason
Receptacles, local, for the insane, 121, 179n.63
Recoveries, colonial vs. Jacksonian-era, 125. *See also* Insanity, reversability of
Reform movement, antebellum, 5, 6, 10. *See also* Asylum movement
Religious pluralism, 127, 183–84n.83
Resocialization of the insane, 120, 133
Restraining chair, 108; 174–75n.9
Restraints, 113, 116, 123, 135. *See also* Chains; Fettering; Manacles; Straitjackets
Returning insane to hometowns, 53–54, 97, 98, 136
Revolutionary war, demand for medical care stimulated by, 66
Reynolds, Edward, 24
Richardson, Asa, 100, 101
Ridicule, as therapy, 109
Rituals, common, participation in, 9
Robinson, Nicholas, 19, 25, 43, 46, 72, 164n.17
Rose, Henry, 68, 107
Rosen, George, 2–3, 63, 139
Rosenberg, Charles E., 186n.8
Rosenkrantz, Barbara G., 188n.26
Rotary swing, 112, 175n.17
Rothenberg, Winifred, 183n.82
Rothman, David, 5, 6, 82, 139, 141n.1, 184–85n.86
Rush, Benjamin, 67, 72–73, 74–85 passim, 108–9, 112, 123, 165nn.25, 27, 28, 166–67nn.35, 37, 38
Russell, Peter, 184n.85

Salem, Mass. 128–29; almshouse, 96, 101, 173n.40; Mary Goose case, 51–52; town response to its insane, 93, 95–97, 101, 102; witchcraft epi-

sode, 14, 33, 158n.58; workhouse advocated at, 81
Salisbury, Mass., George Webster case, 135–36
Salpêtrière, la, asylum, 74, 166n.34
Sanders, Daniel, 72
Satan, 12–15, 16, 65, 145n.18, 146n.21, 149n.33
Schizophrenia, 142–43n.17
Schoolmasters, distracted, 32–33, 34, 35, 36
Scott, Donald M., 147n.23
Scull, Andrew T., 4, 191n.40
Seasickness, simulated, as therapy, 112, 175n.17
Seclusion, 134
Second Great Awakening, 168n.63
Sedation, 110
Segregation of the insane: "furiously mad" from nonviolent, 121, 134; from society, 8, 90, 121, 138–39
Selectmen, 62, 160n.58; as judges of sanity, 57–58
Selement, George, 147n.23
Self-control, 72, 120, 122; loss of, 9, 61, 62, 69, 75, 78, 105
Sewall, Samuel, 44, 45, 49
Sexuality, 88, 169–70n.78
Shame, 86, 160n.59
Shower baths, as therapy, 112
Shryock, Richard, 148n.30, 165n.27
Signs and portents, 16, 146n.18
Sin, 20, 21, 23, 25, 64; madness as punishment for, 15; secularized notion of, 29. *See also* Insanity, moral implications of; Vices
Situational impropriety, 142n.14. *See also* Socially appropriate interaction
Smallpox epidemics, 44, 56
Smith, Lydia, 52
Smith, Peter, 97
Snow, James, 96–97
Social changes in post-Revolutionary Massachusetts, 125–28
Social control, 122, 128: Jacksonian-era need for, 6, 8
Socially appropriate interaction, 120. *See also* Situational impropriety
Societal stress, insanity induced by, 82–83, 117, 133–34

Somes, Abigail, 49
Soul, 73
Souther, Capt. Daniel, 50
Speare, Samuel, 38–39
Spleen, 18
Springfield, Mass., 62, 63; commercialism in, 158n.58; economic development of, 161n.61; Solomon Griswold case, 102
Starr, Paul, 148n.31
State and the Mentally Ill, The (Grob), 5–6
Stedman, Charles, 132, 185n.7, 186n.11
Sterling, Mass., town strong room at, 136
Stigma, post-treatment, 142n.16
Stoddard, Simeon, 27
Stoughton, Mass., Joseph Belcher case, 27, 35
Straitjackets, 91, 108, 110, 135, 166n.34. See also Restraints
Strangers, 128, 155n.20, 160n.58, 180n.76; distracted, 52–55, 62
Stratification of wealth, 126–27, 157n.45, 46
Strong rooms, 113, 116, 135, 190n.35.
Submersion, 110–11
Sudbury, Mass., sends East Sudbury (Wayland) man to Ipswich jail, 99–100
Suicide, 146n.21; attempts at, 172n.18; sermons following, 24–28
Superior Court of Massachusetts, 79, 80
Surveillance, community, 160n.58
Swift, John & Mrs., 39

Taunton State Lunatic Hospital, 131, 185n.1
Therapeutic nihilism, 187n.18
Thompson, Benjamin, 144n.6
Thompson, Joseph, 144n.6
Thompson, William, 13, 44, 144n.6
Three Hundred Years of Psychiatry, 1535–1860 (ed. Hunter and Macalpine), 3
"Tobe," pauper at Concord, 52
Tomes, Nancy, 7, 8, 47, 141n.13, 166n.36, 191nn.39, 40

Topsfield, Mass., Rev. Gilver case, 35
Town life, 61–63, 128, 157–60n.58
Towns: autonomy of, 162n.62; confinement of the insane by, 90–105; economic growth of, 161–62n.61; legal responsibility for own insane, 50–57; question civil rights of the insane, 80–81
Townshend, Mass., Anna Valkins case, 53–54
Tracy, Patricia, 146n.18, 158–59n.58, 160n.58, 161n.61, 181n.80
Traitement moral, 74, 75. See also Moral treatment
Trask, Kerry Arnold, 159n.58
Trumble, David, 25, 26–27, 69
Tucker, Ichabod, 81
Tuke, Samuel, 77, 111
Tuke, William, 76–77, 78, 79, 109, 111, 112, 123
Tukesbury, Andrew, 91

Underfunding and understaffing of asylums, 132
University of Pennsylvania, medical school at, 67
Unreason, 2–3. See also Irrationality; Reason, loss of
Utica State Lunatic Asylum (N.Y.), 168n.60

Vascular theory of insanity, 72–73, 108, 165n.25
Vendue, see Auction of pauper insane
Vices, 117. See also Insanity, moral implications of; Sin
Vinovskis, Maris, 188n.26
Violent insane, 40, 47, 61, 91, 152–53n.40. See also Furiously mad
Virginia, housing of insane in, 138
Voluntary associations, 181n.79

Walkins, Anna, 53–54
Wallis, George, 107
Ware, Caroline D., 183n.82
Warham, John, 15, 45
Warning out, 37, 53, 56, 180n.76
Warren, John, 66, 67, 76, 77, 112
Water, cold, as therapy, 107–8, 109
Waterson, Robert, 190n.34

Watertown, Mass., Samuel Coolidge
case, 31–33, 52, 55, 155n.11
Waughan, John, 71–72, 107–8
Wealth, distribution of, 126–27,
162n.61. *See also* Almshouses; Paupers, insane; Workhouses
Webster, George, 135–36
Wells, Daniel, 100
Westermeyer, Joseph, 180n.71
Westhampton, Mass., nonfamily
home care at, 136
Westminster, Mass., jails Thomas Ball
of Concord, 99
Wigglesworth, Michael, 18
Will, 133, 164n.14
Willard, Dr., private asylum proprietor, 110–11
Willard, Samuel, 144n.11
Williams, Solomon, 24–26
Williamson, Jeffery C., 182n.81
Wilson, John, 100
Winchester, Mass., Belknap case, 42
Winthrop, John, 149n.41
Wintrob, Ronald, 180n.71
Witchcraft, 12, 16, 43, 71, 144–

45nn.8–13, 153n.47; Salem Village
episode, 14, 33, 158n.58
Witches, 42, 43
Witty, Goodwife, 38–39
Wood, Gordon S., 151n.57, 170n.81,
181n.78
Woodward, Samuel, 83–85, 115,
116–18, 123, 168nn.60, 64, 177–78n.40, 178n.47, 185n.7, 188n.20
Worcester State Lunatic Hospital, 11,
83, 93, 103, 114–34 passim,
185n. 1, 190n.33; trustees' reports,
86, 87, 89, 115, 116, 117–18
Work: incapacity for, 26; productive,
as criterion of sanity, 120; as therapy, 116. *See also* Workhouses
Workhouses, 55, 81
Wyman, Rufus, 113

York, Maine, Rev. Moody case, 33–34
York (England) Retreat, 76, 77, 111

Zuckerman, Michael, 162n.62
Zukens, George, 144n.9

.